SEC*ND THOUGHTS

COLIN BAKER

Colin Baker : Second Thoughts
First Published September 2010
by Hirst Publishing

Hirst Publishing, Suite 285 Andover House, George Yard, Andover, Hants, SP10 1PB

ISBN 978-0-9566417-6-2

Copyright © Colin Baker 2010

The right of Colin Baker to be identified as the author of this work has been asserted by him in accordance with the Copyright, Designs and Patents Act 1988.

The articles in this compilation originally appeared in the Bucks Free Press between 1995 and 2010.

All rights reserved. No part of this publication may be reproduced, stored in or introduced into a retrieval system, or transmitted, in any form, or by any means (electronic, mechanical, photocopying, recording or otherwise) without the prior written permission of the publisher. Any person who does any unauthorised act in relation to this publication may be liable to criminal prosecution and civil claims for damages.

A CIP catalogue record for this book is available from the British Library.

Cover by Robert Hammond
Compilation by Louise McDonald.
Typesetting by Elise Hattersley
Printed and bound by Good News Press

Paper stock used is natural, recyclable and made from wood grown in sustainable forests. The manufacturing processes conform to environmental regulations.

This book is sold subject to the condition that it shall not, by way of trade or otherwise, be lent, re-sold, hired out, or otherwise circulated without the publisher's prior consent in any form of binding or cover other than that in which it is published and without a similar condition including this condition being imposed on the subsequent purchaser.

www.hirstbooks.com

This book is dedicated to my wonderful daughters Lucy, Bindy, Lally and Rosie who have each in their separate and very different ways provided me with inspiration, motivation and most importantly of all – pride.

Contents

	Introduction	5
1.	Topical Issues	7
2.	Baker Towers	17
3.	Eco Warrior	28
4.	Colin vs. Public Transport	34
5.	Doctor Who	47
6.	Foibles, Friends and Fancies	55
7.	Little Britain	71
8.	The Beautiful Game	92
9.	Abroad	103
10.	Education	114
11.	Light Relief	129
12.	More Mundungus	141
13.	Election 2010	148
14.	10 Years Ago	156
15.	It's *"Would have"* not *"Would of"*!	174
16.	Dicing with Death Wearing a Safety Helmet	180
17.	Your Call is Important to Us	195
18.	Wycombe Man	214
19.	Acting Up	231
21.	Season's Greetings	250
	Afterword	261

Introduction

August 2010

It's all your fault, dear reader. Or, if by any chance you have happened upon Volume 2 without having experienced Volume 1 of my musings, then shame upon you for being so anarchic – but thank you for investing your wages or a part thereof on this book without having sampled its predecessor. .

Why is it your fault? Well, enough of you generous and discerning folk have seen fit to purchase Volume 1 of my articles written over a decade and a half for the Bucks Free Press, as to persuade Tim Hirst, the publisher, to risk his yacht, private jet and, more importantly, his rapidly growing reputation as a publisher in asking his colleague Louise McDonald to select more of my opinionated ramblings for your entertainment.

I have been heartened by the reaction of those of you who have read the first volume and been kind enough to give me feedback. This can be summed up as 'I may not agree with everything you wrote but I enjoyed reading it.' Some of you have been even kind enough to say that I have occasionally made you smile or laugh. What more could a columnist ask for? If everybody agreed with me, then I suggest that I would not be doing my job properly and if I can stir the occasional chuckle of recognition or sympathy then I am more than content.

I hope that Louise's selection is as warmly received.
It starts with some glimpses of my take on what is happening in the news and the world in general.

As usual, Political Correctness in its many pernicious forms figures along with the ever extending desire of government, both local and national, to control every waking moment of our lives.

5th February 2010

Many of my contemporaries have been sending me copies of their autobiographies, some actually written by them and others, shall we say, 'assisted'. I suppose it is now de rigueur for any self respecting actor who has achieved even a modicum of notoriety to write about their lives. Indeed, I recently read one such by an exact contemporary of mine who has appeared in not one but two very high profile series over the last few decades; and it was a very good read indeed. He had worked and played with many household names and film stars. The stories of his (failed) marriages were similarly revealing and his exes will either be picking up the phone to speak to their solicitors or keeping a low profile in the event that the wonderful defence against libel (i.e. truth) prevents them from doing anything else.

I have been approached, I admit, to write my own story. My reticence thus far has principally stemmed from the fact my life has been spectacularly uninteresting compared to those of my peers that I have thus far read. The very few diaries I have ever kept contain information along the lines of got up, had breakfast, took the dog out, watched Coronation Street – possibly not the kind of stuff that would ensure the book would disappear off the shelves faster than a premier league footballer's reputation. Add to that my disinclination to dish what little dirt there is in my distant and barely remembered youth and it may well be that, when written, any memoirs of mine would lie unpublished on my computer hard disk for ever.

However, I did succumb to the invitation of a young, up-and-coming publisher to make a book out of the articles that I have been churning out weekly in this paper for nearly fifteen years now. He had been reading them online, and was kind enough to think a selection of them worthy of sharing with a wider audience than the population of South Bucks. So, I have yet another thing to add to that list of 'things I never dreamed could ever happen to me when I was a child' – I am a published author.

Should you wish to find out more and even (dare I hope?) get your very own copy of 'Look Who's Talking' – details are to be found at www.hirstbooks.com.

No pressure!

1. Topical Issues

25th June 2010

I have a friend in Yorkshire who has worked for BP in Saltend for the last thirty years. Amongst his other duties, he is charged with the safety of the workforce in his department and tells me that for as long as he has worked for the company, safety has always been the number one consideration. They work in an industry where the consequences of shortcuts or the tiniest error can be catastrophic; and they all know that. He tells me that every time he goes on shift his main priority is to ensure that everyone on site leaves to return to their families as they arrived, safe and well. He says that everyone from CEO, Tony Hayward, down to the technicians is devastated by what has happened on the Deepwater Horizon platform but they all also believe that until a full investigation has taken place it is deeply unjust to point the finger of blame in any direction.

He points out too that the company is now an international one and has been 'BP' rather than 'British Petroleum' for ten years. He and his colleagues share the uncomfortable feeling that many of us had last week at the undignified spectacle of their CEO being treated like a common criminal by members of the congressional committee.

One cannot help but wonder whether an American CEO would be asked to, or indeed agree to, endure a similar grilling were there a comparable incident in our waters. In fact, back in 1998 when the Piper Alpha North Sea oil and gas rig exploded catastrophically with the tragic loss of 167 lives, I don't recall the chief executive of Occidental Petroleum (Caledonian) Ltd. - an American Company - facing anything remotely comparable. And even after that company was found guilty by the Cullen Enquiry of having inadequate maintenance and safety procedures, no criminal proceedings were ever brought. It would be tempting to conclude that lives matter less than millions.

It is undeniable that something went wrong somewhere in the Gulf of Mexico and those who suffer any loss as a result should be compensated, but it would be absurd to imagine that all concerned are not well aware of this and keen to minimise the damage and consequent loss to all parties as soon as possible. All the sabre-rattling and unseemly Brit-bashing comments emanating from certain quarters in the United States are neither helpful nor fair.

6th November 2009

It is heartening to see how many people still wear their poppies with pride, in an age when some may be inclined to forget the huge debt we owe all who serve and have served in our armed forces, past and present. However much some may disapprove of what our servicemen have been called upon to do in our name over recent decades, the last people who should bear the brunt of that disapproval are the soldiers, sailors and airmen who put their lives on the line every day in places far away from the support of their families and friends. Servicemen and -women who die in Afghanistan or Iraq are just as dead as those who laid down their lives in the trenches of Ypres or the Normandy landings. Objections to our participation in those current theatres of conflict should never lead the objectors to do other than support the men and women who signed up to defend us and their country and are thereafter obliged to go wherever they are sent.

We hear daily stories of enormous bravery on the part of our troops who sacrifice their lives for their comrades and to help the oppressed citizens of other countries. It is as much for them as for our fallen ancestors in the two World Wars that I wear my poppy with pride. It is a small gesture but it is one that, I am delighted to say, is holding firm across all ages. I believe that as long as we honour those who fought and died for our survival and freedom, then we will continue to value that freedom both for ourselves and others.

My father survived the Second World War. He was a non-commissioned officer in the Royal Army Service Corps. While doing some research, I recently found the supporting documentation for the British Empire Medal he received in 1943. It read "In the early stages and throughout the North African campaign he set a very fine example of hard work and cheerfulness under all conditions and even under heavy bombing." He was no different to thousands of other servicemen who simply got on with it then and get on with it now, because to do otherwise would be to let their colleagues and their country down. Let us wear our poppies for them as well as those who have gone before in our name.

26th March 2010

We need to update the law on trespass. Householders no longer feel that they have any protection at all if, in the absence of any police support, they are brave or foolhardy enough to attempt to use the 'reasonable force' that is permitted by law to eject trespassers from their property. Combine this legal minefield with the fact that the trespasser is usually much better informed about his rights than the landowner whose rights he so cavalierly ignores and the situation becomes even more desperate. The police are currently powerless to intervene until a breach of the peace or other more serious criminal offence is committed. But if a clued-up and determined trespasser restricts his activities to merely being on your land, there is absolutely nothing the police can do to remove him. The owner of the land has to apply for relief to the civil courts, thereby affording the trespasser weeks or months making whoopee in his back garden. And you can bet your mortgage that the moment an evicted trespasser bleats to the authorities about an over strenuous summary eviction, then the mighty hammer of the law will descend upon the beleaguered landowner.

There were reports this week of gangs of immigrants who have built what is nothing less than a shanty town on gardens and private land in Peterborough. Apparently, the area is a rich source of casual vegetable picking employment. One resident has had a Czech immigrant living in his coal shed for three months. The police can't help; the local council say that they can't do anything beyond advising and helping the people sleeping in residents' gardens 'to access the services available to them.' They suggest residents should employ a solicitor and take the intruders to court. Great.

Is this really how we want the authorities to whom we pay or taxes to act? I suspect not. So why is it beyond the wit of Parliament to formulate a simple law whereby the blindingly obvious cases of trespass can be swiftly remedied? If a homeowner can demonstrate that he is the tenant or owner of land (and in the majority of cases that will be fairly simply done) then the local authority and/or the police should be empowered to enforce the law of trespass in the same way and with the same degree of assiduity as they do when a car owner leaves his car in a prohibited place.

1st August 2003

Last week a very good friend of mine had the steel shutter of his locked barn forced open during the night and, for the second time in as many years, had the tools of his trade purloined from its interior. He will now spend a large sum of money that he can ill afford supplying the barn with electricity so that he can then spend even more money installing a system that will deter and/or identify the greedy scum who systematically deprive decent hard-working people of their property and livelihood. Were my friend to do what I would be sorely tempted to do and employ the anti-personnel tactics of the designers of the pyramids, then he would run the risk of incarceration, while the thief would get counselling and compensation.

There has been widespread sympathy for Tony Martin's desperate protection of his home; but we have all learned the bitter lesson that the burglar is more likely to be treated with kid gloves than is the violated citizen.

Hence booby-trapping your property with devices that lop off the hands of the miscreant as he reaches out for your treasured possessions would result in the immediate prosecution of the householder. Rigging your tractor so that it sent a few thousand volts through the taker and driver-away of same would be similarly punished, as would leaving your pet cobra coiled menacingly on the driver's seat.

To compound the frustration of the robbed citizen, the police have to try to recover the stolen property without having the case thrown out of court because of the alleged infringement of some regulation regarding the acquisition of evidence that would be seized on by defence lawyers (who get a much better hourly rate for finding ways for the ungodly to evade retribution than the police do for identifying and arresting them).

And you can bet your last pound of bail money that the miscreant knows the law in the tiniest detail and will exploit its weaknesses to the full at every opportunity.

The police failed to attend the scene of a series of attacks on cars and property in Seer Green last week. It's not the fault of the police that their new "state of the art" (huh!) telephone system isn't working, but the police are the ones whose image is going to suffer if we don't very soon make it clear to the government what it is that we want from our police forces. At the moment they seem to believe that we want a policeman in every car, issuing us with fixed penalties every time we transgress one of the myriad of arbitrary speed limits and parking restrictions that have been imposed on us.

I drove back from Malvern on Saturday night and passed through many small Oxfordshire towns and villages in the wee small hours. I saw at least five police cars tucked away by road junctions and roundabouts, each with two policemen aboard watching us motorists as we desperately scanned our surroundings in case there were driving restriction we had not noticed among the panoply of painted lines, warnings, restrictions and road signs that festoon our roads.

Twenty years ago, when I saw a police car, I felt protected and reassured. Now I check my car for missing light bulbs. Twenty years ago felons saw a police car and legged it. Now they carry on a-burgling, secure in the knowledge that they're after motorists.

7th March 2008

Whilst we all know that parking restrictions, planning regulations and byelaws generally are designed to be for the benefit of society at large rather than the individual, there are occasions when citizens who try to circumvent the rules earn our sympathy and grudging respect.

I suspect that I am not alone in harbouring such feelings for Robert Fidler, a farmer in Surrey, who evidently believes that an Englishman's home should be his castle.

Wearied by years of frustration in his attempts to persuade local planners to sanction a home for him and his family on his farmland, he devised what Blackadder's servant Baldrick would undoubtedly describe as a cunning plan. He built a castle. He built it behind a forty foot barricade of hundreds of bales of straw. He then lived in it for four years with his wife and baby son, who grew up looking out of his bedroom window at – straw. That is until his resourceful papa removed the bales and exposed to the gaze of the world the castle that was now his home. Naturally, outraged locals informed the local authority. There will always be someone who is outraged, whatever you do. Mr Fidler (even his name brings a smile) was served with a demolition notice.

He declined on the established legal basis that it had been "substantially completed" for four years. He applied to the council for a Certificate of Lawfulness, which can be sought after a development has been in place for at least four years without planning permission. The council however ruled that the bales had prevented them from knowing it was there, and therefore he has to demolish it. A neighbour predictably and inarguably, declared, "Everyone else has to abide by planning laws, so why shouldn't they?" Yes, that is true. But wouldn't the world be much more fun if the occasional fiddler attracted the occasional official blind eye and sense of humour. I believe a "straw" poll of citizens might well consider that our intrepid farmer has earned a little admiration and deserves some leeway. The castle, judging from the photographs in the press, is undeniably splendid and invites very favourable comparison with some of the awful residences that planners do sanction throughout our rural landscape.

But sadly, we all know deep down that he can't win. As the saying goes – "You can't beat city hall." More's the pity.

4th June 2010

Watching *Britain's Got Talent* this week with my family, we all got similarly amazed and emotional about Tina and her dog Chandy. If you haven't seen the programme you won't know what I'm talking about. In précis – a lady and a dog both so mutually devoted that the dog willingly and lovingly dances with her in a way that would not disgrace the prima ballerina-ette of Twinkletoes Junior Academy of Dance. Audience, voters and jaded Simon Cowell all melted with a collective 'AWWWW' and the delightful duo is through to tomorrow's final with the chance to appear at the Royal Variety Show later in the year. I suspect that Her Maj, who is allegedly not a great fan of the performing arts, preferring the racecourse to the stage, would be right-royally delighted to see this beguiling refugee from the dog pound strutting her happy, doggy stuff at the Palladium. With due deference to the superb athletes, dancers and singers all vying for that honour, I believe the nation might well share my hope that Chandy will get her moment of glory.

This tale coincides with Baker Towers acquiring a rescue dog. Suzie, the gentle and sweet ex-racing greyhound, may not be able to do a soft shoe shuffle nor do her eyes never leave those of us, her adopters, in grateful adoration. Indeed, she has taken to the life of luxury now afforded to her with consummate ease, it seems. Her eyes never leave the fridge door, nor the cupboard that contains the dog food. She has learned that chasing the cats is a no-no swiftly enough and even tolerates the goat swaying across her recumbent form in search of something edible only by goats.

I have investigated, via the tattoos in her ears, the history of our new resident. She was bred in Eire (where else?), and raced in this country three times, coming sixth in a field of six in each race, the last of which was in January this year. Two months later she was handed in to a dog-warden by a man who left a non-existent phone number, whence she eventually arrived in Stokenchurch.

At least her treatment was somewhat better than that meted out to other less fortunate canine rejects, including a dog with its ears cut off to avoid identification, and then just dumped. If only we were the people that our dogs think we are.

24th August 2007

Anyone who has any doubt at all that the lunatics are now running the asylum need only scan the daily papers for a few moments.

And I am aware that those key words in the last sentence will probably attract the attention of the PC PCs.

In the last few weeks alone the following incidents have taken place in the UK:

A clerk working for the RAF has been awarded £484,000 for straining her thumb while inputting data on her computer. Compare this with the £57,000 awarded to a serviceman who loses a leg in action. How much would we get for strained credulity?

A pensioner in Wiltshire has been told she can no longer tend a small flowerbed in Urchfont, where she lives, unless she puts out three warning signs, wears a fluorescent jacket and employs a lookout.

Bournemouth Council has banned its swimming pool employees from loaning armbands to children in case they catch something nasty while blowing them up.

A Jamaican-born dustman has been ordered not to wear a St. George's Cross headband at work on the grounds that it is racist. He now sports a skull and crossbones headband which is considered acceptable by his worryingly blinkered employers. I like his style.

In the same week as we read of the appalling behaviour of a minority, but a sizeable minority, of young people, there is a story of mother in Bedfordshire who was being investigated by the police for inappropriate parenting. When her child had a tantrum in a shop she took her outside, put her in the car, closed the car door and stood a few feet away watching until the toddler calmed down.

To me that sounds a rather good strategy.

And, unbelievably, an 18 year old science student from Bedfordshire has been banned from applying for an Environment Agency flood management training course because she is English... She was told that only applicants from ethnic minorities could apply. Apparently Irish, Welsh and Scottish would be acceptable.

In an age when most local authorities and government departments are struggling with diminishing budgets, may I suggest that a very good way to save a shed-load of money would be to release onto the job market the bureaucrats who make all these ridiculous and irritating decisions? Though, heaven knows, I would be hard pressed to think of any useful contribution they could make in any capacity for anyone else.

5th June 2009

The debate over politicians' expenses rumbles on fuelled by the gleeful media.

The whole farrago started when the government of the day lacked the courage to present to the public salary increases for MPs that might appear excessive to the man on the Clapham omnibus but which, in the world of business, would have been considered modest.

It is pointless to compare the salary of your elected MP with that of a nurse or teacher, however tempting it can be to highlight the difference in their perceived contribution to society. The blunt truth is that an MP does have to maintain an office with staff and in many cases does have to run two homes in order to function in both constituency and Parliament.

However, in a pusillanimous attempt to disguise what was intended to be a salary increase, an expenses system was constructed with 'nod and a wink' encouragement to claim expenses up to an amount that made the total salary acceptable. A culture then developed in which, as long as you had a bit of paper with proof of expenditure on it that fitted the jigsaw of the claimant's intended total payment expectation, then you just chucked it at the appropriate office and waited for the money. Some, but not all, of the utterly preposterous were rejected.

It may well be that any reluctance to appear dishonest was quietened by the belief that they were merely receiving their proper salary via a different mechanism, but if a better honey trap could ever be set up, I don't know what it is. And the thing that this ludicrous bait threw up with clarity beyond the greatest anarchist's possible expectation is just how stupid these people are whom we have elected to represent us in Parliament. No one thought about the possible reaction of a citizen whose tax office had disallowed as an expense the newspaper on his hotel bill. No one said (loudly enough, anyway), "Hang on, not only is this ridiculous, it is suicidal." And if they weren't bright enough to see the potential electoral meltdown ahead of them, then they simply aren't the right people for the job.

Maybe this self-inflicted cull will leave us with the MPs who have that winning combination of intelligence, dignity, principles and scruples.

The inner London ones are just lucky, despite what they may have thought originally, as the gravy train chugged by!

23rd November 2007

There was a story in the papers last week that highlighted two points very starkly for me, one of which was depressing, the other uplifting.

It concerned a postmaster in Rochdale, the town in which I spent the first twelve years of my life. A thief stole the British Legion poppy collection tin from his post office. The theft was recorded on the shop's CCTV system and the police were informed of that fact. But no-one from the local police station, which was 300 yards from the shop, came to review the tape and a week later he received a letter informing him that "all lines of enquiry" had been investigated and the case had been closed.

This was a depressingly familiar story, of which I have heard many similar versions over the last few years. Petty crime has little chance of being investigated when dwindling financial and manpower resources are available to investigate them. I still find it hard to understand why this should be the case when we are, as a nation, better off and subject to higher taxation than we were when I was a young man and when a policeman on the beat was a welcome and familiar sight in those same streets, and when the smallest offence was worthy of rapid and effective attention. Could it be connected with the time dedicated to paperwork, targets and policies, which have gradually replaced beat work and policing? Anyway, the worst thing about the story, apart from the despicable nature of the crime, is the fact that we are probably less surprised than perhaps we would like to be to hear it.

The uplifting part? Well the postmaster's name is Harbinder Singh Dhillon. He was so incensed by the insult to his country's war dead that he has replaced the amount stolen from his pocket and sent stills from the CCTV footage to the national press in the hope that the culprit could be identified by the public. Perhaps then the police might be persuaded to act? At a time when immigration is a hot topic and its beneficial effects might be overlooked, it is heartening that a man who is either a recent immigrant himself or whose family have only within a generation or two been living in the UK should identify so strongly with those who sacrificed themselves for this country and care so passionately about remedying the situation.

2. Baker Towers

I have dedicated this book to my daughters because they and my wife Marion have been the keystone and motivating factor in my life for the last three decades. I do not pretend that I am in any way unique in this, but that does not make it in any way less true. I have greatly enjoyed my career, and have been lucky to have earned my living doing a job that I love, but it all makes sense when I close the door behind me at the end of a day, week, or months work and rejoin my family.

I have referred to my home as Baker Towers for many years, both in my writing and elsewhere. It is slightly tongue in cheek of course, but it is also a very real reflection of how I view my home. There is a notional drawbridge and portcullis and my home is both my sanctuary and my inspiration.

The following selection offers you a glimpse of what goes on in the inner keep – and the dungeons of course.

18th September 1999

When I was growing up there was always at least one animal in our home. I am grateful to my parents for that, because I learned to value the company and beneficial effect of pets. Occasionally, we have small visitors at our house who have not so benefited and are consequently mortally terrified by a friendly dog or inquisitive cat. Clearly, a sensible respect for unknown animals is advisable, but leaping up and down, screaming with terror in front of an otherwise amiable sabre-toothed terrier could provoke said STT to respond unthinkingly and painfully stop the irritation and noise.

Just as dangerous are the children who erroneously believe that all animals are as docile as their parents' toothless, overweight Labrador and therefore attempt to tie knots in a sleeping beagle's ears.

There are few animals, however well-trained, who would fail to snap if rudely and violently woken from dreams of pursuing king-size tins of Marrowfat Doggo across a field populated by cats the size of horses.

Those who have lived with dogs and cats all their lives make no assumptions about the behaviour of animals based on their superficial appearance. Indeed, a disgruntled miniature poodle could take out a whole class of Rising Fives, whilst that slavering beast with the spiked collar that resembles something out of an early evening Channel 5 epic, might just as easily roll over in gooey ecstasy to have its tummy tickled by a toddler.

Many of my clearest and happiest memories from my childhood are connected to animals. The rabbits – one black and white and the other brown; Parker the aristocratic cat who refused to enter the house when we suddenly acquired a bull terrier called Bonzo. At more or less the moment that poor old ugly-but-lovely-with-it Bonzo kept his appointment with destiny and a Hillman Minx, Parker, after months of self imposed exile, returned to his favourite chair in the kitchen, a good half hour before my father returned home with news of the dog's demise.

You know I am hard-pressed to bring to mind the name of a single child that was in my class in the first two schools I attended up to the age of 9, but all the pets are still frozen in the aspic of deep affection in my mind's eye. They never let you down and they were companions, confidants, and playmates. Dogs are better at the latter as their companionable nature enables them to fulfil the roles of armies, Indians, detective's bloodhound, dinosaur. Cats tend to have their own script and a lofty disdain for the plans of others.

From the age of 12 my soul-mate was a Dalmatian called Barney. He saw me through the anxieties and crises of puberty; he calmly endured my despair at the inability of my parents to cherish their own resident teenage alien. He understood me. I took him for long walks that enabled me in later years to loiter near the homes of certain teenage girls in order to feign casual surprise at meeting them on passing their bay-windowed semi for the umpteenth time. He was my best mate, my excuse for almost everything and occasionally my counsellor. He wisely let me do most of the talking.

Wind forward thirty years and we seem to have rescued a female Dalmatian.

She is young, sassy and beautiful. But she is stone-deaf, chases cats, is greedy, irritates our Jack Russell and is oh so energetic.

Just how do you train a deaf dog?

17th July 1998

When we built a new kitchen onto our house ten years ago, we were steered by the company providing the units and fixtures towards the purchase of a new and rather expensive European fridge/freezer and dishwasher. An attractive discount, coupled with the fact that the company's fittings were designed to accommodate this particular brand, was persuasive.

I suppose ten years is not a bad life span for a fridge and ours has started to show distinct signs of fridgezeimer's disease. It forgets to get cold and then when it suddenly remembers what it was designed for, it goes berserk. Clearly, despite the fact that this summer hasn't been too much of a threat to the freshness of unrefrigerated food, when the butter is continually wrapped in soggy paper and the interior is reminiscent of a Santa's winter wonderland in the Chiltern Centre, then the time has come to take action.

I telephoned the manufacturers and a helpful engineer identified the compressor as the likely culprit. A new one would cost at least two or three hundred pounds. Furthermore, - if it was not possible to effect a repair - I would have to pay a call-out charge of fiftyish pounds for the luxury of being informed of that.

"You'd be better off getting a new fridge, sir, after all ten years' use is not bad, you know."

This didn't sound too unreasonable, I thought, until I made a couple of calls to find out how much it would cost me to replace it. The only one that would fit was - surprise, surprise - the current model of the larder fridge presently in place. A few phone calls later I plucked my lower jaw off the floor and went in search of the smelling salts.

The cost of a replacement would be in the region of £700 to £800 pounds, inclusive of fitting.

So I returned to the phone and the manufacturers' repair agents in Uxbridge.

A repair, if possible, would not only cost between two and three hundred pounds for parts but there would also be a £47.90 call out charge for the first 18 minutes, with an additional £3.17 for every six minutes thereafter

And I still hadn't been able to put my hands on those smelling salts. I decided to shop around. A few phone calls to friends and a recommendation or two later, I was able to get some competitive quotes for expert assistance. I am amazed that there are presumably people out there who are prepared to pay the sums now required from the big, brand approved repairers for the privilege of simply turning up. A friend of ours had a recent experience of similar charges per minute for a domestic repair job and said that she couldn't even bring herself to offer the chap a cup of tea, as it would cost her a tenner for him to drink it.

I contacted a well-recommended local firm. For a little over fifteen quid, after a quick inspection of the offending refrigerator-turned-humidifier, I learned that new compressors in sludged-up old fridges were really not a good idea and that replacement was the only real option. This is when you suddenly realise that the fitted unit that seemed such a nice idea in those distant rosy 80's, doesn't leave a lot of manoeuvring space in the priced-by-the-minute 90's.

Yes, we have computers, CD's, digital mobile phones and the Internet, but there are also no more proper hardware shops where you can take in the item you bought twenty years earlier and get a similar one from a cardboard box on the top shelf. Everything is blister-packed, homogeneous and oh-so-disposable now. And money is clearly considered the most easily-disposable commodity of the lot!

25th February 2000

I freely admit to having many strongly held views that cause embarrassment to my family. I believe, for instance, that if you are paying for something you are entitled to have and, when appropriate, express an opinion about the service you are getting.

Therefore, it is only after a small struggle, that I overcome my native English reticence and tell it how it is, usually to the accompaniment of urgent, whispered entreaties from my family not to cause a scene. Clearly, I should regard those twenty long minutes before a waiter ambles nonchalantly over, to ask whether we would like to order some drink or food, as a welcome opportunity to spend quality time with my family and work up an appetite.

When a shop assistant tells me that there is no demand for something that I have just asked for, at least I don't succumb to the overpowering temptation to perform exploratory surgery to see if they are in possession of what might pass for a brain. But I do point out, as mildly as I can in the face of such provocation, that there clearly is some demand; am I not standing there, flesh and blood, with legal tender in hand, asking for it?

This is the point where they suggest that I write to their chief buyer, who is at that moment away on an inter-personal skills-development course, learning how to pacify customers who want to purchase things that they don't want to sell. Apparently Tesdasafesainsrose don't make enough profit stocking items just for me and the handful of other deviants who want Vegemite or chilli burgers.

All parents are also familiar with the desperate entreaties not to cause a scene at school - when a child comes home and says that Wayne Thug set fire to their school bag, and then the teacher shouted at them for handing in charred homework.

My current battle is with Microsoft and the supplier of my computer. I don't balk at the big ones, do I? One of my delicate offspring has trodden on a computer disk containing all the graphics in the publishing programme they use. I thought that I would be able to purchase a replacement disk. Oh no. Hollow laugh.

Microsoft says I must contact my original computer supplier, who no longer supply that programme. Apparently I am supposed to buy the whole package again – all three disks.

I shall set about these institutions with all the weapons at my disposal – interminable whingeing, moaning, sarcasm, e-mails, whispering campaigns and pins in wax dummies.

No-one can be bothered to stock or sell spares of anything any more. Try and buy the flange grommet from the bracket that secures the car's back seat and you'll be told that you can only buy the seat with bracket assembly as one item, which will set you back more than the cost of a second hand Austin Allegro.

Another embarrassing burden that I heap on my children is a disinclination to break the law by letting them join friends whose parents apparently allow children as young as 13 and 14 to watch films certificated 18.

My children do however, I believe, ultimately reap the benefit. They get to see the films when they are equipped to understand and derive enjoyment from them, rather than be confused and struggle to appear worldly-wise ahead of their years.

Yet again I find myself pleading for children to be permitted to have a childhood before they're subsumed by the stark though celluloid realities of a far from child friendly world.

22nd August 2003
I remember first visiting London Zoo decades ago and spending an uncomfortable few minutes watching Guy the Gorilla and not really being sure why those minutes were so uncomfortable.

It is perhaps fanciful of me to suggest that Guy was reproaching us, the onlookers, for the mind-numbingly miserable existence he had to endure. But he would have been perfectly justified in doing so. In fact, Guy became emblematic of all the traumatised victims of what was, in the bad old days, nothing more than a public parade of captured trophies. We have moved on considerably since those unenlightened days, when animals were collected together in inadequate, undersized spaces with little thought given to their physical or mental health.

I visited Whipsnade this week and was hugely impressed by its evolution into something that transcends the Alcatraz style of zoo of my childhood. The modern zoos are, in many cases, the only hope for the continuation and preservation of endangered species that otherwise might vanish all too soon. Even the apparently omnipresent chimpanzee is now officially classified as being endangered, as their natural habitats are reduced and they continue to be hunted for the bushmeat trade. Now, instead of being encouraged to "ape" human behaviour by having parodies of tea parties, the chimps live in a stimulating environment with plenty to occupy them and in which they forage for food that is hidden in logs around their enclosure, or frozen inside blocks of ice.

We are, as a species, beginning to recognise the responsibility that goes hand in hand with the advantages that we have been able to enjoy as a result of being the winner in the evolutionary lottery. I derive great satisfaction from the knowledge that the Zoological Society of London, that runs Whipsnade and London Zoo, are collaborating with zoos worldwide to institute breeding programmes that are proving so successful as to be able to re-introduce into the wild species that had recently only existed in captivity.

I felt privileged, rather than embarrassed, to see a European Brown Bear investigating the interior of an orange in the sunlight, or an elephant playing, like a child, in its own version of an Olympic swimming pool. Even the tricks performed by those old stagers, the California Sea lions, were designed to replicate the skills they would have to demonstrate in the wild in order to survive, rather than simply to entertain their human visitors.

I like the human race better when I can see it valuing the wonderful diversity of the world we have been given to strut our stuff in. Even the children whose parents think discipline is a proprietary brand of painkiller and who as a result feel free to pursue and screech at the small animals that roam freely in the park, were unable to dampen my sprits for long. If you were put off zoos in the bad old days when rows of sullen creatures cowered behind iron bars, give Whipsnade a visit and see what they're doing to redress the balance.

And you can learn a thing or two. Not just about rhino horn being made of hair, or giraffes having the same number of bones in their necks as us.

Our goats (Dusty McSporran and Rusty Brown, named in honour of the Wycombe Wanderers' players!), will be the beneficiaries too, when we've built them the cleverly designed stepped goat platforms we saw in the children's farm.

13th July 2007

It is not just because I was once a time traveller that I have an active interest in the past. I started to investigate my ancestry a couple of years ago and found that I was not alone in doing so. The increase in revenue to the various record offices supplying birth certificates, census records, etc. has been exponential, apparently. We may be the first generation that has been so actively curious about their ancestors. Perhaps it is because, as a society, we are becoming more fragmented and feel an increasing need to establish any kind of roots... After a couple of years of intermittent foraging for information I have managed to get back as far as seven generations along some lines. I find it fascinating, even though my ancestors were almost without exception of the humblest labouring stock.

The researches of course leap to life when there are photographs to accompany the names. Clearly this is only available to a limited extent. But how those faces, poses, clothes speak volumes.

That is why I am delighted to have been invited to assist in the launch of an exciting project in Wycombe this Friday evening - sharing Wycombe's old photographs – otherwise known by the acronym SWOP. The Library Service has managed to access Lottery Heritage funds to catalogue and digitise around 18,000 photographs which are now online for public access via the internet on the Bucks CC website.

A search engine offers a wide variety of categories and I spent a fascinating hour or so this week discovering the history of theatres in Wycombe. Residents who have lived in the area longer than my meagre three decades will doubtless remember the Intimate Theatre in Temple End, where it appears the late Jack Hulbert appeared in 1960. It is not mentioned whether his wife Dame Cicely Courtneidge accompanied him on that occasion. But how many recall The Electroscope Theatre, later the Electric Theatre and Skating Rink in Frogmoor?

Or the Majestic Theatre in Castle Street? Or the Primitive Methodist Chapel that became The Palace Cinema, next door to the old Swimming Baths?

Local Studies specialist Chris Featherstone and Project Manager Mike Dewey have gathered together a phenomenal and precious archive which anyone with even the slightest interest in local history will find fascinating.

I particularly liked a stunning colour photograph of the fountain (yes I said fountain!) in Frogmore in 1910.

4th July 1997

In common with hundreds of others in the Wycombe area , I have the misfortune of living in close proximity to the M40. When the motorway was upgraded, widened and extended to Birmingham, compensation was very properly payable to those whose adjacent properties were blighted by the works carried out. However, when it came to assessing the amount of compensation due, the levels of settlement were by no means generous.

The law apparently provided only that we should be compensated for the extra traffic carried as a result of the widening of the section between Cressex and Stokenchurch and not for the vehicles attracted to the road as a result of its extension to the Birmingham Motorway interchanges with the M6, M5 and M1. The justice or logic of this arbitrary apportionment has never been explained. If the principle of compensation is accepted, it is patently absurd that it should not be awarded honestly, on the basis of actual compensation for actual loss. The reason for the reliance on this arbitrary apportionment is however all too clear. It is to save money, by making the inhabitants of Cressex, Lane End, Wheeler End, Bolter End, Cadmore End and Stokenchurch subsidise the construction of the very road which is blighting their lives. And that is too much to bear.

Most of us believe that we cannot have the intended benefits of a motorway system without a corresponding diminution in the quality of the countryside through which it passes.

However, it is unfair to compel a few people to carry a loss greater than that borne by the rest of the motorway using population. We are in effect paying twice. Once - with everyone else - through our taxes, and again through the demonstrable and quantifiable loss in value of our properties. Some homes are frankly unsellable and yet their owners have been paid only a fraction of the amount they have actually lost. Having exchanged letters interminably with the Dept. Of Transport and the Valuers appointed by the Department I was offered a fraction of what even the negotiating agent acknowledged I had lost. But as soon as one house owner accepts a package of compensation, with whatever justice, then the negotiators use the device of linkage to keep all other awards down. Your neighbour accepted x, you have a similar house; we cannot therefore in justice give you more than x. The logic is devastating and effective. Divide and conquer.

There is an appeals procedure via the Lands Tribunal. But the sting in the tail is that the Tribunal has the power to award costs. So, even if you conduct your own case against the might of a Government Department, on the basis that you cannot afford the services of a barrister, in the event that you lose your claim, you could and probably would have to pay the costs of the Department's lawyers, which might be measured in tens of thousands of pounds.

This was the Hobson's Choice that prompted me along with hundreds of others to accept an offer at least 60% below the actual loss in value of their homes, and that is before taking into account any compensation paid for air and light pollution.

The Stokenchurch Village Protection Society, those stalwarts who have fended off several attempts to build Motorway Service Areas in their village, have taken up cudgels again to persuade the Department to take another look at the justice of the levels of compensation they have paid. Their MP David Liddington is supporting the re-opening of the claims on the basis that compensation should have been paid for the full effects of upgrading the M40. I urge everyone who feels they have been inadequately compensated to contact their MP, the Dept of Transport and the Stokenchurch Action Group, c/o 3, The Dell, Stokenchurch. I'm going to.

29th August 2003

I am about to enter a new phase in the process of easing my children out of the nest into a turbulent and uncertain world. University looms. My oldest daughter is off there any minute now, lugging shed loads of cash with her for the privilege.

If I were to have a chip in the area of my shoulders, it would be that my father, for reasons that seemed good to him at the time, refused to allow me to join the ranks of a group of young people for whom he had little time – students. And that, perversely, was in the age when grants were available for further education.

I am therefore delighted that my daughter will have the opportunity that I was denied. But I must confess that I am somewhat miffed that my reluctance to stand up to a strong father resulted in my inability to avail myself of the state-funding investment in my and the country's future that was then available, and that I find myself today faced with an unenviable alternative. Either I sell all the Baker family treasures (there goes the dog, my Harry Secombe autograph and collection of Dalek salt cellars) or I sell only some of them and my daughter starts her working life with the repayment of a student loan hanging over her for a decade afterwards.

And thus far no-one has explained to me why we could afford to support the education of our young people three decades ago, but cannot now.

And it's not just the £1200 share of the tuition fees. There are innumerable extras. Memberships, bonds, deposits, insurances, registration fees, landing fees and heaven knows what – and that's before the student even begins to think of accommodation or food. And the same government that has put a price on further education has added a straw on the back of this particular camel that, for some reason, has really hacked me off. When I drop my daughter off in a couple of weeks' time, if she has a television with her, then I will have to also pay another licence fee for that television, even though it has hitherto been covered by my licence at home. No compromise here. Every student in a hall of residence has to have one; and the welcome literature warns of detector vans that roll into the avenues of academe within milliseconds of their arrival. Now is that mean or what? When you have no income and might be very grateful for the telly sometimes for free entertainment in between your studies, then the state makes you pay a fiver a week more for the privilege (university terms being as short as they are).

I have discovered that there is a loophole. If the television is solely battery-operated, then for some undisclosed reason it is exempt from the licence fee. Three years of licence fee is about £400, so a portable telly costing less than that would result in a net profit and leave us with an asset, should any of my other offspring opt for university.

But, dear reader, can I find one? Not in Wycombe. Not even for ready money. And the internet has thus far proved unhelpful too, for anything other than the tiniest of pocket sets. And why hasn't someone invented a wind-up telly?

Someone will tell me there's no demand. I may throttle them.

3. Eco Warrior

I am not alone in thinking that we humans are often more of a blight on this fragile planet than we are a benefit. And there are many, many more people who really do a substantial amount of very good work in counteracting our deleterious effects on the environment than I do my merely whingeing about it on a regular basis in print. But every little helps.

Every day there are new examples of the profligate consumption of our natural resources and despite all the posturing of the commercial giants about their green policies – every time I look at what is left behind when I remove the thing I have actually bought from its layers of protective, decorative or size enhancing packaging, I realise that we still have a long way to go. We all agree. Or so it seems. So why is progress towards a less wasteful consumer society so slow?

12th June 1999

I cashed in some points on my credit card this week in return for a computer programme for my children.

It came in a large cardboard box, inside which was another cardboard box, inside which there was an elaborate origami construction made of – yes – cardboard. This held a plastic CD case, snugly encased in cellophane – to protect it from harmful cardboard emissions, I suppose.

The fact that the outer box was probably large enough to contain a hundred CD's is probably a direct result of the desire of the manufacturer to have the maximum surface space upon which to emblazon improbable claims for the product inside.

They don't trust us to understand that size really isn't everything and that something as small as a computer disk might actually have a lot of useful information on it, so they dress it up in fancy clothes, several sizes too big.

This rampant waste is matched in profligacy only by the extra price our noses have to pay for them to be able to contribute so lavishly to the headlong consumption of our finite resources.

(Why exactly are we said to "Pay through the nose" for something?)

I am a born again re-cycler and would never dream of throwing bottles, cans or recyclable paper into my domestic refuse bin. So now the discarded packaging which encases almost any purchase is forming an ever-increasing proportion of our weekly garbage. And all of that bubble wrap, expanded polystyrene packaging and cellophane is going to be a long time biodegrading down the old infill site!

A small percentage of the packaging is inevitable, for reasons of hygiene, for instance.

But who reading these words does not mourn the passing of the hardware shop, where you could buy the exact quantity of nails, screws, brackets and hinges you needed instead of those awful blister packs? Do ballpoint pens have to be individually packaged? Or birthday cards? Even wrapping paper is sold wrapped!

Developing my theme of rubbish, I still find it more than frustrating that the only day on which I, as a driver of a 4x4, can take my excess domestic waste to my local tip is a Saturday. As well as being the busiest garbage dumping day, this is more often than not, in my job, the only day I actually can't get there.

As I write this article I am looking out of the window at a pile of rusty old garden chairs, and other accumulated bulky refuse which on this particular idle weekday I am unable to take to the tip, unless I am prepared to lug each item under the height restriction barrier and incur consequent damage to my middle aged vertebrae and the wrath of my osteopath.

There is still a nasty little voice whispering in my ear urging me do wicked things.

It tells me to tip the said rubbish on the doorsteps of those councillors who voted for the wretched barrier and then realised that they had thereby alienated a powerful and vociferous chunk of the electorate. They then did some vote-saving wriggling and thought that the Saturday opening sop would restore their image. Wrong! It just serves to constantly underline the fact that I am paying for a service to which I do not have the same access as everyone else.

And don't give me that childless taxpayers still pay for education and people without cars pay for roads claptrap.

Everyone was a child once and everyone needs the products that are delivered by roads. And everyone generates rubbish.

And some councillors talk it too!

26th January 2007

We are all being encouraged, quite rightly, to recycle. The residents of Baker Towers are getting better at it all the time. The contents of our wheelie bin are dwindling weekly. Paper, cardboard, glass, metal, plastic bottles are all deposited at one of Wycombe's many recycling points – and never a special trip – always when we are going to or past that place anyway.

It is tricky sometimes to get full information. This week, for instance, we learned that the tetrapaks that contain fruit juice are not required on voyage in the cardboard recycling skip because they are waxed and therefore not recyclable. Oops! Sorry.

But the more we do our bit, it seems the less effort the retail outlets and manufacturers make. The packaging in which goods are sold gets steadily more comprehensive, to the point now of ludicrous excess.

Why do computer programmes on a CD have to be packaged in a box that would comfortably contain another hundred of them? Why does glass have to be smashed and reconstituted before it can be used again? Why can't we re-use them – a practice to be seen frequently in Europe? And what about bananas sold in a plastic tray covered in cling-film and then placed in a larger plastic bag?

The debris left after Christmas, when goods are given yet another layer of wrapping, was phenomenal and completely dwarfed the pile of goodies carried off by my children. All right, I am honestly not being Scrooge here, but if the goods themselves weren't already triple wrapped, then the festive tradition of wrapping gifts in colourful fancy paper wouldn't jar quite as much.

I bought a replacement ink cartridge for my printer recently. I opened a cardboard outer box, a foil bag, two outer plastic trays surrounding the replacement cartridge – and then, like a goodie in a lonely game of Pass the Parcel, I discovered the cartridge itself.

The manufacturers will only change their current practices if they feel we really mean it when we say "Enough."

I still mourn the departure of the old hardware shops when the blister pack was not in evidence and you could buy as many loose washers, screws, brackets and nails as you needed and pop them in one brown paper bag. And the friendly man selling them knew about his products and you could handle them before buying.

"Wake up Mr Baker – you're dreaming again."

19th September 2009

I am lucky enough to serve as a school governor in both the primary and secondary school sector. I say 'lucky' because, despite the work and responsibility involved, having continued access to the thoughts and aspirations of the next generation is a privilege.

However much we hear about the small disaffected minority of young people, the majority is much more tolerant and concerned about the future of the planet than our generation can claim to have been.

I recently visited a Primary School in Brill, Oxfordshire where a wind turbine and ground source heat pumps had been installed. They have reduced their power costs and now sell surplus electricity to the National Grid. This remarkable initiative by a small rural school has also had considerable educational benefit, the whole school being involved in the daily monitoring of the generation and use of energy.

I was saddened therefore to read of the reaction of some neighbours of Highworth School in Wycombe, who are objecting to the school's application to erect a similar wind turbine in their playing field. They object to the visual blight, although we have all lived with pylons for decades in order to obtain a domestic electricity supply. Turbines do not, I would suggest, blight a panorama any more than any other man made construction; I would go further indeed and say that they have a certain grace and majesty. There is a phalanx of turbines astride the moors west of Bodmin that are far more pleasing to the eye than any power station. When my family go down to Cornwall, we eagerly anticipate the sight of their graceful demonstration of man's quest for clean energy.

Much too is made of the wind farms' impact on bird life. The RSPB itself concludes however that there is no evidence of "any major adverse effects on birds associated with wind farms" in the UK and has even backed the siting of a nature reserve in Wales adjacent to a wind farm. It is worth adding that it is estimated that 10 million birds are killed by cars in the UK every year. The effects of climate change and the exhaustion of fossil fuels however will inevitably adversely affect birds and humans alike.

It was the children of Highworth School that instigated this initiative. They are the ones who will have to live in the post-carbon world that will be the legacy passed on to them by previous generations.

26th September 1997

When I was visiting friends recently while working in the North East, I presumed to instruct them on the proper disposal of one of those plastic frameworks of circles that are used to connect six cans of beer or fizzy drinks for easy carrying. I had been told some years ago that small animals foraging in waste disposal sites were getting their snouts and heads inextricably caught in these things which, as a result, rather restricted their ability to do any further effective foraging. The remedy, I was told, was to cut up these six plastic racks into pieces that did not contain any potentially dangerous holes. Being a born again re-cycler I have scrupulously done so ever since.

By one of those extraordinary coincidences that make life so unpredictable, whilst I was in mid-educational flow, the telephone rang, much to the probable relief of my enforced audience. It was my wife to tell me that I had been invited to open two newly built rehabilitation pools at St. Tiggywinkle's Wildlife Hospital in Haddenham, of which I am honoured to be a vice-president. The money for the pools had been provided by the very company that manufactures these plastic whatsits. I was diverted to learn that this company is called the Illinois Tool Works - a title that offers plenty of opportunity for ribald jokes, hence I imagine their abbreviation to the acronym ITW. They have now introduced a re-cycling scheme which involves asking schools to collect these things - there must be a name for them, I'm sure, but I have failed to discover it - using Safeway Stores as a collecting point. The money raised by re-cycling the plastic is to be used to contribute to the funding of the construction of a much needed visitors' centre at St. Tigs.

It has long been a source of frustration to many hundreds of well meaning supporters of the Wildlife Hospital that they are not able to visit the animals in situ. Most people understand that this is not possible, when it is explained to them that an endless flow of benevolent humanity is not conducive to the speedy recovery of a badger with gunshot wounds, a deer that has been injured in a road traffic accident, a brain damaged hedgehog or a swan that has swallowed several metres of fishing line with hooks on it. Indeed, any hope of an eventual return to their natural habitat is eroded by any non-essential contact with humans. A continuing suspicion of our species has, alas, to be encouraged if the animals are to be returned safely to the wild, where not all human beings are as concerned for their well being as the Stockers and their helpers. Les, Sue and Colin, their son, with the help of their staff and loyal volunteers, have pioneered techniques for the treatment and care of animals which could not have been helped to recovery twenty years ago. They are a remarkable family and Les Stocker's MBE a few years ago was very proper recognition of his enormous contribution to the understanding and care of our indigenous wildlife. Indeed, vets world-wide now turn to Les for advice on the treatment of injured and sick wild animals.

It is good news that this imaginative initiative which is worthwhile in itself for finding a use for redundant plastic is capable of having the added benefit of creating areas around the Hospital where schools and other groups can learn more about its work and see some of the patients from purpose built vantage points that do not disturb the animals. Added value is very much a buzz phrase at the moment. I can think of no better example of real added value than this project.

And Les Stocker's book "The Complete Fox" is a must for anyone who really wants to know everything about that much maligned animal.

4. Colin vs. Public Transport

I should never have handed back the keys of my Tardis. (Not that I actually had much of an option there really!) As travel goes, despite the occasional - no who am I kidding – frequent navigational errors, there wasn't a great deal of other traffic around to cause a problem, and fuel, apparently, was not a problem. Zeiton ore lasts a long time it seems. And if you don't know what I'm talking about, you've probably been far too busy to watch television on a Saturday evening – or are very young. For the rest of us, whether it is by rail, road, air or motorised pogo stick, travel is invariably fraught with pitfalls, delays, frustrations and, most of all, expense.

It is interesting that all fictional depictions of future travel tend to reflect this desire to escape the awful truth – that travel is inevitably a tortuous, painful and costly enterprise. Will we ever have the individual, noiseless air car? Or be beamed up like good old Scotty? Who knows? But wouldn't it be nice?

16th July 2010

I'm sorry. It's my fault that the recent spell of hot weather has come to an abrupt end. I got my car's air conditioning fixed. It was only when this long hot spell started that I realised that it wasn't working. To be honest, there aren't that many occasions when its absence would be noted in the UK. But, we visited friends in East Sussex last week and sweltered both ways on the M25. Open windows on that particular tarmacadamed hell's highway would expose you to the risk of terminal carbon monoxide poisoning to add to the already mind-numbing tedium of the miles of crawling traffic. Anyway, the replacement pipe has been fitted and I collected my car just in time to see the thermometer plunge.

Another certainty, to accompany that fickle-finger-of-fate moment, is that most information displayed on motorway gantry signalling systems is out of date. I hope that is the case, because the alternative is that someone is having a laugh or incompetent. The long term messages tend to be accurate – for the very reason that they're there for a year or two, caused by those road works where there are sporadic flurries of nocturnal activity.

I returned from London earlier this week just as the evening rush hour was starting and the gantries proclaimed that there would be queuing traffic on the slip road going up to Handy Cross, so if we were leaving the motorway there we should be jolly careful. And quite right too, if that were the case. That slip road can get quite tricky at the best of times, given its strange and illogical lane subdivision.

However, I am sure that those of you who drive regularly will not be surprised when you hear that this was the first and only occasion that I have ever driven up the slip road and around Handy Cross without stopping anywhere along the way.

The omnipresent cameras along the motorways have the capacity to record average speeds in order to prosecute us for speeding offences. Why can't the cameras that watch the traffic network be similarly responsive? Why can't we get consistent, accurate and current information about traffic, so that we don't have situations where several hundred cars are creeping along at 40 mph on a trouble-free motorway because no one has cancelled a warning about a long remedied problem?

28th October 2005

We all do stupid things sometimes. Some of us stretch the definition of "sometimes" towards the outer edges of "often." I exceeded myself last week.

I should start by explaining that the worst crime in the actor's pantheon of misdemeanours is not, as you might think, overacting or even bumping into the furniture and failing to know your lines – it is being late. If you are late in the theatre the audience is left in those uncomfortable seats wondering why nothing is happening and wishing they were at home watching Celebrity Chiropodist Challenge. In film and television it is even worse. The expense of keeping a whole film crew standing around because you are stuck in traffic or didn't get your alarm call means that the producers will be very unlikely to see you as an essential part of any subsequent venture unless you are Marilyn Monroe – and even with the divas the balance sheet has to end up in the black most of the time.

So, having spent four decades working in a profession where being late is roughly comparable to offering garlic bread to a vampire, I found myself doing that stupid thing last Wednesday.

I was working in Birmingham, recording an episode of the BBC daytime soap Doctors. I left home at 5:45 a.m. to ensure being on set three hours later in Selly Oak. As I reached Oxford Services on the M40 I noticed that I was low on petrol and filled up. Thirty miles further on I noticed a smell of petrol and realised that I had already used half a tank. I was losing petrol somehow but instead of stopping and summoning assistance, I reacted only to the actor's imperative to "get me to the set on time" and carried on my journey, filling up one more time and then watching the petrol gauge move steadily and visibly back towards the empty mark. I worked out afterwards that my fuel consumption for the journey was around two miles to the gallon.

The breakdown man who replaced the faulty jubilee clip on the flexible fuel hose that was casting my gasoline recklessly to the tarmac told me that I was lucky to be alive. Had the fuel pipe been on the same side of the car as the exhaust pipe I would, in his opinion, have deprived the crematorium of the opportunity to supervise my immolation.

Next time I'll risk the endorsements on my equity card I think.

15th August 2008

In bringing up the issue of the hounding of the motorist, I will inevitably provoke the "Well if you don't want to get caught, then don't break the law" response from the ranks of the righteous. But – to save them writing in – I will tell myself that, okay?

But - when I started driving, many moons, suns and galaxies ago, there were just two speed limits – 30mph in built-up areas and whatever you liked really everywhere else. There weren't signs every two yards changing the speed limit or warning you about bus lanes, cameras, freeways, congestion zones, etc.

Most of us drove well enough back then and did so by reference to the road conditions and common sense. Yes, there is much more traffic on the roads now, but do we really need the profusion of road traffic signs that now clog up our roads? Come on, admit it – how many of you, after seeing a speed camera on the roadside ahead, have desperately looked in every direction to check the speed limit and slowed down to thirty just in case, only to discover the limit is actually fifty, after you have passed the cash generating yellow box?

Driving is now comparable to a computer game, where you have to pick up information every few seconds in order to avoid falling foul of the law.

Take bus lanes. You see a sign indicating a bus lane is ahead. Then, travelling at 30mph and keeping an eye on the road, you have to find the sign that tells you the times of this particular bus lane. Because if, unsure of the finer detail, you sit in the outside line to avoid the risk of prosecution, you will provoke the irate motorist behind you, who travels that road regularly, into overtaking you on the inside lane. On the other hand, if you take your eye off the road, in order to read the fine print, you run the risk of missing a real hazard in the road ahead.

In the good old days it was - lampposts? 30. No lampposts? Use your common sense.

A friend was recently prosecuted for driving at 32mph in a 30mph zone.

Our fear of racking up too many points is resulting in motorists spending too much time flicking anxiously between their speedometers and the roadside traffic signs, rather than looking at the road ahead.

19th June 2009

As I am currently not allowed to drive because I have been speeding, I am trying to minimise the inconvenience to my family and friends, who are all otherwise very generously suffering for my misdeeds. Whenever there is public transport available, I am using it. I am as a result experiencing what many suffer on a regular basis.

This week's joy came when I timed my business in Wycombe so that it finished in time to catch the 3:45 Carousel bus that would take me half a mile or so from my home, as opposed to other more regular buses that deposit me a mile or more away. There is only one of these buses in the afternoon.

I waited at the designated door and bay, having checked the display board first and seen that it confirmed the information in the timetable. I waited in vain. Three forty-five came and went. I was then informed by two ladies who had also been waiting for that bus that they had been told that it had already gone – from a different bay at the other end of the bus station.

I found a Carousel employee, who explained that the bus had 'probably not been able to get onto the allotted stand because the bus station was very busy at that time of day.' Why, I asked, had the illuminated display board not been changed to reflect that? Believe it or not, the departures board is pre-programmed and cannot be changed to reflect actuality, rather begging the question why, given this patent absurdity in a new state of the art bus station, there couldn't be large notice somewhere explaining that the display board might be telling porkies.

I then asked why an announcement couldn't be made of the change of stand for the bus. He said there was no public address system available to them. So given that there are several bus companies operating within the bus station, there must be many occasions where the first time user of a service is completely stranded by an unannounced changed departure point.

They even have notices telling us not to go outside, but to wait inside until the bus arrives – thereby ensuring we can't see the bus pull into a bay fifty yards away, if we happen to know what it looks like and our view isn't obscured.

Everything of course is done in the interests of the passengers – for our safety and convenience.

13th November 2009

Those of you who have followed my six months of enforced public transport as a result of my failure to obey speed limits and my glee at being restored to the convenience of car travel again will doubtless be diverted to read that I have already being reminded of the downside of driving. Last week I worked for four days in North West London. I decided to pay the congestion in advance, knowing my pre-disposition to forget to do it afterwards and incur penalty charges. I discovered that the website was out of action while they did mysterious things to it. As a result, I couldn't pay until my return home on Monday evening. The online service was still unavailable so I paid the £32 for Monday to Thursday using the telephone payment line. On Wednesday, I received an emailed receipt, dated that day for Tuesday to Friday, the Tuesday being charged at £10 as a 'late payment'. I immediately rang and pointed out that I had phoned on Monday and paid in advance, not arrear. The operator told me that there had been problems that week, so I could pay for the Monday at the £8 rate I suggested that the payment that they erroneously had down for Friday – when I would not be going to London – could be transferred to cover the Monday that I had in fact already paid for. They couldn't do that; I would have to pay for the Monday and then write and claim back the overcharge and they would check the original phone call.

I intend to do this, but may well find that days and weeks will pass when I haven't had time to go through the lengthy process that it will doubtless entail. I dare say that Transport for London make a pretty penny out of their failure to provide a proper service to their customers.

They really don't want us up there, of course, so it's not in their interest to make it easy. The consolation is that the studios in Ladbroke Grove that I visit frequently are currently in the outer London charging zone that the mighty Boris intends to unfetter from the congestion charge during the next few months.

And the reason I do not use public transport is that it takes me under an hour by car, and at least two hours by train/tube/bus. That's two hours of precious time each day.

6th April 2007

I make sporadic forays to London, never from choice but under circumstances of duress, like employment. I am currently rehearsing a play that will be touring the country from May to August (for culture lovers, it is *Bedroom Farce* by Alan Ayckbourn – at Wycombe Swan the week commencing 14th May!).

The producers - in their wisdom - have decided that the optimum spot to rehearse, being central for all participants, is Leicester Square. So I have discovered the joy that is the Oyster Card, a technology that had mercifully escaped my attention hitherto. Fortunately, there were sympathetic members of the public around to guide me, as I was jabbing the thing ineffectually at the wrong contact point, and to inculcate me into the mysteries of the 9:30 a.m. price barrier. I am already wondering how long it would take to walk.

In my section of the Piccadilly Line carriage there were five people shouting into mobile phones. The other passengers seemed oblivious or past caring. It would be slightly less tedious if the conversations that they were having were remotely interesting to anyone other than the direct participants, and I was staggered that even they felt them worth having. No details of corporate mergers or exciting indiscretions, but endless banalities. I resorted to popping in my earphones and listening to the radio but could still hear the girl sitting next me. When she bellowed "I knew you were going to say that!" followed by a manic cackle, I involuntarily muttered to myself, "No need for the phone call then!"

Well, I thought I muttered it. But you know how headphones can lull you into thinking you're whispering when the actuality is otherwise?

Suffice it to say that the West Indian lady sitting opposite me got a fit of the giggles and nodded in conspiratorial and sympathetic agreement. Her subsequent attempts not to laugh were infectious and the people either side of her started to smile too. Megaphone Mary sitting alongside me was mercifully oblivious, so immersed was she in her tedious cataloguing of what she said to him and what he said to her.

But that brief moment of catharsis was not enough to make the experience other than barely endurable. And some people have to do it every day. My heart goes out to them.

Today I am going to try the train. I hear hollow laughs from seasoned commuters.

1st March 2002

Undoubtedly, the steady forward crawl to gridlock on our roads is something that needs urgent attention. And on first glance, Ken Livingstone's decision to impose a £5 toll upon those who enter London in their cars seems to have the potential of going some way to reducing congestion and raising much needed funds for the revitalising of London's creaking and inefficient transport system.

However, it is an inescapable consequence that those with money will grit their teeth, pay up and benefit from the less congested roads that result from the absence of those cars whose drivers simply cannot afford to pay a fiver for the privilege of driving through road-works and carbon monoxide fumes.

I am an unashamed car lover. That is not to say that I have the slightest interest in discussing torque, new styling, badges, acceleration or spec. I am only interested in comfort, reliability and mobility. My affection for the motorcar stems solely from the fact that it liberates me from dependency on the unreliable and unappealing alternative.

Furthermore, my job makes it impossible for me to use public transport on any but the rarest occasion. The hours that I work are almost invariably well outside the normal parameters of the 9-to-5 commuter. When I am filming for television, I would normally be expected on location between 6 and 7 o'clock in the morning. The venue could be almost anywhere, as the days of television studio based programmes are long gone, with the exception of the soaps that have purpose-built lots. Otherwise, most filming takes places in "real" locations. In order to ensure the minimum of disruption to filming resulting from noise pollution, these are, wherever possible, well away from buses and trains. My last location was a house in the outskirts of Birmingham. In my car I was able to be there by 7:00 a.m. after a ninety-minute journey. In order to travel there by public transport, I would have had to leave the day before and book into a hotel.

I am currently touring with a theatre production of the Terence Rattigan play, *Flarepath*. When the curtain comes down at around 10:15 p.m. – in Basingstoke this week – were I reliant on public transport, I would have no means of getting home at all. In my car, I am home not long after 11pm. I value my home life and am happy to commute distances up to a hundred miles in order to be able to spend time with my family and sleep in my own bed. Clearly, if the proposed satellite charging for the miles I travel in my car were to come in, I would have to pay a premium for this.

I recently had no choice but to use public transport, as I was picking up my car from a garage on the south coast near Bournemouth. I got a lift into Lane End, my nearest village two miles from my home. I then caught a bus into Wycombe at around 8 a.m. Four and a half hours later I arrived at my destination in Hampshire at a total cost of just over £40.00. I drove back in 1 hour 40 minutes. The petrol cost me twelve pounds.

Give us decent, reliable and affordable public transport and we might be tempted to venture outside our mobile cocoons. The carrot always works much better than the stick!

5th March 2004

Either something happens to people when they find themselves in positions of authority, or only people of limited imagination and robotic tendencies seek employment in jobs where they have to exercise common sense. There are examples everywhere of a world significantly madder than anything Lewis Carroll ever came up with; you know that, I know that and almost everyone who can tell a hawk from a handsaw knows that. But nothing changes.

An off-duty policeman gets a parking ticket in Wycombe when he leaves his car in a disabled parking bay in order to apprehend a wanted criminal whom he has spotted. He tells his son to explain the situation to any ticket-issuing warden. The son does, to no avail. The ritual dance must be danced until all the participants are dizzy, bureaucracy has ground them into the dust and public money has been poured down the drain of stupidity, yet again.

Many years ago I was working in Hull. My car had blown up, the repairs had been botched once, and the manufacturers had accepted responsibility for the faulty engine that caused the second failure. When I picked it up two months later, I discovered that the tax had run out that day. I rang my flatmate in London to ask him to post me the documents I needed to renew it. I then (I thought sensibly) called in to the police station to tell them of my temporary problem and assure them that I was doing everything that I could to comply with the law, but that I had nowhere off road to put my car until the documents arrived. Not only could they offer no friendly reassurance, but when I arrived at the theatre that night a policeman stepped out of the shadows, headed straight for my out of date tax disc and issued me with a ticket.

I am cursed with what my critics might see as foolhardiness but I would characterise as a passion for justice. I spent more money going back up to Hull months later to explain my technical rather than premeditated offence. I summoned the officer whom I had asked for help at the Police Station as a witness; he confirmed that I had indeed gone to seek their help. The magistrates gave me an absolute discharge and expressed their irritation at the waste of time incurred in prosecuting someone who was clearly doing his best to comply with the law.

This week I have again been unable to renew my car tax because it appears that I never received the registration papers back from Swansea when I bought the car a year ago, as I discovered when I didn't receive the expected renewal form. I presented money, insurance certificate, MOT and old tax disc at the local post office but apparently they're not allowed to renew without the registration document any more. I telephoned Swansea in the hope that they could help. I offered immediate payment by credit card; I offered blood. I should have known better. I could either write to ask for a replacement for the documents that they never sent me (enclosing nineteen pounds) and wait a week or so – or go to Reading or Oxford in person – but not in my car, of course, as I would be committing an offence.

Oh, and the Buckinghamshire sturmbahnfuhrer of parking has refused to rescind the conscientious off-duty policeman's ticket. Malice in Blunderland.

23rd October 2009

Readers will react in a variety of ways, no doubt, to the news that I am back behind a wheel again. Reactions to my occasional musings about my enforced period of carless (sic) rapture (or is that 'rupture'?) have varied. There's the flawless citizen's "If you hadn't been caught speeding four times in three years, you wouldn't have been banned; no sympathy…" and the "There but for the grace of God…" - more sympathetic response. The former is undeniable; the latter offered more consolation, as I endured the vagaries of public transport, including the omnipresent mobile phone users.

I finally cracked last week when a middle aged man spent practically the whole of his journey from Wycombe to Marylebone arranging an event for the following day, over half a dozen phone calls, loudly enough for people at the other end of the carriage to hear how important he was. As we shuffled off the train, I thanked him for the thirty seconds of the journey that he was not bellowing down a phone. He did, I must own, apologise – but then went on to say how busy he was and how he couldn't afford to lose the opportunity to work on the train. I pointed out that he clearly thought his work was much more important than anyone else's, as his stentorian tones precluded the opportunity for anyone else to do anything other than listen to him. He shrugged and walked off. To put it in perspective, on another day another man had quite a long conversation – very quietly – on his phone and disturbed no one. It's not the use of the phone – it's the failure to adjust the volume to the surroundings.

But, my long-suffering wife no longer has to turn out at all times to pick me up from the station when the next bus isn't for another hour or so; or from the bus stop two miles away on the other occasions. She does not have to do all the school runs, all the shopping, all the visits to friends – and she will be able to have the odd drink too now, while I return the compliment and chauffeur her on social occasions. In most senses she has suffered much more than I have – and endured my grumpiness as I have been 'stranded at the drive-in'.

I take the opportunity therefore to thank her through this column.

19th October 2007

Driving back from rehearsals in Birmingham this week after dark and through teeming rain, I encountered my first major, seasonal outbreak of rear-fog-light-itis. It continues to astound me how many drivers are sufficiently incompetent to fail to judge the appropriate conditions in which these potentially lethal hazards should be used.

The law, as contained in The Highway Code, states that front or rear fog lights should only be used when visibility is seriously reduced. This is apparently interpreted as meaning that they shouldn't be employed unless you cannot see further than 100 metres (328 feet); it goes on to say that they must be switched off once the visibility improves. Certainly, using rear fog lights when visibility is greater than that can not only make it difficult to see the car's brake lights but can also dazzle the drivers following, thus increasing the risk of a rear-end collision rather than reducing it. In the case of my journey down the M40 this week, all those glaring rear fog lights did was reflect and magnify the spray thrown up by the vehicle illuminated and almost blind the drivers behind them. Once past the offending vehicles, the visibility reverted to the half mile and more that it would have been had they been more considerate, or if they had the wit and imagination to consider the effect on others of their knee-jerk reaction to the weather…

Because I was blinded, I was unable to check whether the drivers were also displaying those helpful little signs that inform other vehicles that they are carrying children in their cars - and which are designed to achieve precisely what?

Are we expected to have a look as we drive by and wave to the little darlings? Or perhaps we are being invited to congratulate the driver on his or her demonstrated ability to procreate?

I suspect that the idea is that having been tempted to drive far too close in order to read the wretched sign, we should then change our appalling driving habits in order to protect the very offspring that they have endangered by putting the blessed warning there in the first place.

I passed a car bearing one of these badges of parental prowess recently and noted that the driver was talking on her hand held mobile phone.

So much for caring for the safety of her child!

30th June 2007

If Ken Livingstone's intention is to stop people wanting to go to London, he has succeeded in my case. I have been working in Richmond every evening this week and have also been obliged to travel up on three days respectively to Westbourne Park, Putney and Kensington to do other work in assorted studios. I am not complaining, I insist, when I say that work for actors is like the proverbial buses; none turns up for what seems an eternity and then everyone wants you at once.

Ken's extension of the Congestion Zone further west has resulted in an exponential rise in the volume of traffic attempting to avoid entering the zone, which in turn caused a mind numbing one and a half hour journey from Chiswick to Putney – some four miles – for no reason that I could discern other than sheer volume of traffic.

A later journey from the BBC to Richmond – six miles – took an hour and a half. Were there a viable public transport alternative that would enable me to get home at all the same day, let alone in less time, and for less money and at the times I needed to get there, then I would have seized that golden alternative with both white-knuckled hands.

What is going to happen when millions of sports-loving tourists descend upon the capital in 2012, unless the transport infrastructure is radically overhauled and improved? Gridlock, I suspect.

Then I had the joy of visiting Westbourne Grove to record a Doctor Who audio adventure – yes, I am still allowed the keys of the TARDIS from time to time – not in vision mercifully, as the infamous multicoloured coat would probably be unable to take the strain.

My transport of delight was intensified when I returned to my car to find it had been clamped. I had bought a parking ticket for five pounds that covered the period for which I was parking (and more) but my mistake was clearly popping a spotted dog dashboard magnetic toy on top of it to hold it down. In any event, the attendant, doubtless ticketing me in the torrential rain, failed to spot it. One hundred and fifteen pounds and ninety minutes after discovering my first ever yellow boot, I was released and made it to the theatre for my evening show by the skin of my teeth.

How I envy those who can work from home.

5. Doctor Who

Even though I only spent three years as Old Sixie – 'the half way Doctor' (as I now am), I am happy to reflect on that time as one of the best and most exciting of my life. I was the Tardis key holder at a time when the poor old Doctor was not held in such high esteem as is enjoyed by the incumbents of the second millennium. Comparisons of actors and their respective charisma and abilities aside, the BBC itself was, it appeared, slightly embarrassed by this strange programme that was being kept alive, at the point at which I became involved with it, only by the single handed and determined efforts of John Nathan Turner.

He was a lone voice echoing insistently in the corridors of Threshold House in Shepherds Bush in the face of a management back in the 80's who neither understood nor sympathised with the appeal of a programme, that may well have needed a re-think and re-look, but was nonetheless beloved by enough viewers to invest the time in doing just that. When John eventually relinquished the reins it lapsed into the temporary obscurity of the television archives for more than a decade before the great Russell T Davis (who, I believe, would have found he had a lot in common with dear JNT) rescued and re-imagined the programme so dramatically.

It remains a large part of my life; and many of you who have bought, stolen or borrowed this book may well have done so because of an affection or dedication to Doctor Who.

I am still privileged to attend many events that celebrate the programme's past and present successes and I make no excuse for the fact that it has filled a few column inches over the years in my weekly contributions to the Bucks Free Press.

13th November 1999

When I sat in the office of the BBC's head of series and serials in the summer of 1983, he went to great pains to ensure that I fully understood the implications to my future life and career of taking on the most famous role on British television – the Doctor in Doctor Who. I, however, was made of the stuff that could not resist the opportunity to play intergalactic Cowboys and Indians for a few years and was unashamed to surrender willingly to the lure of temporary fame.

Even though I knew that there would eventually be a price to pay for my brief time in the spotlight, I am still proud that from 1983 to 1986 I was a hero to a generation of children who dived behind the sofa when the Daleks trundled on screen, waving those sink plungers from their pepper pot casings and, against all logic, striking absolute terror into audiences of all ages. At this point, I must pay tribute to Raymond Cusick, the BBC staff designer who responded so imaginatively and brilliantly to the one line description of those alien creatures with the obsessive drive to EXTERMINATE. Without his three dimensional realisation of the ominous and implacable Dalek - hate on casters - it is truly arguable that the programme itself might have fallen at the first hurdle. It was only when they appeared, in the second story in 1983 that the nation became glued to their screens every Saturday evening in a way that has never happened since and, indeed, in the age of multiple television channels and videos, never will again.

Perversely, Ray Cusick, being a salaried, contract employee at the BBC, never received another penny for his inspirational design, unlike Terry Nation, who wrote the first script and coined the word "Dalek," thereby securing ownership of the rights to all things Dalek in perpetuity. 'Twas ever thus.

This weekend sees a long overdue re-examination by the BBC of its most famous and successful family entertainment programme ever.

My namesake Tom, the oldest surviving Doctor, is hosting a programme this weekend in which there are contributions from many of us who have over the years played a part in the Who legend. Even though science fiction has undoubtedly moved on and expensive special effects are considered by some to have made the BBC's trailblazing time traveller look a little outmoded, nonetheless I still think that it is a great shame that we have a generation of children today who have never had "their" Doctor.

But when the plug was pulled on Sylvester McCoy in 1989, I doubt that many would have predicted that ten years later, when the BBC wanted to convince us all, via advertisements, that it is worth keeping, licence fee and all, the good Doctor in his TARDIS and the Daleks are the flags that are unfurled to trumpet Beeb excellence. In the BBC's annual Red Nose Day charity fundraiser, twice in ten years

Doctor Who has been seen as the perfect vehicle to engage a national audience.

Some might think I am engaging in special pleading, but so far down the line, it could even be disadvantageous to me if Doctor Who were revived. But for my children and for all those future generations who might just love to surrender to the delicious thrill of terror at Saturday tea-time after the footie results, there is surely still an opportunity for the TARDIS to *vwo-orp* into life again, with well-constructed, imaginative plots showing that hi-tech effects are not essential for good story telling.

I vote for Dawn French as the Doctor!

21st December 2007

I was invited last week by the good citizens of that lovely old coastal town, Cromer, to turn on their festive lights with my old friend Terry Molloy, who played Davros, the evil genius creator of the Daleks when I was Doctor Who. We are both appearing in panto down the road in Norwich.

The Cromer lights are entirely the work of a dedicated team of volunteers who fundraise throughout the year and supply and install the impressive festoons of light over a series of Sundays throughout the winter.

This unpaid dedication to their local community was, I thought, worthy of "bigging up", so I deemed it appropriate in my short speech to indicate that I had a few weeks earlier seen the lights in Blackpool and the Cromer illuminations were - I paused for effect - infinitely superior!

Everyone was happy with my unashamed hyperbole and we adjourned for a sandwich and mince pie in a local hostelry.

When I say everyone was happy, I am sadly excluding the press in Blackpool, who somehow heard about this distant but monstrous insult to their sea front attraction and pursued me relentlessly for three days via telephone and email.

As I was in the throes of dress rehearsals for Dick Whittington, I declined to respond to their plaintive requests for a justification of my hideous and offensive slur to their town.

A Blackpool councillor even suggested that I would benefit from a word with my successor David Tennant, who turned the lights in Blackpool on this year and had declared them to be superb.

Oh dear!

I am now worried that a remark I made to a friend that her house was more desirable than Buckingham Palace might provoke questions in the House and a letter from the Lord Chamberlain; or that Brad Pitt might come and sort me out because I think my wife is more attractive that Angelina Jolie!

Clearly the local press in Blackpool are for some reason a little more sensitive about their town than, say, we in Wycombe who know we live in a town that is regenerating and improving year by year.

And if anyone who had a working fountain in their town were to try to belittle us because we don't, I like to think we would rise above it.

Anyway, a happy Christmas to all you sane, well adjusted and non-politically correct readers, near and far.

16th September 2000

It would be surprising, I suppose, if I did not comment on the recent poll conducted by the British Film Institute to find the members' choice of the 100 best programmes ever seen on British television.

When you see the list, the first thing that leaps out is just how many wonderful programmes have been made and shown over the last thirty or forty years. It was no surprise at all that seventeen of the top twenty programmes were made by or for the BBC, the first being the peerless Fawlty Towers, of which only 14 programmes were ever made, each one a classic piece of television comedy in its own right.

In second place was Cathy Come Home, Ken Loach's ground breaking drama, made under the prestige Wednesday Play banner in 1966. Highlighting the plight of the homeless, it led directly and swiftly to the founding of the charity Shelter shortly afterwards.

The members of the BFI decided that third place in this list of the all time televisual elite should be occupied by Doctor Who. I am particularly pleased at news of this, frankly rather unexpected, accolade because for a long time it has been widely believed that the regular success of Doctor Who in viewers' polls has been due principally to some sort of reckless repetitive voting frenzy on the part of the loyal fans of the programme, somewhat patronisingly regarded in some areas as being obsessive and therefore to be disregarded.

However, the BFI members are producers, directors, critics and other professionals involved in the film and television industry. Their assessment of a half a century of television is clearly, given the quality of the company the good Doctor is in, based on something more than a sci-fi fan's obsession. I am proud to have been involved, albeit for only three years of the programme's long history, in something that is clearly held in such great affection by so many people.

I suppose it could be seen as simply a reflection of the age and generation of the BFI's members that there are only two programmes in the top 20 made in the last ten years and you reach No17 before you encounter one of them (Ab Fab).

However, I would argue that it is more than that.

Leaving aside my special connection with, and arguable bias for, Doctor Who, the quality of some of the programmes of the 60's and 70's was simply magnificent, judged from any standpoint – Boys from the Blackstuff, Yes Minister, The Naked Civil Servant, I Claudius, Morecambe and Wise, The Singing Detective, Edge of Darkness.

Eleven of the top 100 are that modern rarity, the single play. Made as the Wednesday Play, Play of the Month or Play for Today, they frequently attracted great writers of the day to produce remarkable work for that huge, growing and hungry audience of ordinary people, who would never dream of going to a theatre but avidly watched Bar Mitzvah Boy, Edna the Inebriate Woman, The War Game and Abigail's Party.

They perhaps thought that television would always be that good. I know I did.

Then along came more and more channels, satellite and cable, all competing for the same viewers, with the finite funds available to make them being spread more and more thinly.

So the fly on the wall replaced the writing on the wall.

Pass me the swatter.

8th May 1998

The actress Drew Barrymore was reported last week as having such a strong affection for her cat that in the event of her predeceasing it, she wishes to have " a little of my ashes put in his food, so that I can live inside him." I suspect that this bizarre desire says more about the particular woman in question than it does about cats or indeed actresses in general, but it is certainly true that some people find it a lot easier to relate to cats or dogs than they do to others of their own more complicated and dangerous species.

Even the great Albert Schweitzer is on record as having said "There are two means of refuge from the miseries of life - music and cats."

The cat versus dog debate goes back into the mists of antiquity where each species has at various times been accorded divine status by different civilisations.

I have never seen the need to declare myself as either a dog or cat person. They fulfil separate and quite distinct needs. Although I did make the mistake when I was playing Doctor Who of taking liberties with the Kipling quote and suggesting that the good Doctor was a bit like the "cat who walks by himself and all times and places are alike to me." This idea was seized upon and I found myself with a cat badge on my lapel and cat silhouettes inside the lining of my jacket. My predecessor, Peter Davison, had had a stick of celery on his lapel, so I think I got the better deal in the symbolism stakes. I certainly found it easier to justify mine, even down to the nine lives bit. But having nailed my feline colours to the mast, I then found myself the lucky recipient of caterphernalia from all over the world from generous people who shared the Doctor's affection for cats. Recently I had to institute a cull. Some several dozen pottery cats, pictures of cats and books about cats joined other household items at a table top sale at a local village hall. Intriguingly the cat items were snapped up at such an alarming rate I wished I had been a little greedier in the pricing of them.

The first cat that can remember as a child was a superior black and white neutered tom named Parker, I think because of his nosiness. When we had had him for some years my father decided that we should have a dog too. We acquired a bull terrier called Bonzo and Parker made no effort to tolerate the newcomer, he moved out. He didn't go so far as to put the stick with the spotted hankie on the end over his shoulder and head off into the sunset, but he declined to enter the house but would only deign to sit on the garden wall so that we could bring food out to him and then disappear again until hunger enforced his return.

Then one day while I was in the kitchen with my mother, Parker leaped through the open window, strolled indolently across to an armchair which he gave a considerable seeing to with his claws before stretching, and settling down for a nap. Half an hour later my father came home and said that Bonzo had been run over and was dead.

Parker, of course, knew before we did. He was perhaps an associate of T S Eliot's Macavity the Mystery cat who was "not there" when crimes were committed. Someone recently suggested that it was unwise to meddle in the affairs of cats "for they are subtle and will pee on your computer"

"Cats are smarter than dogs - you can't get eight cats to pull a sled through snow" - Jeff Valdez.

15th February 2008

Given the many and varied opportunities now available to inform and educate, one might be tempted to think that our young people would be better informed than previous generations. After all, this generation has had the benefit of not only television and radio, but now the limitless, if variable, access to knowledge offered by the internet. But it would appear that the information age has failed to deliver to a significant number of young people.

It was reported this week that 58% of the British teenagers surveyed believed that Sherlock Holmes was a real detective who lived in Baker Street; one in two thought Robin Hood really did live in Sherwood Forest and 65% were convinced that King Arthur was real. Even Biggles was considered by some to have contributed to our victory in the last war. Of more concern is the fact that one in five thought Winston Churchill and Florence Nightingale were fictional characters and two in five thought Richard the Lionheart was the stuff of myth. They were also under the impression that Charles Dickens, who created some of the most vivid fictional characters, was one himself. Gandhi, Cleopatra, Sir Walter Raleigh, The Duke of Wellington, General Montgomery and Boadicea were all thought, by some, to be characters created by authors or screenwriters.

The poll of 3000 teenagers was conducted by UKTV Gold who, with good reason, concluded that their programmes about history were not a major attraction to the youth of Britain.

What is most alarming is that, when around half of the population were alive when Winston Churchill was our prime minister, anybody could be unaware of his contribution to modern history. Even the rather plodding talk and chalk history teacher, who sadly failed to enthuse me with an interest in his subject, wouldn't have deprived me of that information. Mind you, Churchill was still around then.

It was only later I discovered that there was more to the study of history than learning the minutiae of the Reform Acts 1832. Mercifully, history teaching has improved greatly since my school days, as I have discovered with my daughters' education, but clearly there are still pockets of resistance out there.

Mind you, perhaps I can persuade someone that Doctor Who is real. Can I interest you in a used TARDIS? Only ten previous owners, deceptively roomy interior and only slight exterior damage?

6. Foibles, Friends and Fancies

Any regular reader of my weekly contributions to the Bucks Free Press would very quickly deduce that I have quite strong feelings, in the Grumpy Old Men territory about many matters. And I suspect that many others of my generation would share the majority of those opinions, when they touch upon the vexed areas of manners, discipline and the continuing battle between private freedom and public responsibility.

The following eclectic selection has gathered together some of my reflections on both my own particular foibles and some of the events in my life that have given me an insight into what it is that makes me tick. One of the articles that I wrote over a decade ago, I was interested to note, has subsequently proved to be rather prophetic. No prizes offered, I'm afraid, but should you spot the unintended bit of lower league Nostradamus stuff, do tell me what you think it is if ever we meet up.

14th September 2007

I suffer from queue blindness - the affliction that makes it impossible to predict which checkout queue will take the least time. Obvious strategies, like assessing the quantity of articles in other people's trolleys and the number in the queue, never prove effective. The moment I attach myself to the rear of what appears to be a short line, the people in front of me discover that blackcurrant juice has leaked all over a bag of doughnuts, can't find their purses or, being close friends of the person at the till, discuss the barbecue they were both at the previous weekend, or worse – they ring the dreaded bell of doom.

As soon as that happens, you know that you should have brought a good book with you. Invariably, the supervisor for whom the bell tolls is at the furthest corner of store showing another frustrated customer the secret location to which they have moved light bulbs this week... I am sure they relocate products regularly to ensure that we have to scan all the shelves looking for them, thereby stimulating impulse purchase temptation.

She will then slowly walk down the line of checkouts, which almost disappear into infinity in some of the bigger gigastores (or whatever they call the aircraft hangers that pass for shops these days), stopping intermittently to deal with all the other flashing lights.

Bitter experience has taught me too, that queue switching never pays off. Once the queue-inertia virus has struck it will follow you, even if a new checkout opens beside you and you're lucky enough to get there first. The till roll will inevitably commit instant hara kiri or it will be the assistant's first day and they don't know what an aubergine is.

Post offices and banks now operate a single queue feeder system, but even then I find that a thitherto swiftly moving queue grinds suddenly to a halt soon after I join it. You can tell you're in trouble when a teller starts to look perplexed and goes to fetch a colleague, who is similarly perplexed by whatever mysterious challenge has been passed through the metal airlock under the reinforced glass. What arcane business other customers have I have never been able to deduce, as I invariably conclude my business in twenty seconds flat. I can almost feel the scorn of other customers, as I creep away after completing my very dreary business.

23rd January 2004

I do not subscribe to the view that the crimes committed by burglars, muggers and car thieves are somehow morally excusable if they are deprived or poor.

I was brought up in Rochdale, a Lancashire mill town that may become familiar to Wycombe Wanderers supporters next season if the lads don't manage to turn things around sharpish. We were surrounded by cobbled streets, back-to-back houses and massive unemployment as the mills closed and there was hardship that makes some of today's problems look like minor inconveniences. The children with whom I was educated had no televisions, no CD players, designer clothes, skateboards or games consoles. Most homes had outside lavatories and crowded conditions with no fridges, convenience foods or microwaves. Yet crime was as rare in those streets as weapons of mass destruction are in Iraq. We never locked our doors. It simply never occurred to us that anyone would want to come in and steal anything. Arguably, of course, there was very little worth stealing – at least by today's acquisitive standards – but the ethos of community and mutual trust and support was so strong and prevalent that any potential miscreant would be instantly identified and sternly dealt with. And here comes the other old chestnut. We knew our local bobby – a wise non-PC PC - and he would mete out summary justice for any minor infringements that were committed. And if I ever came home and said that the teacher had administered a salutary clip round the ear for misbehaviour, then I got a further dose of the same from my parents. Today, parents storm the palisades of educational establishments bristling with indignation and lawsuits if teachers raise an eyebrow let alone a hand at their little monsters.

Many cultural and social shifts have intervened. Not only has that sense of community evaporated with increased mobility but the ability to buy on credit, the proliferation of expensive in-home entertainment, the media explosion that shows the have-nots exactly what it is that they have not, the universal expectation of instant gratification and the powder keg of drug addiction have despatched that world of my childhood to the history books. I used to hang around street corners, with the handy excuse of my dog, to meet girls and talk to my friends. We were not preyed upon by drug pushers, or viewed with suspicion as potential car thieves.

It is impossible to turn the clock back, alas, but it is possible take steps to restore at least some sense of community; and many valiant citizens in our area are working hard to do that. On Monday at 12:30 I shall be at the new Lane End Youth and Community Centre to help celebrate its handing over to a local management committee by the District Council, who deserve considerable praise for having the vision to provide the wherewithal to build an activities centre and meeting point in an area almost completely devoid of such facilities. The opening of the centre will demonstrate to the young people of Lane End that their community does care and it will hopefully provide a focal point for the rebuilding of something we used to take for granted – a sense of mutual support and pride. If the whole community gets behind it not just on Monday - when I hope the whole of Lane End will turn up - then maybe we can turn the clock back in that respect at least.

29th March 2002

Last Friday I accompanied a friend, Tom Smith, to the Nojo Awards in London. The charity, Help the Aged, was celebrating those who help to improve the lot of a generation often dismissed as "past it." Tom had been nominated, along with hundreds of others around the country because at the age of 86, he spends most of his life helping others. If I am lucky enough to reach that age with my faculties intact, I strongly suspect I will feel I've done my bit and batten down the hatches. Not Tom. Despite being severely restricted in the use of his arms, hands and legs by arthritis, he has had a van adapted, so that he can drive it around Wycombe and surrounding districts collecting unwanted furniture, clothes and other personal effects on behalf of Wycombe Aid, which in turn passes them on to those in need, whether it be the homeless or a battered wives refuge or, alternatively, sells them to raise money for local charities.

The nominations in the category of Charitable Hero Award had been whittled down to just two people, Tom and an 85 year old lady from the Retired and Senior Volunteer Programme.

None of Tom's family were able to make the journey to London with him, so he asked me if I would accompany him. I was luckily free and delighted to escort Tom.

Newscaster Moira Stewart read out the nominations and Claire Rayner, one of the judges, informed the several hundred supporters and friends who attended the Dorchester Hotel luncheon, along with the charity's patron Cherie Blair, that the award had been made this year to Tom Smith – someone who had overcome his own severe handicaps in order to help others.

For most of the occasion, despite the ceremony and great honour, Tom would, I suspect, probably have been happier doing what he normally does on a day to day basis in Wycombe, serving the community and keeping busy. However, he had to emulate the Oscar winners and make the long walk up to the stage to collect his award – a rather striking engraved, elongated glass pyramid. Despite having a ready turn of wit and wicked sense of humour, he was, I knew, relieved that no speeches were expected.

I hope Tom will forgive me for telling you that he had a childhood that is not given sufficient justice by words like "tough" or "deprived." I mention this because his van, which displays clear disabled stickers and obvious indications that it is being used on charitable business, was broken into recently. His tax disc was removed and his petrol tank siphoned, while he was – as usual – doing something for others. The sociopathic morons who could see no reason not to rob an elderly, handicapped driver would probably, if caught, have their poverty and deprived upbringing dangled before the courts as a justification for their petty and disgusting crimes. Yet their victim's own childhood, I would guarantee, was demonstrably and significantly more deprived than theirs. And it never occurred to Tom to do anything, after serving his country at war, other than work for his living and continue to keep busy helping others after his retirement.

Tom, I salute you. You've been honoured by a National Charity. I rather think it would be appropriate if our community too should find some way of honouring a man who has served his town and community so well that it has been recognised nationally.

30th August 2002

Three decades ago (or more if I'm honest), I was a law student living in Bayswater. One afternoon, returning home from a lecture, I was crossing Hyde Park on foot and saw a small child standing alone, crying, in the middle of a vast expanse of grass. After only the briefest hesitation to establish that she was truly on her own, I walked over, knelt down and asked her why she was crying. She was about five or six years old and she had lost her mummy, she told me, even though it was, in fact, clearly the other way round! I took her by the hand and chatted reassuringly to her, while we went in search of her mummy or some help.

Back in those halcyon days, there were such things as bobbies on the beat – and we called them bobbies too – not the less user-friendly nicknames that the police have to endure today. I found one quite quickly and he and I were doing our best to pacify the poor child when her distraught mother turned up. After the tearful reunion and exchanged thanks and reassurances, we all went our separate ways, with our various reactions to an incident satisfactorily concluded.

It is the sign of a long past innocent age – both mine and society's - that I don't recall being worried about the possibility that my instinctive desire to help the little girl was either foolish or involved any risk for me. I suppose, even then, if the mother had happened upon us before we had found the policeman, there could have been the potential for misunderstanding. Nowadays, alas, it would be difficult to both ensure the child's safety and avoid prejudicing one's own.

I imagine today one would quickly engage the active participation of whomsoever else was around; there's safety in numbers, I suppose. On that occasion in the 1960's, however, there wasn't anyone else around.

I suppose today, if one had a mobile phone, one would immediately phone the police to ask for guidance; but in the absence of a phone, one would just have to risk one's own behaviour being misunderstood, in order to safeguard the safety of a child. It's an awful sign of the times that we are all frightened of doing ordinary, everyday human kindnesses to one another for fear of those actions being interpreted otherwise, or indeed giving rise to future litigation. Not only are we all seen as potential abductors, but also as insurance risks. Members of the caring professions run the constant risk of their behaviour being perceived awry. When I was first at school, I remember very clearly how important the comforting hugs of my primary school teacher were on all sorts of different occasions – homesickness, grazed knees, simple anxiety. Sadly, from all sides, teachers today are warned not to touch children at all. Indeed, even the administering of the most basic of first aid is fraught with the possibility of subsequent complaint or litigation. There is a prevalent culture of claim, blame and suspicion that the motives of others are less than worthy and we, the vast majority who are blameless and benign, have been robbed, as a society, of the chance to give or receive the simple human gestures of caring and nurture because of the tiny percentage who are not.

Wouldn't it be nice to turn the clock back?

12th September 2009

Of all the reality programmes that currently fill the television schedules, displacing drama from our screens, there is one that even I, an actor who might be expected to whinge about reality shows, cannot fault. The Choir (Tuesdays at 9 on BBC 2) works on so many levels. Those of us that have seen the two previous series, in which the fresh-faced disciple of choral singing, conductor Gareth Malone, has achieved miracles in two schools already, expect him to find nuggets of singing gold in the most unlikely places. The programme works partly because we, the viewers are gently nudged to make the same mistake that society as a whole seems to make in writing off certain sections of society far too easily. If you didn't believe that we all have some musical ability, I would defy you to persist with that belief after watching the residents of South Oxhey sharing the discovery of their untapped musicality. South Oxhey is not a town I had previously been aware of, but it appears that it is one of those drab urban, wildernesses with tumbleweed blowing through concrete shopping precincts, neatly summed up in the subtitle to the short series - Unsung Town. Residents of the surrounding areas in Hertfordshire regard it as quite simply somewhere to avoid – a place with no cultural activity at all. Fertile ground then for the wonderfully empowering and determined Mr. Malone.

All those more glitzy, prime-time talent shows like to tweak our emotional heartstrings with stories of individuals rising above personal tragedy and shining in the face of adversity. The Choir doesn't shy away from showing us how some of the members of the choir have triumphed over their sometimes desperate life situations – and nor should it. This programme clearly demonstrates what most of us know already, that many of society's problems arising from disaffected communities could be swept away if there were more Gareth Malones (in whatever field) who could offer the opportunity to people of all ages - but especially young people - to discover one of the many ways in which they can interact with others creatively, through sport, the arts and a hundred different activities.

Yes, the television cameras are obviously a motivating and enabling factor, but the premise remains the same – give people a way to do something they can be proud of and most of them will eventually take it.

26th March 2004

There is a syndrome for everything these days – no one is lazy or daft any more. I think I'm suffering from Age Related Attention Deficit Syndrome.

I tend to amble around the home barefoot and discovered the inherent dangers of that when I trod on a strip of carpet gripper that has been demanding my attention since we removed the small amount of carpet it had secured, to prevent one of our cats from continuing to regard it as a feline convenience. We solved the Temporary Cat House-training Deficiency Syndrome but introduced a foot laceration problem instead.

I go out to the shed, to get the claw hammer and pincers. While there, I espy the lawnmower, still covered in last year's grass. The time of lawns and the mowing thereof is at hand and I haven't had the mower serviced. Imagining the sucked-in breath of the engineer on seeing last year's caked-on grass and mud, I decide to clean the mower before calling him. Returning indoors to get the mower key, I notice a pile of letters by the front door. I put the key on the table and open them. I consign the fifty percent of the letters that are junk mail into the bin and notice that the bin is full. I take the black plastic sack out to the wheelie bin and return. I cannot find a bag to replace the one I have just removed. A bulb has blown in what, as a child, I would have called the "back kitchen" (it is now a "utility room"). I go back outside to get a bulb from the shed; in clambering over the mucky mower to reach the shelf I dislodge a plastic ice-cream container. It contains screws, thousands of the blighters, which have minds of their own and are now strewn to the four corners of the civilised world (well, the uncivilised shed anyway). I'll deal with them later! I return with the bulb. I shine the light of truth onto the cupboard of despair and find the plastic bin-liners and place one in the bin.

I finish opening the mail. There is a utilities bill; the suppliers hint darkly of dire judicial consequences that I can ignore "if have paid the bill already." I haven't. I go upstairs to get my cheque-book from my trouser pocket. No trousers to be found. Anything washable left briefly unattended in my house ends up in the washing basket. And there they are, complete with cheque-book. An outbreak of money laundering has been averted. I write the cheque and go in search of a stamp. In my briefcase, I find the stamps and the notes of the previous day's meeting for which I was supposed to write minutes. The phone rings – it's a tabloid reporter trying to manoeuvre me to say that just because the producer of the new Doctor Who series wrote "Queer as Folk," I have grave concerns about the possibility of a camp, flower arranging Doctor. I have no such concerns and say so, as neutrally as I can, knowing I'll be misquoted or partially quoted at best. I type out the minutes of the meeting and email them off. I go back downstairs, see the mower keys on the table and remember what I was planning to do. On my way out to the shed, I tread on the exposed carpet gripper.

23rd July 2004

It happened again last week.

I was in Nottingham to launch the pantomime in which I am appearing this Christmas. These annual events, aimed at block-bookers and the media, always happen while we're all innocently enjoying the long light evenings and serve as a heady reminder that before you've shaken the seaside sand out of your swimwear and are contemplating the subsequent credit card bill, there will be fireworks and Christmas trees lining the supermarket isles.

But I digress. What happened?

Well, this strangely unseasonable event was attended by some local competition winners, who had been presented with a question along the lines of, "Which of the following famous people have never been Lord Mayor of London – Ken Livingstone, George Bush or Dick Whittington?" I suspect that they were the only entrants, so the accuracy of their answer was not an issue.

I don't know what they said to Kevin Kennedy or Chris Gascoigne from Coronation Street, but I was greeted with words that are now becoming familiar to me, though I remain at a loss to understand the thought processes that lead the questioner to feel that it is okay to address a stranger with the words, "My God, you've put on a lot of weight since you left Doctor Who, haven't you?" Bad enough, dear reader, but when accompanied by an admonishing pat on my stomach, it amounted, I would suggest, to sufficient provocation to justify stapling the patter's tongue to his roaming hand. I resisted the urge to say "Good Heavens, you're as stupid as a lobotomised bedbug." When my torturer asked if he could have his picture taken with me, I asked if he had a sufficiently wide angled lens. He looked confused. A minor victory. I wondered briefly whether I should comment on his defective oral hygiene, ludicrous comb-over and lamentable taste in trousers, but I rose above it and simply blinked when the photograph was taken. Another small victory.

And yes, I'm on a diet again. My children are helping. They have stuck signs in the fridge saying, "You're not hungry, Daddy." This statement is demonstrably false, but it's the thought that counts. Then one of them appears behind me and solemnly and kindly hands me an orange.

Much as I love Harry Potter and share my children's enjoyment of the books and the films, I do wish that, during the first ten minutes of each film, we were not subjected to the inevitable loathsome fat boy and fat father who are objects of hatred and ridicule. Their behaviour may be odious, but it is their girth that we are invited to ridicule and identify with their unkind treatment of our hero. Too easy JK, too easy! Otherwise, top marks.

I don't want to suggest for a second that obesity is not a health problem. I would certainly be doing myself a favour if I were to shed a stone or three and am determined to do so, somehow. But I am beginning to resent the underlying implication that those of us who are, after all, more efficient at processing and benefiting (in survival terms) from our intake are somehow less acceptable socially, less worthy of esteem than our slimmer less energy efficient fellow citizens.

I am in Cornwall this week and will be negotiating with my benevolent teenage jailors. If I surrender a Cornish pasty, I might be allowed a glass of scrumpy.

13th October 2000

Recently, someone I had never met in my life before, but who believed she knew me because she had seen me on television, approached me at a charity event I was attending with my family. I will leave it to you, dear discerning reader, to determine whether you think the manner in which this woman, I repeat – a total stranger, made my acquaintance was appropriate.

She advanced towards me, prodded me in the stomach several times and said "My God, you've put on weight since Doctor Who, haven't you? Where's all this come from, then?" To the open-mouthed astonishment of my wife and children, the prod then evolved into a double handed pat on either side of my admittedly far from anorexic midriff.

It is undoubtedly true that since she had last seen me slipping easily in and out of the TARDIS, I have succumbed to middle age and even those who love me most would not claim that I was a sylph. Truth be told, I never have been, apart from the time in the eighties when a rude article in "that" redtop provoked me to challenge them to sponsor me to lose weight. The fifty pounds I did lose earned five thousand pounds for charity. But despite my deep love for the new moody, slender CB, it all crept back inexorably, over the next few years.

I admit that my genetic make-up converts the food and drink, that I consume in moderation, into more of me and less disposable energy than some other lucky gannets of my acquaintance who shovel the starch and slurp the stout whilst remaining "the same weight as I was when I was 17." Don't you just hate them?

But not as much as I hated the jolly bonhomie of the ghastly woman and her grinning family, who felt able to casually provoke in me such an overwhelming desire to punish such presumption by chaining her to Kate Moss for a month with a notice round her neck reading "Now who's fat, birdbrain?!"

Even though being a recognisable face does seem to make the less intellectually gifted feel able to be so familiar, it is also a crime committed against men rather than women. I can't imagine many people who would refer to the physical appearance of a woman in quite such a derogatory way. But men tend to get more unsolicited remarks about lack of hair and increasing girth than women do about their unwanted baggage of increasing years. Given the fact that, despite their protestations to the contrary, the media constantly, by implication at least, demonise the non-slender woman, it is rare for a woman to be accosted in quite the way I was.

I finally cracked once at a reception in Stockholm, where I was working. A Swedish woman, whose English was perhaps less good than that of the majority of her countrymen, of all the politer options available, chose to greet me with "Oh my goodness, you have become very much fat since I saw you on the television."

I replied, "And you, madam, have a very large bottom."

She was deeply offended and complained bitterly about the rude English actor.

I warn anyone tempted to believe that they can say whatever they like to one more fleshily endowed than themselves, try it on with me and your Achilles heel, hairy wart, big ears or scrawny neck may not escape my eagle eye.

16th July 1999

In my thirty years of acting on television I have never played a policeman. I have always hankered after being a Morse, Wycliffe or a Frost – not just because it is a very good living for several years – but so that I could solve all those murders, infuriate my superior officers, irritate my peers and be gruff with my dogged underlings.

If we were to base our understanding of the real police force on the picture painted by these programmes, it would appear that murder occupies the majority of any police force's time, especially serial murder. They are usually committed by geniuses whose ability to plan intricate alibis is matched only by their tendency to crumple into involuntary confessional mode (shades of - "It's a fair cop, guv!") when confronted with the truth by our hero.

The detective will, of course, only be able to solve the case after his superior has suspended him from duty. The latter will have been promoted to Chief Superintendent precisely because he suffers from apoplectic rages, has the man management skills of a steamroller and is incapable of recognising the ability of the only officer in the force who has ever brought a single murderer to justice.

Despite the fact that the brilliant detective is frequently boorish and ungrateful, he will have one sidekick who is tolerant of his excesses and who will, albeit reluctantly, do the legwork for him when he has been suspended for the umpteenth time.

Most murder investigations will necessitate our fragile hero losing the possibility of a companion in his empty private life, when a romance turns sour because he treats his new potential ladylove as a suspect. And most enquiries will involve visiting a strip club at least once.

But they are still the most popular programmes on the box, because they are superbly made, exercise our grey matter in the quest to get there before the detective and our families and because they really are nothing like real life.

Films have their own absolutes too.

In America, detectives always live in strange vast apartments at the top of downtown high rise blocks – accessible by a lift which opens directly into the apartment and which would be outside the price range of any employee of any police department in the world. He will show minimal reaction to pain when shot or beaten to a pulp, but wince when an attractive woman cleans the wound.

American cops work in pairs. One is always loyal, hard working and incorruptible and therefore gunned down two days before his retirement, particularly if he has just shown a picture of his happy, decent young family to his moody, authority-hating colleague. The replacement will then be selected on the grounds of his, or more often her, complete incompatibility with the survivor of the original pair. They will only bond as the rookie is lying in a pool of blood near the end of the movie.

The film industry has introduced us to many such insights.

Most lap top computers are capable of infiltrating and immobilising the systems of any invading alien fleet. All planes can be landed by anyone safely because they can be talked down from the control tower. And good guys need never worry about fighting against impossible odds. The baddies will always wait patiently to attack you one by one, dancing around threateningly, until you have disposed of their predecessor.

And my personal favourite - if you decide to dance down the street, everyone around you will know the steps.

If only life were like that.

16th December 2005

As a boy, growing up in post-war Rochdale, the public library was for me a treasure trove of excitement and imagination. I devoured books in much the same way that children today devour television, DVDs and computer games. But I don't subscribe to the hard-line view that the latter are intrinsically bad. Like any activity, provided it does not preclude additional elements of physical activity and social interaction, then anything that stimulates the brain or the imagination or has the potential to offer insights into other peoples' lives and other ways of thinking can only be beneficial. I came from a generation that did not buy books but used public libraries. That has changed to a certain extent, but not as much as some may think, and the public library remains an invaluable resource for all of us. The first thing I do whenever, as at the moment, I am working away from home is to sign up as a visitor at the local public library. The research resources are unparalleled even by the Internet, which can frequently offer only a time consuming trawl through irrelevant dross of variable reliability. But even for that erratic, etheric tool, the public libraries are my first port of call to collect emails and send these articles to the Bucks Free Press.

It is therefore with a leaden heart that I view the closure of any library, so the news that we may lose as many as eight libraries in Bucks is very depressing. I spent a very pleasant morning in Micklefield recently to help publicise a new drop-in facility for local residents. I saw how welcome and necessary that opportunity was for the local community. To learn a very short time later that the nearby local library is on the closure list was doubly depressing. It is hard to imagine that all of the Micklefield residents who used their library will be willing or able to brave the London Road trip into the library in the town centre. Indeed, had there been no library in Micklefield, I find it easier to imagine the logic of an initiative to open one there in order to provide a focal point and resource for that particular community than I do the current and depressingly familiar evidence of a culture of making us all travel further and further afield for resources we had hitherto taken for granted.

Extend it and improve it rather than remove it.

22nd May 1998

Since I began writing this regular column, I have had a varying level of reaction to the subjects I have touched upon. Some provoke little or no response either way. Others seem to hit a raw nerve, whether it be pro or anti. Until last week, I would say that my preference for the life-style and habits of the fox as opposed to those of the hunter had provoked by far the strongest reaction.

Over the years, I have fulminated against cuts in Education spending and the intolerable pressure on our teachers to create trophy children from a gene pool not of their creation.

I have railed against the jobsworth mentality in many areas of public service. I have voiced my despair at the continuing rise in the universal acceptance of self interest as a way of life and the erosion of decent standards of behaviour. I have moaned about the abuse of our language which results in such linguistic untruths as "positive parking," "for the convenience of our customers," and "rationalisation," which, in fact, really mean, respectively "no parking," "for OUR convenience," and "wholesale redundancies and increased profit."

Yet nothing I have written has resulted in quite so many fulsome messages of support and thanks as I have received in the last week from other people who cannot now deposit their domestic refuse in County Council Refuse Disposal Sites. Friends, who had never felt moved to mention my column before, have seized my hand with tears in their eyes, muttering, "Thank you! Thank you!"

I have been approached in the street by tax payers who share my frustration at the cavalier disregard for them shown by the County Council and are relieved to realise that theirs was not a voice crying alone in the wilderness.

Clearly I tapped into a well of silent majority outrage, when I highlighted the casual attack by the County Council on drivers of vehicles higher than five feet nine inches.

The reason that they are not welcome at South Bucks waste sites is that their vehicles are similar in height to those used by tradesmen who wish to avoid paying the charges levied by the County Council for depositing trade waste. The supreme tactician at County Hall, who shares Marie Antoinette's legendary flair for empathising with the needs of the populace, clearly has a desire to incur the loathing of every 4x4 and MPV owner in Bucks. Seemingly, it has not occurred to him that it will pay the trade tipper to attach a tow bar to one of his other vehicles and deposit his contraband waste from a trailer. But someone, say, with more than three children who has acquired their larger vehicle to accommodate their family - as well as the extra volume of garbage generated by a larger family - is not quite as likely to have a fleet of vehicles and/or a trailer to enable them to deposit their otherwise acceptable waste at the site.

I am emboldened by the extraordinary level of approval for my words last week, therefore, to bang on about this topic again. I am sure that the dozens of people who have voiced their gratitude to me for airing the subject will share my interest in seeing if anyone from the County Council can, through this paper, offer us a sensible suggestion as to our future strategy for the disposal of those items which until a fortnight ago we were able to take to the Waste Sites.

And when the fly-tippers deposit their building rubble, mattresses and old fridges in country lanes, bridle tracks and areas of outstanding natural beauty where householders are not allowed to put up so much as a garden shed without getting planning permission, will the Local Authority come and clear it up?

And who will be paying for that?

7.   Little Britain

The title of the following chapter has a double or even treble resonance for me. Little Britain is, of course, now mainly known by most people as a very funny and inventive television programme starring two remarkably gifted and original performers. I was delighted to be asked to participate in one sketch in the show a few years ago. It was one of the 'two ladies' scenarios and I played a raffish roué who was rather taken with one of the eponymous cross dressers despite the fact that he/she had provided incontrovertible evidence of the actuality of his/her gender.

It was, a 'Nobody's perfect' moment with an unconscious (?) nod to the blissful final moment of one of the best films ever made – 'Some Like It Hot'. It just occurs to me in writing this that the title – that we all know so well – is actually a rather strange one to modern ears. But we are so used to it that we simply accept it as the title of that film. Sorry! Rambling again.

Aficionados of the programme who have only watched it on screen may be perplexed by my claim to have been in it. Sadly the episode with which I was involved and the scene that contained my contribution was cut. I was assured that this was not because of any deficiencies in my performance; but one is always paranoid in these matters. However, the DVD of the third series does contain these discarded pearl, should you feel curious enough to delve.

But the title of the show was of course coined because of the 'Little Englander' expression, that dates back, apparently, to the Gunpowder Plot, and neatly encapsulates the importance that we have traditionally attached to ourselves in this 'sceptered isle' – an importance that is completely disproportionate when you look at any map of the world for more than a second.

The third connection. Well of course one of my august predecessors in the Tardis and sonorous part namesake plays a significant though unseen role in the aforementioned television programme.

But it is the vagaries of our country and its traditions and regulations that I expatiated upon in the following pages.

18th August 2006

Whilst any form of vigilante action is, of course, to be discouraged, nonetheless it is hard to resist the urge to enjoy a little unholy glee when clampers get their come-uppance. We live now in an environment where clamping is such big business (as a quick internet search of "clampers" will reveal) that, believe it or not, those with an urge to clamp cars for a living are able to study for a B'tec qualification in "Vehicle Immobilisation," for which examining board Edexcel expected 1,500 potential students.

In Chalk Farm in London last week, Camden Council's clampers returned to find their own van clamped. It had been parked on double yellow lines for some time when an anonymous champion of the people decided to employ the immobilising embrace of an abandoned clamp that he had acquired at some time previously. He felt, and you may share his opinion, that if clamping is, as it seems to be, considered a proper way to discourage illegal parking, then that discouragement should be applied to all who transgress without fear or favour. The Camden Council clampers returned to their van to find that the biter had been bitten and then had to endure the unbridled delight of passing citizens who not only shared merry witticisms with the red-faced officials but filmed, photographed and otherwise celebrated their very public embarrassment.

A press official for Camden Council displayed unusual official sangfroid about the incident, thereby at least deserving some Brownie points. He said, "We are ending the use of clamping in Camden after residents told us they felt it was an unfair and overzealous response to minor parking infringements." Power to the people!

Would that other official bodies were more responsive to the public's dislike of their overzealous actions. Then, speed enforcement would be targeted where it was demonstrable that lives would be saved. In other words, not on Marlow Hill where the uphill speed trap is tantamount to shooting fish in a barrel and there is no history of accidents or a credible danger to other road-users.

The continuing disinclination of Thames Valley Police to say how much revenue has been raised by this occasional police trap serves only to prove that valuable law enforcement resources are being diverted away from much needed protection from thugs, vandals and thieves towards cash gathering from the motorist, a much softer and easier target.

3rd April 1988

On a recent trip to America, I was staggered to see the enormous differential between the cost of petrol in the States and over here. In some places, you can get a gallon of gas - as the Americans, quaintly and with little regard for scientific accuracy, call what is incontrovertibly a liquid - for just under a dollar. That's something in the region of sixty pence a gallon, or twelve pence a litre. And that, don't forget, is in a country of traditionally big cars, where journeys are measured not in miles but hours. No wonder Kuwait was worth protecting at the time of the Iraqi invasion...

The other thing I discovered is that speed limit enforcement cameras have been tentatively discussed in America but the general feeling is that, in the land of the automobile and the drive in cinema and hamburger joint, the majority of the population would not tolerate such an infringement of their right to do pretty much whatever they dang well please as long as it doesn't stop anyone else from being able to have a beer while watching the world series on TV.

In fact, one American I spoke to was visibly shaken by the notion that spy cameras could be placed on the public highway with the sole intention of trapping speeding motorists.

I felt just a little miffed that here in England we are being bled dry by punitive petroleum taxes on the motorist that still don't result in decent roads.

(I still can't believe that John Prescott blocked the final stage of the A40 widening and improvement just outside London - especially after they had compulsorily purchased all those houses at White City, just two traffic lights away from unblocking that awful crawl out along Westway, to Acton and the flower sellers and windscreen washers, that can take an hour and a half on a Friday night.)

And I am still grumbling about the three points I picked up on the M25 when I was doing 72mph at 1 a.m. when, apparently, the 60mph lights were showing.

So they say! Hurrumph.

As mine was the only car in the photo in four lanes of empty Motorway and it was the middle of the night in clement weather, I could see no reason why they might have a reduced limit. But I was advised that as I was 2mph over the maximum permissible speed anyway, I didn't have a wheel to stand on.

So speed cameras are not my fave rave either.

While I was still casting envious looks at the freedom enjoyed by the American motorist, news reached England of the school shooting in Arkansas.

Freedom in the States includes the constitutional right to bear arms. Freedom means not only that you get cheap petrol and no speed cameras, but it also means that children have fairly easy access, in many cases, to an array of weaponry that would be envied by many terrorist organisations. The facts clearly have yet to be established. But it seems beyond doubt that a boy who was barely a teenager and his even younger accomplice have been able to get their hands on a selection of assault weapons legally owned by a relative.

So perhaps I'll grin, however fixedly, and endure the speed cameras and continue to pay through the trunk for petrol. At least the morally bankrupt, deranged, or simply bad or stupid can't get their hands too easily on such weaponry over here.

I spoke last week of a memorial bench in a quiet rural spot which had been smashed by unknown vandals.

Since I wrote about it, the destruction of the wooden bench has continued apace.

Thank goodness that the tragic zombies who are capable of such furtive, petty and utterly pointless destruction can't get their hands on guns.

16th June 2006

The outbreak of St George's flags fluttering from the windows of cars seems, perhaps rather ironically, to have divided the nation.

Some people of my acquaintance find it unbearably jingoistic, whilst others dismiss the practice as, quite simply, "common."

Now there's a word that has changed in its meaning over the years, like "gay" and "bad" – but that's another column, another day.

"Common" used to describe a characteristic shared by all; now it is regularly used as a means of describing people to whom the speaker wishes to feel superior, whether that superiority comes from the way they speak, the possessions they own, the clothes they wear or even how they name their children - Arabella and Oliver or Kylie and

Jason? Those who occupy the highest ground of disapproval of things common have a distaste for displays of emotion of any kind, which has given rise to the perception that the higher up the social pecking order you get, the less you are able to demonstrate affection for anything or anyone. It is a particularly British affliction; and, admit it, when you are watching the news on television and you see the citizens of a third world country screaming, beating their breasts and tearing out their hair after the loss of a loved one, you feel embarrassment as well as a sneaking envy for their ability to give vent to their emotions. As global warming bites, maybe we will adopt the habits of those residents of other hot countries and allow the world to see that we have feelings too. Supporting our country in the World Cup at least enables us to show approval of something that our government is up to on the international stage, which many find otherwise quite difficult.

We have allowed our flag to be hi-jacked by a xenophobic minority for too long and it should be reclaimed by the majority. We should stop being embarrassed about being English. It's okay to support your own nation and doesn't have to imply a corresponding antipathy for the rest of the world. Indeed, just as in relationships with other individual human beings, it is much easier to relate positively to others when you are at peace with yourself. So in the face of the sneers from the uptight descendants of the "U" and "Non U" brigade, I am going to attach my flags to my car and be happy to be English, whatever the outcome of the football in Germany.

15th Dec 2000

I succumb instantly to cynicism when politicians start referring to family values, because it usually indicates some governmental wringing of hands and a refusal to take much-needed measures to control the growing minority who agree with Mrs. Thatcher's famous and shocking assertion that, "There is no such thing as society."

Theories abound as to why a significant number of people, from all sections of society, feel so detached from the rest of us that they are unwilling to conform to minimum standards of decent behaviour, let alone stretch a hand out, or smile at another human being. But there is one thing that it certainly isn't. It is not a simple issue of the haves and have-nots. All of us who are over forty (oh alright - fifty) can remember a time when doors really did not need to be locked, when people who had little of what today would be regarded as the necessities of life, were nonetheless fiercely proud of their decency, their honesty and their dignity.

It is the very family values themselves that are changing. My bugbear is the parent who remonstrates with a badly behaved child but fails to follow up when the child persists with its unacceptable behaviour. What on earth is the point of telling a child not to do something and then tacitly condoning the unacceptable behaviour by failing to deal with subsequent disobedience?

And what about those parents who smile benignly when their uncontrolled and noisy toddlers amble around destroying an environment in which other people and their well behaved children are trying to enjoy themselves in less selfish ways?

We visited some friends a while ago. They have two sons who are privately educated, have most things that young pre-teenagers might hope to have and then some. Despite repeated exhortations from their very pleasant, well-meaning but ultimately ineffectual mother, they continued to do exactly what they wanted to do, which included forcing my daughters to watch them driving around on their garden tractors, crawling under the table during lunch and going off to play on their computers whenever they felt like it. My girls were perplexed and amused in the same way that we are entertained when the chimpanzees in the zoo jam their food dishes on each other's heads.

They agreed that they had no desire to be seen as quite so uncaring for others themselves.

The same family visited us some months later. The boys climbed out of a bedroom window onto our conservatory roof, necessitating the replacement of several sheets of corrugated plastic.

Their mother threw her hands in the air in a gesture of world-weary helplessness, as if to indicate that she could not possibly be expected to rein in these interesting free spirits to which she had given birth.

They have not been invited back.

But their unruliness is no less worrying than that of the roaming gangs of youths from somewhat different backgrounds who shout obscenities at one another in the street without caring about the sensibilities of those around, who push past you in doorways, who leave their drink cans in your garden and chuck their fast food containers out of the windows of cars.

They have never seen discipline in action and have no concept of how it might improve their lives. All they have learnt is that they can do what they like; small wonder that they persist in living down to our expectations.

22nd June 2001

As the Foot and Mouth crisis fades from the front pages, we are turning our media-led attention to other 21st century blues – the crumbling railway infrastructure, our fracturing national health service, a demotivated education system. The images that dominated our screens of the charred corpses of farm animals with their legs forlornly sticking up into the air will begin to fade as we enjoy the freedom to rove the countryside again, a freedom that many now realise they value considerably.

We had a brief glimpse of the way that our food is produced. We learned of the cruel absurdity of live animals' transportation over vast distances to be slaughtered or sold, sometimes passing on the motorways lorries carrying others of their species in precisely the opposite direction for the same purpose. The closure of hundreds of local abattoirs has been partly responsible for these tumbrels crammed with poor creatures being transported unnecessarily vast distances; but also responsible is mass buying by supermarkets who dictate where and when animals should be slaughtered. Hence, cows from Devon are taken to Scotland for slaughter and return south as Scotch Beef.

The virulence of the Foot and Mouth outbreak is a direct result of this cross-contamination.

And who is to blame?

We are. We expect and demand ever cheaper food. We are bombarded by television programmes that suggest we have the most refined of tastes, telling us how to cook exotic dishes with the finest ingredients. But we spend less per head on our food than any other European nation. And, despite the fashionable cachet of organic food, 75% of it is bought by 7% of the population and the proportion of fresh food we buy drops every year.

Farming is no different to any other commercial operation. Farmers, whatever size their farm, need to make a profit. It would be ludicrous to expect the producers of our food to improve farming practices and animal husbandry unilaterally, when the supermarket giants won't pay the extra cost of higher veterinary bills, higher feed bills, lower yield and more environmentally friendly practices that might actually produce better food.

And they won't pay because we demand ever-cheaper food. Just look at he advertising of the supermarket chains. "Prices slashed", "Buy two get one free" etc., etc.

Until the harrowing pictures were broadcast on our TV screens this spring, despite the omnipresence of Messrs Harriot, Oliver and Smith, our interest in food has been restricted to the cost and the ease of preparation and consumption. Six out of ten children never eat with their families. Only the USA and Japan own more microwaves per family than us.

Until we lose our obesity-inducing, health-damaging, environment-sapping addiction to cheap food come what may, we will continue to succumb to outbreaks of pestilence of biblical proportions. We will continue to decimate our once thriving and self-supporting farming industry and turn the countryside into a factory.

The farmers can't do it alone and the supermarkets and MAFFs, NAFFs or whatever department is cobbled together in the future, won't do it unless they are responding to a strong message from us that we want better food, not cheaper food and that we are prepared to pay the cost of better farming practices and decentralisation of the food chain.

Popular pressure is the only way to bring about change. While we demand cheap food, we'll get it, with all its social, environmental and nutritional disadvantages.

4th October 2002

The issue of foxhunting is one that arouses passions on both sides of the debate. I always get an increased reaction to this column, and indeed abuse, when I declare myself to be one who believes that a civilised society can no longer condone the pursuit of an animal to its death in the name of sport.

And despite all the arguments about rural livelihoods, ancient traditions, towny prejudice and thin ends of wedges, that is what the "sport" is about.

The history of fox hunting is often overlooked. Until a century and half ago, it was largely confined to upland Scotland and Wales. Jack Russell, of the terrier fame, worked hard to introduce the hunt to England, when a shortage of deer demanded a replacement quarry. By the middle of the 19th century, a dearth of foxes actually led country folk to protect them, for subsequent hunting. One record explains "...so far from persecuting the fox, many a moor farmer would rather have lost the best sheep in his flock than see the gallant animal killed in any fashion except by hounds." The foxes that are hunted today are predominantly direct descendants of the foxes imported from France to compensate for the dwindling numbers of quarry in this country. Were it not for the hunt, many parts of rural England might arguably now be foxless.

So, is it about controlling "vermin" (defined as "small animals that carry disease or damage crops") or is it about sport? For the record, foxes predate on the rats and small rodents that do eat crops.

The need to (humanely) cull species is clear. I, and many others, am not convinced that the vast sums of money spent maintaining hunts, horses, hounds and the support trades would not be better spent in other ways in maintaining the countryside and its way of life, which is undeniably under threat. I would have joined the march two Sundays ago, had the proposal to end fox hunting not been falsely presented as the key symptom of a neglected rural economy.

There are approaching 200 hunts in England and Wales, but the number of foxes they kill is relatively insignificant. On one 2,500 acre Hampshire estate last year the tally of foxes killed was "Hunted 2, trapped 30, shot 180." The commonest and most effective way to dispose of unwanted foxes is by "lamping." A bright red lamp, hung from a vehicle, transfixes the fox, which is then shot between the eyes by a marksman.

Demonising an animal as some sort of furry Jack the Ripper is ludicrous. In nature it would never meet a hundred chickens in a pen. If it grabbed one for food the others would all fly away. Man has put the poor birds in close confinement and the hunting fox is presented with one after another flapping, squawking fowl and does what a fox does. Just as a squirrel collects nuts for a rainy day.

Hunters resist the suggestion that they could continue to have exciting rides across the country, with everything except the (occasional) kill, by drag hunting. The reason is that farmers will only allow the hunt on their land to get rid of foxes. I spoke to a farmer recently who agreed that he wouldn't allow the hunt on his land if they weren't after foxes – unless, of course, they offered to pay him!

25th January 2008

Whenever I write in this column about the current levels of antisocial behaviour in our streets and the violence that seems to be the inevitable result of law abiding citizens' attempts to protect their families and properties from marauding youngsters, I am thanked by scores of strangers in the street, as well as my friends and acquaintances.

It seems everyone is of a like mind. It cannot go on. People of my generation share a memory of parents who were universally mortified if their children behaved badly in any way, however minor by modern standards. Not just middle class parents either. The working class and even those who would fit into a group that we would today categorise as "poor" shared similar values. Decency and honesty were not just ingrained but a matter of pride for the vast majority of the population.

We can discuss forever how the slide into near anarchy has happened, but one central theme that keeps recurring is discipline. Early discipline in the home, in the schools and in the streets.

The fact that many people have become terminally outraged by the current level of antisocial behaviour is evidenced by the increasing number of otherwise civilised people who are calling, quite seriously, for the re-introduction of the stocks as a means of deterring crime and shaming perpetrators. Stocks were not needed or even mentioned when I was a young man.

This week, three youths were convicted of kicking and beating a man to death outside his own home after a seven-hour drinking binge. Garry Newlove had challenged them while they were vandalising vehicles outside his house in Cheshire. The assault was witnessed by his family. His widow delivered a very moving tribute to her husband and a plea that should resonate across the land. Somewhere between the justice of Iran, where two rapists were recently given a hundred lashes and then thrown off a cliff, and the UK's current culture of, "You can't touch me, I'm under age (or deprived) and can do what I like!" there must lie a happy medium.

Garry Newlove could have been you or I. I don't think I could stand by and do nothing while youths came onto my property or threatened my family.

We must refuse to vote in, locally or nationally, politicians who continue to equivocate on this subject and do nothing. I want the streets to be ours again.

6th October 2006

I spent a week in Glasgow last month and was delighted to be able to join the rest of the cast of the play in which I was performing for a drink or two after the show. Nothing remarkable about that, I hear you saying. But there is.

I suffer from asthma and within ten minutes of being in a pub I react to the smoke in the atmosphere. If I soldier on and use my puffer in order to be sociable, then the following day my lungs invariably pay the price. And my clothes reek of tobacco smoke, which as non-smokers will attest, is unpleasant. And I am only mildly asthmatic. In a population where there are now hundreds of thousands of reactive and allergic people, there must be a vast number who would visit public places more often if the experience were more pleasant.

I now avoid pubs unless I can sit outside or there is a genuinely smoke free area. And we have all been to bars or restaurants where the smokers and non-smokers are only nominally separated by a sign that implies that smoke drifting in the air can not only read but somehow stop in its polluting tracks.

In Scotland all public places are smoke free – and how pleasant it was to be able to have a drink with my colleagues after work without impairing my health in the process and contaminating my hair and clothing. Scotland the Brave!

I am also surprised that, in a political climate where anything considered potentially dangerous is banned, restricted or controlled, no one has seen fit to legislate about smoking while driving a car.

The use of mobile phones in the hand is forbidden while driving, yet you can drive while having a lit cigarette in your hand or mouth. If a mobile phone is dropped it causes no problem to the driver, but a lit cigarette falling on to the floor or the driver's clothing could very easily cause the driver to react violently and lose control of the car. Yet I have never heard any mutterings from officialdom about a proposal to ban smoking while driving. But there are frequent rumblings about enacting a complete ban on the use of mobiles while driving, whether hands-free or not, despite the fact that when talking to someone in the car, you may occasionally glance at them. That is not an issue with a hands-free mobile.

It couldn't be anything to do with the tax revenue on cigarettes, could it? Surely not.

24th November 2006

Combating anti-social behaviour is becoming more and more difficult. This is partly because we are, as a society, less willing to challenge it.

For many years, I have found it impossible to resist the urge to confront loutish behaviour. I remonstrated with two teenagers recently in a high street bookshop whose conversation was not only conducted in Anglo-Saxon profanities, but also delivered at a volume that even their limited awareness must have told them could be easily heard by everyone in the shop, let alone the young mother and daughter standing immediately next to them. Their reaction was predictably truculent.

In common with many of my friends, I have asked people to put their casually discarded litter in the bin; I have urged people in the cinema to bellow their conversations later; I have challenged queue jumpers and people riding bicycles on the pavement. You will, dear reader, no doubt have your own story to tell.

But it may be that we are in an ever-dwindling minority, and for very good reason. A friend of mine, a retired BBC producer, recently paid a high price for remonstrating with a youth cycling on a pavement in London. On being challenged, the youth leapt off his bike and delivered a violent blow to the stomach of my 70-year-old ex-colleague and rode off. My friend died later that day as a result of undiagnosed internal bleeding.

He remembered a time when most unacceptable behaviour could be dealt with swiftly by any passing citizen, most of whom were prepared to take on troublemakers. A word of rebuke and, in most cases, the miscreant would acknowledge the error of his ways.

In a world where discipline is simply a ten-letter word and the rights of the victim seem to be given less weight than those of the aggressor, more and more of us are keeping our heads down. You only have to travel on a train late at night to witness one drunk, drug addict or lout creating a situation where thirty or more people are desperately burying their heads in their papers praying, "Don't let it be me!"

Parents, who passively, and occasionally actively, encourage loutish behaviour in the home, deliver their children to schools where teachers have the unenviable job of nudging them towards civilised behaviour without the back up of many real or effective sanctions.

The good Samaritan would need a bodyguard today.

29th October 2004

The activities of a tiny percentage of the population are beginning to have a vast impact on our lives. And I am not talking about politicians.

The criminal and the deviant have had such an effect on our lives that we have to spend hours proving who we are and that we don't have criminal records. If for no other reason, please bring on the identity card with all its coded information about me. There is nothing about me that I don't want anyone else to know (apart, perhaps, from my weight or waist measurement – and even then it might shame me into tackling those witnesses to my weakness of will).

I am a member of several voluntary organisations that require me regularly to offer my credentials to be checked by the Criminal Records Authority. I have to take my passport, a recent utilities bill and assorted other evidential sundries to an office at the local council where a young lady who doesn't know me from Eve let alone Adam solemnly checks them to confirm my identity and then that confirmed identity is checked against a computer containing the murky details of the ungodly. Thus far I am delighted to say I have come through unscathed. Understandably, some upright citizens who are perfectly well known to the previously mentioned young lady are irritated by the need to go through the first part of the ritual dance. "She has known me for years and I have to show her my passport!"

In the wake of Soham, such checks are to be expected, although clearly in that case checks failed to reveal the actual danger. But given the number of people now being checked, the potential to delay a large number of people from getting on with jobs they have done perfectly well for years is growing. A local school was without a caretaker for half a term while they waited for a satisfactory result; as a result teachers and support staff felt obliged to clean the school every day themselves. Not within their job description, but what could they do if they were not (as few teachers are by nature) dogged jobsworths?

It's bad enough that our society has hidden within it those who seek to harm children and who use positions of authority to achieve their base desires. We see daily examples of those people and no profession is free from them, the church, the police, education and medicine have all produced from their midst people whose appetites are depraved and who prey on the weak. The sad result of this tiny number of the subhuman is that the rest of us are obliged to prove repeatedly that we are not of their number. The presumption of innocence has gone to hell in the same handcart that carried off discipline, good manners, consideration and respect for others and honour. And it is hard to argue against the checks. If one child's life is saved because a potential killer is identified and prevented from being given the opportunity to kill, then your and my irritation is a small price.

But I wish I could get away from the nagging little voice in my ear that whispers, "But they'll lie and cheat the system somehow and they'll still get those jobs in sensitive areas."

At least the ID card with iris, DNA or fingerprint analysing capability will slow them down for a while.

13th April 2002

A week or so ago I was standing in the car park behind Easton Street in Wycombe, with only a five pound note and insufficient small change to pay for a parking ticket. I considered finding somewhere to purchase a small item and thereby get some change. But I knew, as sure as tumbling toast always lands buttered side down, that I would return to find a penalty ticket on my windscreen. I couldn't see a warden, but a sixth sense alerted me to the vibrations of an excited presence in the vicinity, as he or she lay in wait behind a nearby van or 4x4, stealthily unbuttoning a breast pocket containing those little plastic bags.

I was already a little late for my appointment and was weighing up the likelihood of there being any spaces available on my return were I drive off in search of small change, when a young girl approached the ticket machine, getting coins out of her purse. It was worth asking at any rate - so did she by any chance have change for my five pound note?

She didn't, but asked me how much I needed. I needed 45 pence. "Here," she said, passing me the money. "Oh, I couldn't possibly," I demurred. "Please," she replied, "After all, it's no more than the cost of a can of cola." It is, I suppose, a sign of the times (or perhaps of my middle-aged cynicism) that I was quite so surprised by the generosity of a stranger.

I felt the need to show her that, even though the gift of 45p was no big deal to her (it was nine shillings to me!), I valued her kindness. So, I asked her what her favourite charity was - and I will therefore make a donation to Breast Cancer Research at the next opportunity.

But the point is that I left this chance encounter with a spring in my step and feeling warmly disposed to the rest of humanity. This feeling was modified some time later when a teenage boy casually jettisoned into the street a polystyrene carton and its limp lettuce contents, after he had polished off most of its meat-effect polystyrene contents. The obverse side of my desire to thank my earlier benefactor surfaced swiftly.

"And just who do you think should pick that up and dispose of it for you?" I Meldrewed at him, with my eyes undoubtedly bulging in the manner frequently identified and derided by my daughters.

He looked blankly at me, but wasn't so far gone down the cul de sac of truculence or sociopathy as to challenge me or demonstrate his generation's familiarity and ease with Anglo-Saxon. He managed to grunt "Uh?"

I seized the initiative. "Pick it up and put it in that bin over there!"

He did so, but as if he was the one having to deal with an antisocial casual encounter, and slouched off.

A minor victory for civilisation, but by no means as uplifting as my earlier experience.

But when that enemy of gentleness and civility - political correctness - prompts otherwise intelligent people to object when younger third parties stand up for them in trains or open doors for them, as happens all too often, then we can only marvel at the few who do cling to that, alas now old-fashioned, virtue - Good Manners. They really do cost nothing - or 45 pence at most.

25th July 2008

There is a late night fly-on-the-wall programme that follows a group of Thames Valley Police mobile patrols. Initially, I wondered why the police would want to expose themselves to the possible disadvantages of co-operating in the making of such a series, particularly as the ungodly seize every opportunity to feign injured innocence and agony when an officer comes anywhere near them.

But I think I see their strategy now. Offenders drive at breakneck speed through estates and city streets, often on the wrong side of the road, crossing pedestrian areas and wrecking cars and property, knowing that the police will be mindful of the risks to the public of similarly headlong pursuit. One such commences when an officer recognises a disqualified and uninsured driver from three previous offences. When eventually cornered, the driver decamps from the car and is tracked by a helicopter with heat-seeking cameras. We learn that he was later ordered to pay a fine of £250 and had six points put on his licence. What?! Er – what licence? Or is that when he gets it back at the end of the previous disqualification? Those of us who have received similar penalties for driving our cars at 85mph on the motorway may well feel a tad aggrieved; not because we have been treated unfairly necessarily, but that those whose offences are massively more heinous are treated so leniently. Young thugs and criminals know for a fact that there is nothing to be lost in reckless flight because the punishment will be barely more severe than if they meekly surrendered when approached.

The police put up with horrendous abuse from drug-addicted hoodies, dealers and drunks – and the voice-over blithely informs us that the screaming, kicking, foul-mouthed youth was 'later released without charge.'

Could it be that the police have allowed the cameras to follow them in the hope that we, the public, will see this for the rank absurdity that it is and batter at the doors of the legislators who hamper the magistrates and judiciary in the same way as they do the police? People who steal cars and drive them at dangerous speeds to avoid arrest should never be allowed to drive again and should receive penalties considerably harsher than those meted out to those of us who insure and tax our own cars and occasionally get caught breaking a speed limit.

20th Sept 2002

In 1868, public execution was abolished in England. A century earlier you could be hanged if convicted of shoplifting, arson, burglary or forgery.

During the decades that led to the abolition there were doubtless many who protested at the erosion of their civil liberties and way of life and threatened to march on Parliament to protest. Indeed, they were probably only prevented from doing so by the fact that such a protest might be considered a riot, and its perpetrators liable to execution by one of the many inventive methods of cruelty that human beings are uniquely capable of devising.

One can imagine their arguments.

Hangmen and torturers, who have devoted their lives to public service, will be deprived of the ability to support their families by following their trade. The manufacturers of gibbets will have to lay workers off. Smiths, whose livelihoods had already been severely damaged by the abandonment of traditional methods of warfare since swords, axes and suits of armour are no longer used, now face bankruptcy as iron maidens, presses, racks and shackles are being phased out.

Peddlers and merchants, who supply food, mementos and knickknacks (all made by local craftsmen) to the massive crowds who bring their families to these traditional public events, will have to endure penury and hardship, if they lose their traditional marketplace.

Rope manufacturers admit that the volume of their product used in execution by hanging is only a small part of their total output, but are concerned that future research and development of better, stronger rope will be adversely affected without the public platform on which to demonstrate their wares. Bow street runners, who police these potentially explosive public occasions, will lose overtime and will therefore, understandably, very soon be pressing for a raise in their basic salary. This will in turn create a drain on the public purse that can only result in the creation of extra, unpopular taxation.

Town and city dwellers see this as yet another example of the inability of those who live in the affluent countryside to understand the traditional urban lifestyle. The wealthy landowners and their employees not only enjoy a higher standard of living than the town and city dwellers, but they also have a disproportionate say in the affairs of the rest of our country. But it is the townsmen of England who fell at Waterloo to defend liberty. And now the privileged shire-dwellers are threatening to deprive us of our traditional entertainment. It is the thin end of the wedge. It is public execution that they are threatening to ban today. But tomorrow it will be our other liberties that will be eroded. Flogging, the stocks and pillories will be next on these "reformists"' agenda. Then penal servitude and even simple imprisonment will be banned. Where will the soft living country gentry stop? It will be our inns and taverns next.

And what will happen when children who have never seen an execution themselves peek through the windows of a prison to get a glimpse of a hanging? Will they be criminalized simply for doing something that has been acceptable for generations?

And it's not as if they actually hang that many felons anyway. Most of them get away.

And those that don't know it will be quick and clean, if it is done publicly, rather than hidden away.

Anyway many of them seem to rather enjoy their moment of fame.

25th November 2005

Why am I still surprised when a school is broken into and robbed of its computers and petty cash? We live in a world where octogenarians are mugged for a handful of coins and where children are knifed for their mobile phones, or because they're simply different. Each time most of us are appalled and find it hard to imagine how any human being can be so devoid of imagination and compassion as to intentionally prey upon the weak and the infirm. But we have daily proof that they exist, even though their humanity may be questionable. We all know too that it is nothing to do with poverty or deprivation. I was brought up in Lancashire, where as the mills closed there was widespread, utter poverty and minimal social welfare, but not only were schools and the elderly safe from robbery and violence, but even the comparatively well off could leave their doors unlocked without the inevitability of thereby guaranteeing a criminal invasion by the then very real "have-nots."

Last week, while members of staff at a local rural primary school were still on the premises working in the late afternoon, intruders ransacked the office, stole laptop computers and cash and left a mess in their wake. As there was no sign of forcible entry, the insurance company won't pay out, so the school's budget will have to bear the cost. This happens on a regular basis all over the country. At the same time as an apparent and probably drug-related moral vacuum exists in certain sections of society, we also have an undermanned and under-funded police force at a time when we need the reverse more than ever before in my lifetime. The school was told not to touch anything until the police came. It isn't the fault of the police that they weren't able to get there for thirty six hours, but that made it harder for them to collect evidence as things simply had to be touched to enable the school to function. Non-violent burglary from a school is understandably a little way down the queue, given the huge demands on the Police.

But it left the children feeling not only vulnerable, but in receipt of mixed messages about the consequences of crime. The reassuring and benevolent presence of the police is not necessarily hard on the heels of criminal activity, which can only encourage potential young miscreants and further discourage the law-abiding.

20th August 2004

A councillor in Princes Risborough was reported last week as having recommended a spell in the stocks for vandals who had destroyed a twenty-year old tree in the King George V recreation ground. The report suggested that this radical sanction for antisocial behaviour was advocated "jokingly." Clearly, the current caring and sharing mindset that is perceived as sending young thugs off for character-building holidays while their victims languish in hospitals has resulted in this councillor, or the journalist that reported his suggestion, seeing the need to tread carefully. But I'll bet he meant it really, deep down. In fact, many people would advocate politically incorrect solutions to socially incorrect behaviour privately, but hesitate to do so publicly.

But, would it really be a retrograde step to identify and vilify those who share and embrace Margaret Thatcher's infamous (or perhaps ironic?) suggestion that there is no such thing as society? Why shouldn't those who repeatedly demonstrate a complete disregard for the rest of us be subjected to public scrutiny and forced to face up to the consequences of our contempt for their behaviour?

It is arguable that actual, physical stand-there-with-your arms-through-holes type stocks might not necessarily work every time. Today's Neanderthals are less prone to conscience than those of yesteryear and might even see the ritual indignity as evidence of their status as a really effective thug. They would possibly also later visit their sociopathic wrath on everyone who came and gazed upon their unlovely countenances, as they stood pilloried in the High Street. But for those whose actions are generated by stupidity rather than wickedness, or who are weak enough to be led astray by others, the threat of a podium of odium might just serve as sufficient deterrent to reduce the number of offences.

It is certainly true that what we are doing now is not working. Yes, it would help reduce antisocial behaviour if we provided adequate opportunities for young people to channel all that testosterone, angst and hunter-seeker energy. But inadequate social provision is not an excuse or indeed a reason for vandalism or antisocial behaviour. Otherwise the generation of my childhood would have pulled down the entire fabric of society. The problem is more complex than can be solved by simply bribing the malcontents to behave better. And as for paying truants to go to school, well, I can feel my blood pressure rising when I consider that particular initiative, so I will forbear to comment on that or the apparent inability of the government to find a way of ensuring that rapists' lottery wins are re-directed swiftly towards their victims.

The modern version of the pillory and the stocks might be to use the media to regularly name and shame. CCTV footage of offenders committing their offences could be transmitted, without any of that Data Protection Act nonsense of protecting the identity of the criminal. The commission of an offence and subsequent conviction should automatically nullify any protection for offenders afforded by that clumsy and ill-drafted act. It is time that we started to find ways of protecting the law-abiding majority without at the same providing the opportunity for the thug and the criminal to hide behind that protection.

But in a country in which the Department of Constitutional Affairs translates a leaflet offering advice to asylum seekers into Welsh to comply with the Welsh Language Act – we shouldn't expect too much.

8. The Beautiful Game

Bill Shankly, the late, wonderfully idiosyncratic manager of Liverpool once stated "Some people believe football is a matter of life and death. I'm very disappointed with that attitude. I can assure you it is much, much more important than that."

This is clearly untrue, a fact that should be underlined to provide a sense of perspective for some of the football fans who might be tempted to allow their passion to spill over into aggressive behaviour to those who support a team other than their own. But we all know exactly what Shankly meant. There are very few other things that I am so desperate to hear at the earliest possible opportunity that we lead me to ask fellow actors to convey the latest information to me via signals while I am on stage.

And similarly I have entered the stage myself with my fingers arranged on my lapel as an indication of the current score in a key football match. For some reason we do care about our football teams. It has been suggested in some quarters that football stadia have replaced churches as focal points for community cohesion. I wouldn't dare to comment on that, but it is undeniable that, in terms of weekly attendances nationwide, I suspect that the figures would compare very unfavourably for the churches. And it is undeniable that the latter have better architecture and attract a less volatile audience/congregation.

I have supported Manchester United since I was a child in school in Manchester, (will there ever be a player to rival the magic and charisma of Eric Cantona?) and Wycombe Wanderers since I moved to live near that town twenty or so years ago. For home matches I can walk with my wife along a leafy lane and down a hill to the stadium , where we sit with people we have now known for many years, on a two weekly basis, and groan, cheer, exult or deflate together as the Chairboys battle away for our entertainment. I find it both relaxing and exhilarating and a complete change from the professional world I inhabit. That is not to say that I do not find the need to grump and grumble about various things from time to time, but it all stems from a love of the game of football and my two teams in particular.

28th March 2008

Player behaviour and respect for referees has hit the headlines again this week. I am amazed that there are still those who are prepared to defend actions that are steadily eroding the respect the game once had throughout the country. The apologists for the louts who gather mob-handed to bellow obscenities and abuse at referees talk about "passion for the game," "the heat of the moment," etc. Are they suggesting that rugby players have no passion? That cricketers don't care?

Yet these sports seem to produce men who can take even perceived injustices on the chin and move on, with a shake of the head at worst. I heard Tony Hawkes, the comedian, talking about his childhood as an aspiring tennis player this week. He spoke of his youthful emulation of Jimmy Connors, when the latter's fiery temperament led him to hurl his racket to the ground and question decisions – minor stuff admittedly in the context of the recent behaviour of some premiership players. He said his behaviour changed when Bjorn Borg came on the scene and proved that the Ice Man Winneth. Was there ever a better example of the effect that high profile footballers can have on the young players of their generation? Anyone who has witnessed primary school parents and their children hurling abuse at referees would know that something must be done to rescue football.

It is no coincidence that when there was self-discipline on the pitch, when the likes of the lowly paid Stanley Matthews and Billy Wright were playing football, with passion, the behaviour of the tens of thousands who stood in the terraces to watch them was similarly exemplary.

Who would put themselves in the firing line today to referee a grass roots match? No wonder so many referees are walking away from the game they love. Something needs to be done urgently, at all levels. But it is overwhelmingly evident that only a sea shift in the attitude of the League, the FA and FIFA, that empowers and encourages referees to penalise unsportsmanlike and loutish behaviour instantly and effectively, can reverse the trend. Maybe some of Rugby's excellent stratagems could be tried? Only the captain may speak to the referee, a sin bin and ten yard advancement of free kicks for dissent?

No one who has seen louts arguing with police officers in the street can doubt the effect the behaviour on the pitch is having in society.

25th April 2003

The fan phenomenon is fascinating. The fan of yesteryear was a supporter. One who followed his team through thick and thin. If your team lost, you shared the players' disappointment and encouraged them to do better next time. When I was young, my local team was relegated to the then second division, but not one of my friends ever suggested for a second that we should desert them. In fact, the general consensus was that they needed us more. The team was Manchester United. I am sorry that I now have to share my lifetime's allegiance with people in Sumatra, Ecuador and Beijing and incur the sneers of those who don't know my origins and see only a southerner following a fashionable team.

I have lived in Wycombe for 18 years and now also support Wycombe Wanderers. My wife and four daughters have been to every home match, and some aways. I have been to as many matches as I could, given my work commitments.

I have used this column before to express my surprise at the comparatively undemonstrative nature of the Adams Park regulars. I am also amazed at the number of (presumably) unemployed footballers and football managers who populate the stands. As it is so blindingly obvious how the team should be deployed and how they should play, I am amazed that they are all free to watch the Wanderers rather than hurtling up the wing or sitting on a lonely bench themselves.

My family attended the fans' forum (My wife managed to tread on Stuart Roberts' foot to her dismay – but to no apparent ill effect to him, thank goodness). The majority of those who attended were supportive, but some fans seemed to care more about what Mr. Sanchez had said about them, rather than recent form. Lawrie has in the past expressed his frustration (which I understand and share), that fans don't truly get behind the team on a regular basis. Remarkably, he promised that night never to criticise the fans again – if that was what mattered to them. So I suppose I'll have to do it for him, starting as I always do with those who leave before the match ends.

I'm glad that is a rarity in the theatre, although it seems endemic in football.

The news that Glenn Roeder, the manager of West Ham, is currently hospitalised suffering from an enlarged blood vessel in his brain will, I hope, serve as a timely humanity alert to all those fans (and the word "fan" jars slightly in this context) that howled abuse at Glenn before the game at the weekend, which the beleaguered Hammers actually won.

Cardiff City lose three games at the end of the season and despite the fact that they are in contention for promotion still, the fans bay for the blood of the manager.

Whenever the Blues go out on the field there is another team there, with another manager who will be criticised by their fans if they don't deliver. Not everyone can win. And players who get no encouragement from their supporters are less likely to do so.

A second division side with no millionaire patron shouldn't have a hope of getting to the FA semis. We did.

We now have several talented young players coming through. Let's see them develop and start another winning streak.

We'll be renewing our season tickets and cheering the boys on next season.

30th June 2006

The Russian referee, Valentin Ivanov, who handed out four red and sixteen yellow cards during the match between Portugal and Holland this week, apart from doing England a favour by removing a couple of first choice players from the Portuguese line-up against us for Saturday's match, has also attracted a lot of criticism. Some suggest that his adherence to the rules was overly officious and stifled the game. FIFA President, the egregious Sepp Blatter, maintained, "There could have been a yellow card for the referee. He was not at the same level as the players."

And what level is that, Sepp? Diving, shirt pulling, face clutching agonies while feigning injury, snatching the ball up to prevent the other side from taking a free kick and general downright cheating seems to be tolerated by most referees, on the sole basis that to do otherwise would inevitably result in the two goal keepers staring at each other over tumbleweed blowing across an empty pitch before half time.

It occurred to me, while watching the match and listening to the subsequent reactions, that if all referees adopted this tougher approach, the players might, in a very short time, unlearn the bad habits of a lifetime and play the game the way it used to be played – by men who fought to stay on their feet rather than perform a dying swan routine every time someone brushed past them, with sportsmanship and without bellowing obscenities at each other and the referee.

It is ironic that when Stanley Matthews and Nat Lofthouse played football half a century ago, for a wage not vastly dissimilar to that of the working men who watched them, it would never have occurred to them to obtain an unfair advantage by diving, nor would they have tried to pressurise the referee into sending an opponent off. A victory gained by those means would have been hollow for those men.

Yes, there should be consistency in refereeing, but make it a consistency that supports rather than ignores the rules of the game, that rewards good fair play and punishes cheating, that allows the skilful player to dazzle rather than dodge the two-footed, studs-forward challenge of his opponent.

Turning a blind eye works no more on the football pitch than it does in the rest of life. Until that unfashionable word "discipline" regains popular currency, the cheats, thugs and vandals will continue to walk all over us.

27th November 1999

Until very recently, the last football match I had actually attended was Liverpool v Tottenham at Anfield in 1971. I was working at Liverpool Playhouse and was taken to stand in the Kop by a friend and colleague, Tom Georgeson (an excellent actor, recently seen as Samantha Janus' boss in "Liverpool 1"). I recall that after several minutes, he suggested that I might, for my own safety, wish to either swiftly adopt a Liverpool accent or desist from shouting, "Well played you Re-eds" in my BBC tones, which might have been acceptable "Conduct Unbecoming" on the stage but were perhaps ill advised in the midst of that particular red army.

I recently accepted an invitation to accompany a good friend to see Wycombe Wanderers take on Bristol Rovers at Adams Park. And during those decades of only watching football on the television, I had forgotten just how very different and highly enjoyable the live experience can be.

I cannot put hand on heart and say that the match was a classic. The Wycombe squad was depleted to the tune of four of its regular first team players. There was far too much optimistic punting from one end to the other, on the part of both teams, and despite some erratic refereeing decisions, the 1-1 draw was probably a fair result.

Predictably, I kept looking around for the screen on which to watch the instant replays. It was the first time in decades that I hadn't seen every goal and incident from all angles at least a dozen times.

Aside from that, several things struck me very forcibly. I had genuinely forgotten how exciting it is to be there in the flesh, how close to the action you are, particularly at Adams Park and how good it is to choose for yourself what you look at.

In other ways however, the experience was different to what I remember from all those years ago, when we stood as a throng of strangers, albeit like-minded ones, who frequently surged backwards and forwards, whether we wanted to or not, like a stormy sea of humanity.

Seating has made a phenomenal difference This is not just because it is more comfortable or because the crowd doesn't surge and seethe in such an alarming way. What I particularly noticed was the camaraderie that has built up between season ticket holders who come regularly to support their team. There was a distinct family atmosphere, a far greater number of ladies, children and a much wider age range. I resolved to make the effort to come again to see my local team when I get the chance. And rooting for a local team is what it's all about. They may not be Manchester United, which is incidentally the team I have supported since I was aware of football in the 50's, when I lived in Manchester. The Munich air crash devastated us all; I even went to pay my respects at the grave of Duncan Edwards, whose promise to be the greatest footballer ever was so cruelly cut short.

The Wanderers certainly played with commitment and effort; and any team that has a player called Jermaine McSporran deserves our support. He came on as a substitute that day and proceeded to run at the Rovers' defence, a tendency that had been somewhat lacking until then. Clearly one to watch.

I would urge anyone who has thought about returning to Football after years of absence, like me, to give it a try and get down to Adams Park one Saturday afternoon to awaken some good memories.

22nd December 2006

Although it is Christmas, having been at the Valley with around five thousand other Wycombe fans on Tuesday night, it would be unthinkable not to celebrate Easter this week - Jermaine Easter, who scored the winning goal that humbled Charlton Athletic. And not just Easter - but the whole Wanderers' team. Every one of them battled, sprinted and harried the Premiership strugglers for the full ninety five minutes and thoroughly deserved the spectacular win that saw the Chairboys through to their second major knockout cup semi-final in their short thirteen-year league history. An uncommitted casual observer would have been very hard pressed to determine which of the two teams was in the senior division.

Indeed, were it not for Scott Carson, their England world cup goalkeeper on loan from Liverpool, a score line of three or four nil would not have been an unreasonable reflection of our team's effort, commitment and passion on the night.

The Wycombe fans, usually so reserved and slow to ignite at home, were magnificent too. The support was so loud and constant, that at no point did I hear anything from the home fans, who admittedly only outnumbered us by less than two to one.

It was worth the three hours spent in a coach on the way there. It was even worth the two hours on the way back enduring the rowdy teenagers who occupied the back of our coach with scant consideration for we senior citizens at the front.

There will always be a minority of football fans that unfairly tarnish the vast majority who are genuine sports lovers but there were none such in evidence at the Valley. On the way in a Charlton fan, seeing that we were confused, offered his assistance and pointed us in the right direction. And afterwards, despite their own inevitable disappointment, many of them congratulated us on our team's "deserved win" and wished us well in the semi-final.

It is just as well that I am not appearing in pantomime this year – I wouldn't have had much voice left to entertain the audience the following day! Mind you, had I been in panto mode I might have had the inspiration to shout at their goalie, "It's behind you!" when Easter made all our Christmases come at once after 35 minutes of scintillating cup football.

Arsenal? Tottenham? Chelsea? Our semi final revenge on Liverpool? Over two legs?

Bring it on!

9th January 2004

Tony Adams' credentials as a player are peerless. He played for England for over twenty-four years and won more trophies with Arsenal than any other captain of that club, four league championships, three FA cups, two league cups, one Cup Winners' Cup, three Charity Shields and two double winning seasons.

Two months ago this week he arrived at Causeway Stadium full of East End promise.

He had been associated with the manager's jobs at West Ham (which he would have joined had Trevor Brocking agreed to stay on with him), Reading, Brighton and Crystal Palace. He chose to come to Wycombe. Why, he has not yet explained. I have been unable to find anything to suggest that he saw anything in the squad or the town that he admired. He said only that he felt that Wanderers fans would be more forgiving than East Enders who, he claimed, "like knocking their own."

Adams promised that he would try to emulate "...George Graham's resilience, Martin O'Neill's enthusiasm, Arsène Wenger's empathy with the team and his sensitivity and man management, and people like Terry Venables who is an amazing coach and had a brilliant way of putting his ideas across."

Erm, Tony? I know you have apologised for your uncompromising and brutal comments after our defeat at the hands of Rushden and Diamonds, but it's hard to imagine Arsène opting to motivate his players by dismissing quite so comprehensively them as footballers and people. And however much you may try to imply otherwise now, one still feels that those comments about an uncertain future referred to yourself at least as much as the team. They just weren't the words of the fighter that you always were and want your players to be.

This is the second division. Some players are more naturally gifted than others. A few could play at a higher level, though maybe not at the level you did. You praised the loan players last week, quite rightly but, sadly, exclusively. But Darren Currie had provided some quite magnificent crosses to supply those players and Jocky McSporran's volleyed goal was one of the best I've ever seen at Adam's Causeway or anywhere else in the division. The players may not have received the level of support they deserve recently. Knocking them further down just may not be the best way to move forward, if you don't have Russian (or any other) money to buy players.

Yes, we will miss all the loan players; particularly Newcastle and England under 20's loan Steve Taylor. He not only played with passion and commitment for a team that quite frankly he had no reason other than a love of football to care a hoot about, but he also delighted this fan and many others by coming over to us and demonstrating his solidarity and appreciation of our support when we lost, and our evident delight at our victory over Grimsby. Those few extra minutes ensured my lifelong interest in his future career.

The animation that you showed on the touchline on Saturday, when we dominated Grimsby was also uplifting, and what we expected to see from a great and passionate footballer. It contrasted with the body language displayed during the previous match, which reminded us too much of what we had been used to seeing.

Tony Adams is an anagram of "Today's man" – keep us in Division 2, Tony, and be A Man for All Seasons!

20th January 2006

Whenever any young person dies in a road traffic accident it is a tragedy. When that young person had already apparently overcome considerable adversity with courage and cheerful stoicism it is, if that were humanly possible, doubly tragic. Mark Philo was a talented young footballer who had shown enormous promise at an early age and who had been considered to have the potential to figure largely in the future plans of the club that had employed him for six years, Wycombe Wanderers. A succession of unlucky injuries that had effectively delayed those plans by almost a year and a half had apparently not dented his enthusiasm for the sport that he loved, nor his determination to bounce back from injury and fight for a regular place at the Causeway Stadium. His second broken ankle in two years had finally mended recently and he was back in training again and looking for an early return to regular competitive football. In the early hours of Saturday morning in Reading, the car he was driving was involved in a collision with another car, the woman driver of which tragically also lost her life.

In a world in which one encounters glum, dour and sullen faces on a daily basis, it was even more poignant to read in the many tributes left to Mark outside the stadium references to his characteristic enormous smile. I queued there this week and signed the book of condolence in the club reception. Immediately before my contribution, one of the younger squad players had written a very moving and personal farewell to Mark, thanking him for all the help, support and encouragement that he had given him. To be honest, I felt somewhat intrusive sharing his affectionate farewell to his friend, even though it was written in a book made available for public contribution and therefore also for public view.

But reading it served as a reminder that our sadness as fans was nothing compared to the loss experienced by his friends and colleagues and particularly his family, who knowing of Mark's loyalty to the club that he had joined as a fifteen year old, insisted that the team should not be told of his fatal injuries before the game last Saturday and that the match should not be cancelled. They wanted the team to win the game for Mark and they did.

But how sad it is to have so much youthful promise snuffed out so cruelly.

2nd September 2005

There can be few pleasures to compare with sitting in the Causeway Stadium on a late summer Saturday afternoon, watching one's local team playing the kind of football that hasn't been seen in Sands for quite a while. Without wishing to put a jinx on it, under the guidance of John Gorman, the lads are passing like a dream, playing committed and attractive football and making some of the opposition look rather ordinary. Long may it continue. Hopefully the fans, who still look askance at my student daughter when her lone voice rings around the family stand urging on the Blues, will eventually creep out of their habitual shells and give voice. The team deserves no less.

But the enhanced experience of watching the football is still slightly marred by a continuing irritation for this spectator and many others to whom I have spoken. If you buy food and drink at the ground – and that is a traditional part of the experience – the vendors are obliged to remove the bottle tops from our drinks. The reason is apparently to do with notion that Wanderers' fans, who can barely bring themselves to shout support most of the time, might be tempted to hurl missiles at the pitch.

I conducted a scientific experiment today. I removed a bottle top from a 50 cl bottle of water and, using my considerable physical strength (yeah alright...) ...well – I threw it several times. The longest distance I could muster was 35 feet. I then asked a friend to throw one at me from half that distance and felt nothing.

So it's not the bottle top.

Maybe a full bottle, with its top screwed on is the problem? That went about fifty feet.

Then I threw a full bottle of water without the top on – it went about fifty feet and only lost some of its contents when it landed.

Add to this conclusive experiment the fact that when I recently went to see Manchester United at Old Trafford, where the crowd is actually slightly closer to the pitch, the drinks vendor looked at me as if I was mad when I asked him if he wanted to remove my top (actually now I write that, I can see why...).

Anyway, clearly the fans at Man U are less prone to violence!

Is this bizarre and patronising irritation simply a way of ensuring that we drink up quicker (or spill it all?) ensuring an increase in drink sales?

Answers please, Wanderers!

9.   Abroad...

Following on from the earlier chapter on Little England, there is the inevitable connection to be made with the world outside these tiny islands in the North Sea. I have been lucky enough to travel far and wide in connection with my work mainly, though the occasional foray to foreign climes has been occasioned by a family holiday. Having a large family, most of the holidays we have taken together have been in Cornwall, a county that my wife and I are determined to retire to one day, if the vagaries of my profession allow such a luxury as retirement.

Travel is certainly an enriching activity, and I am perhaps guilty of not being sufficiently curious about the big world out there to have availed myself of as many such opportunities as I might. I console myself by watching the world and its many mysteries and exotic peoples on some of the wonderful television programmes that are available from the comfort of my home. It is perhaps a result of my spending so much time away from home and family that I cherish the times that I am there with them disproportionately. I greatly admire people like Peter Duncan, (with whom I worked on the play 'Corpse!' a few years ago), who took his young family on a round the world trip, followed by backpacking through China and India. He and they doubtless benefitted hugely from the experience, which undoubtedly offers a much fuller education than many children get in their schools. But I am not made of such stuff. Travel for me is a necessary activity to get to somewhere where I have to do something. I am not one who can sit on a beach and sunbathe, though I have greatly enjoyed those evening spent with my wife and daughters over a longer and more leisurely meal than we are normally able to enjoy, in a warm and picturesque location.

But the process of travel remains, I think for most of us, something that we have to endure in order to get somewhere else that we need or want to be.
Not my favourite activity.

Friday 30th March 2007

It's high time that we, the British, held a few people to account.

We should start with Margarethe II and Anders Fogh Rasmussen, respectively the Queen and Prime Minister of Denmark. An apology is long overdue for the appalling depredations of the Vikings and their ruthless imposition of Danegeld, a punitive tax, on the peace-loving and docile pushovers that inhabited the rest of Europe a thousand years ago. Any nation that sets up what is no less than an international protection racket should be ashamed of itself. And what about Romano Prodi? I don't think I have heard him apologising for the decades of invasion, conquest and subjugation that resulted in the Roman Empire which subsumed the majority of the known world and imposed Roman values and beliefs on Britain.

There are also the cities and roads that they inflicted on us, without which there would have been no Congestion Zones or indeed congestion, but a perennial rural England inhabited by Angle and Celt peasants with no military or colonial ambition to pass on to future generations.

And then there are the French and Spanish who spent half a millennium attempting, at various times, to invade Britain either directly or by assisting the Scots to do so. So let's be hearing from you, Dominique de Villepin and José Luis Rodríguez Zapatero.

William of Orange may well have been invited by Parliament to come and rule in England instead of King James – but does that make it right? As I always say to my children, "If your mates asked you to saw your leg off with a rusty knife, would you do it? No? Well don't use somebody else as an excuse then. Think for yourself."

So, that means that Queen Beatrix and Jan Peter Balkenende should be considering very carefully whether or not they also owe us an apology.

On the other hand, maybe we can acknowledge that things that happened two hundred and more years ago, whilst objectively wrong, regrettable and occasionally monstrous, were done in a different age by very different people with very different beliefs and priorities. Perhaps we can move on, certainly think about the sins of our fathers and learn from them without indulging in any ritual personal breast-beating for things that people who may or may not have been our ancestors may have done to other people, who may or may not have been someone else's ancestors.

29th September 2001

I am not a vindictive person. Well… I try to suppress it anyway, but I am finding it hard to resist wishing a plague of boils on the execrable worm that stole my camera case in Majorca. I forgot at the time that my mobile phone was in it. Three days later, I realised that the thief had reaped an unlooked-for harvest. I reported the loss immediately and rang my airtime supplier for several days thereafter to see if calls had been made on it. When the answer remained in the negative, I thanked my lucky stars and moved on.

Last week, in the Cornmarket in Wycombe, I tried to phone my wife and was surprised to find I couldn't. Luckily, I was buying flowers next-door to the shop that I have used for some years for my family's growing mobile phone needs (I eventually reluctantly conceded that 21st century teenage girls need the protection the wretched things afford). The helpful chaps who work there told me that my sim card had been blocked because of excessive use. The peseta started to drop ominously, along with my heart into my boots. A faxed printout of the usage revealed that over three days calls had been made costing £432; and my sneak thief was insomniac, or he passed the phone around his North Africa loving friends, because there was only one period of two hours (from 2 a.m. to 4 a.m.) when lengthy calls were not made to Algeria.

In the very small box at the back of my brain labelled "Hope," I thought that I wouldn't have to pay, because I hadn't made the calls. Time for your pills, Colin!!

I telephoned my airtime supplier and spoke to a young man whose customer interface capabilities (as they probably call it these days) came from the "Customers? Who needs 'em?" school.

"As you will recall, if you read the terms and conditions before you signed the contract..."

"You mean those pages printed in a font that would allow the bible to be written on the head of a pin... ...well, actually I didn't read them all."

"Well you shouldn't have signed it, if you hadn't read it."

"Oh come on, do you read the small print on everything you sign?"

"Yes, sir, I do sir." (It's amazing how the word "sir" can take on a meaning precisely opposite to the one it purports to have when spoken by one who knows you can't get your itching hands around his jobsworth neck.)

I shifted into begging mode. Surely a big rich company like yours, with whom I have had a happy relationship for years, will not want to profit from my misfortune? Might they write off the profit element of the calls, if I pay the rest?

You can guess the answer. Furthermore, they wouldn't unblock my line until I had paid off half of the bill, even though the direct debit wasn't due for another three weeks.

There is something almost intolerable about having to pay out a large sum of money because of the criminal act of a third party that has already caused you financial loss.

So be warned by this cautionary tale. Unless you're confident that the ungodly can't run up vast bills on your or your children's phones, use virtual locks or small prepayment packages, otherwise you'll join me in an Apoplexy and Rage Management Clinic.

27th August 2004

I'm off to Canada this weekend for a couple of days' work on a French film. It sounds very exotic, but I suspect that, as usual, I shall see no more of Montreal than an airport, an hotel, a film studio and the roads in-between; and the notion of visiting new and exciting places would be more attractive if the actual process of travelling hadn't become so tedious and fraught.

The queue to check in, when everyone in front of you seems to take twenty minutes but you're done and dusted in as many seconds, the queue to be subjected to the very necessary security checks that involve emptying your pockets into those little trays so that everyone can look askance at the head of Spiderman that you had intended to reunite with his body before you left. He sits, staring accusingly alongside the lip salve, your loose change and keys, as you pass through the metal detector that still reacts because of your belt buckle. Last time, I had the tiny screwdriver that I use to tighten up my spectacles confiscated. Quite clearly, I was just the sort of misfit who would suddenly leap up, brandishing my minuscule screwdriver, and threaten to loosen everyone's lenses, one by one, unless the plane landed – wait for it - at the gate nearest the terminal. I actually suspect that those gates are all dummy ones. Every plane I travel on involves a two-mile hike along identical passageways and past endless suspiciously empty gates. Have you ever landed at a gate near the terminal? I thought not.

Travel may broaden the mind. I wish they would broaden the seats, which in steerage – sorry, "World Traveller" - are really only designed to carry Kate Moss's skinnier younger sister. On a transatlantic hop, one's world-view changes to the extent that it is measurable in inches only. Simple things like reading a newspaper become logistical assault courses, where turning the page can take minutes of precision muscle control that would be the envy of an Olympic asymmetric bars gymnast. The last long-haul flight I endured, I spent sitting next to a young lady who shared my disinclination to risk ten hours' conversation with a stranger, so we occupied our minuscule universes with mutual consideration. Our only interchange was on the subject of the ten-year-old girl in front of us who appeared to have a pogo stick in the seat with her, and the two younger boys behind, who apparently avoided compound fractures of their toes despite kicking our seats relentlessly throughout the journey.

Turning and delivering those looks that we fondly imagined convey an unspoken threat of unimaginable retribution achieved nothing. She snapped first. Muttering to me that they should have been strangled at birth, she glared over the back of the seat and with enough artificial sweetness to put Canderel out of business said, "Do you think you could stop kicking the back of my seat?"

Their lethargic mother said something faintly admonitory in an Hispanic language, whereupon they commenced an all-out attempt to get into the Guinness Book of Records for perpetual motion. Not long later, I cracked under the onslaught and literally begged her to stop them bashing the back of my seat.

Meanwhile the girl in front appeared to be testing the seat recline mechanism to destruction until we de-planed (as the Americans will so inelegantly have it).

I can't wait.

21st February 2003

Very soon after September 11th 2001, I travelled to the United States and was underwhelmed by the level of security that had been put in place to prevent further terrorist outrages. In fact, the only difference I noticed was that I was asked by a soldier, toting an automatic rifle, whether I was carrying any knives, guns or other weapons. You may share my conviction that had I been an armed terrorist, I might also be sufficiently dastardly as to lie about it. Furthermore, the probing question was barked at me with the same degree of genuine interest displayed by those telephonists who thank you for calling them and ask if they can help you, in those dreadful sing-song falling cadences.

Last weekend, I went over there again and was much more impressed with the precautions taken at both Heathrow and Los Angeles Airports. When screening precautions are demonstrably effective, one is happy to endure queues and inconvenience. I had to show my passport at four or five different stages in the process and said goodbye to the little screwdriver that I carry everywhere because manufacturers of spectacles seem unable to assemble them with screws that don't consistently try to escape, shouting, "I've been framed!" I spent a merry ten minutes sharing the contents of my bag, after the X-ray revealed its outline.

I was told I could collect it on my return through the airport. But as it would cost four pounds, it struck me that it would be cheaper to buy a new one. I wonder what they do with all those confiscated screwdrivers? I also wonder how much a small screwdriver differs in lethal potential from a biro or pencil, of which there were also several in my arsenal. But that's quibbling.

On the return journey the identity checks, screenings and baggage checks were similarly stringent and frequent. My suitcase was passed through an X-ray machine at check-in, and hand luggage was thoroughly checked. It is all now certainly more than tokenism. Those of us who can remember when it was truly possible to "pass without let or hindrance," may mourn the passing of those carefree days, but I suspect they will never return.

They may have been national enmities in the past but they are eclipsed today by the fanaticism of the jihad mentality and the terrorist. It was all thrown into sharp perspective by a sight that greeted me on my return. As always, my plane landed at the end of a series of interminable corridors and the motorised walkway was out of commission (do any planes arrive at the nearer gates?).

As I turned my third corner to see yet another long corridor, demonstrating the truth of the laws of perspective, I noticed a row of seats in a transition lounge and wished my camera were in my hand luggage. Four Hasidic Jews with their plaited locks, beards, open-necked white shirts and black homburgs were sitting immediately next to three sprawling young men who lacked tattoos only where their skin was pierced by metal rings, bails and crosses. Next to them were four ladies (presumably) gazing serenely at the world through the letterbox openings in their burkahs. Without wishing to stereotype anyone, I couldn't help feeling that if we could transfer the enforced mutual tolerance in the melting pot of a busy airport into our everyday lives, then we could start to take down the metal detectors again.

5th September 2003

The Roman Empire, we are told, came to an end not as a result of marauding Goths, pillaging Vandals or the Mongol hordes sweeping down the Po; them they could see off in a trice with a couple of legions. It simply self-destructed as a result of moral decay and internal disintegration. I find myself wondering whether a first millennium political correctness was one of the early symptoms of that impending collapse.

The Western world is rife with it, today. Third World countries have enough trouble feeding (or failing to feed) their deprived millions to have the time or the desire to employ focus groups to identify those whose civil liberties might be being infringed by the cultural and gender stereotypes in children's nursery rhymes. If they had time to even notice the absurd paroxysms of their "First" World neighbours, they would find it hard to comprehend us.

And it is not just in this country that the creeping malaise signals the disintegration of common sense on a terrifying scale. In New York a convicted murderer is suing the state for failing to fund the sex change operation that would enable him to transfer to a women's prison. A judge has allowed the case to go ahead on the basis that failure to treat gender identity disorder could be considered to be "cruel and unusual punishment."

An Australian prisoner who injured himself in a fall from his bunk bed, that he claimed had not been bolted down properly, has won more than $100,000 compensation. The Crown decided not to fight the case – believed to be the first of its kind - and now taxpayers will foot the bill. Children in Melbourne have been banned from dressing up as Superman or Batman while at their child care groups, whose organisers have declared them "super-hero free zones," as wearing the costumes might result in aggressive behaviour.

A childminder in Hampshire has been castigated in an Ofsted report on her playgroup for failing to provide play materials that reflect ethnic diversity. Her charges should apparently have been encouraged to play with ethnic minority or disabled dolls. And the hapless childminder who had been looking after children without complaint for more than a decade was berated for not cooking special meals to celebrate different cultural events, like Chinese New Year.

A ten thousand pound grant was offered to the organisers of an annual fête in Dewsbury, Yorkshire on the proviso that they should consider removing the beer tent in case it offended local Muslims. I am delighted to report that members of the local Asian community, who regularly attended the event, were outraged. A spokesman quite rightly pointed out that they were perfectly happy with the way that the fete was run and that such ludicrous and patronising behaviour played right into the hands of the right wing extremist groups.

And now it is proposed that a compulsory language test for foreign doctors wanting to work in this country may be scrapped. Hitherto they had to undertake a four-hour examination to ensure that their speaking, writing and reading skills in English were sufficient to enable them to practise medicine effectively. But it has been suggested that the practice may be discriminatory. Like it is probably discriminatory to prevent blind people from becoming taxi drivers, or to insist that our police force is not recruited from the ranks of the inmates of our penal institutions.

23rd February 2007

I spent the last week in Los Angeles (who's a little jet setter then?) as a guest at a Science Fiction Convention, which meant that I had to fly, as all other options are a little time consuming.

The process of flying requires that you shut all systems down and go into tick-over mode. The less you expect in terms of comfort, food and rest, the more likely you are to survive without running amok with a plastic coffee stirrer.

When I finally staggered back across the drawbridge of Baker Towers, I realised that it had taken me a mere ten hours to cross continental America and the Atlantic but three hours to get from the aeroplane to my home. The first twenty minutes sitting on the tarmac, after we landed, were unavoidable - I concede. A passenger required the services of a paramedic team and we were asked to remain seated until they and their patient had cleared the plane. I need hardly tell you that several passengers declined to accede to this request and dragged their luggage down the aisles seemingly impervious to the hostile gaze of the compliant majority.

The next phase highlighted for me a mystery that has been intensified every time I fly from Heathrow. Does anyone recall ever flying from or landing at a gate that was not at the furthest point from the departure/arrival lounges? I can't. There appear to be planes parked all along the sides but I am beginning to suspect that they are dummies and that every plane flies from the end. Maybe they think that by exhausting us before we get on the plane we will be more compliant, or that we won't realise how long we have actually been waiting for our luggage, if we have walked for half an hour to the baggage hall. This week, despite trudging wearily to the baggage hall from the furthest end of the pier, we still had to wait forty-five minutes for our luggage, due apparently to "staffing problems" that did not seem to have an impact on the ten flights that landed after us.

Then there was the long stay car park with the lowest rates that boasted it was "ten minutes from Heathrow". An unusual description of Southall.

Robert Louis Stevenson advocated "travel for travel's sake." But he didn't have to empty his pockets and take his shoes and belt off before he left.

19th November 2004

A message on my answering machine this week asked me to ring an American friend on a London number.

When I did, I thought I had been misrouted to Rio de Janeiro, when a voice that sounded like Carmen Miranda on speed said, "Ellotenkyouferracallinzeeblankityblankotel- owkinaielpyoo?"

After requesting and receiving two repetitions of this rapidly delivered gibberish, I deciphered that she was thanking me for calling her hotel and asking how she could help me. I told her the name of the friend who had left the message and spent the next minute listening to his room phone ringing out. Then a tape recording switched in, offering me the opportunity to return to the operator.

I keyed the appropriate button.

I was then treated to more than two minutes of a recorded tape exhorting me to spend Christmas at the Hotel, telling me how very a reasonable a three day break would be, that children were welcome and that the chef would be excelling his already impossibly high standards of cuisine on my behalf.

I hung up and tried again.

The "Ellotenkyou..." rapid fire ritual was repeated. I explained that I had just been put through to a room and then diverted to an endless recorded tape and before I could finish, she chirruped "Haiputchoothroosah" and I heard the room phone ring again.

I hung up and phoned again.

"Ellotenkyou..."

I was ready this time.

"Do not put me through to anyone. I have just spent two minutes listening to advertising material as a result of phoning you just now. I do not wish to do that again. Listen very carefully to what I have to say. I wish to leave a message with a human being for one of your guests."

A momentary silence.

I had a mental picture of a female version of Manuel from Fawlty Towers pausing in suspicious incomprehension and struggling with a situation for which she did not have a pre-programmed response available.

Manuella dived for the nearest available exit "Haiputchoothroosah!"

She put me through to the Porter's desk, where I finally got to leave a message for my friend.

Leaving aside the inadvisability of employing telephone receptionists for whom English is a third language, I wish that companies wouldn't insist that their staff adhere to formulaic greetings and valedictions. It is one of those American imports that really do not cross the pond happily.

The first time I was encouraged to "Have a nice day!" by a shop assistant in the States, I was sufficiently charmed to thank her warmly and offer lengthy and warm reciprocation. She was visibly alarmed and clearly thought me deranged.

Now, I am beginning to wonder I prefer the thinly disguised disdain of the archetypal English shop assistant's response, characterised by the studied refusal to terminate her current activity to meet your eye. I am less provoked by that indifference, than I am by being asked, as a knee jerk reaction, if I need help when I am perfectly capable of asking for it if I did.

My preferred English approach is a cheery, "Let me know if I can help you sir," which carries the implication that the assistant is aware of my existence but will not hassle me.

And why, oh why, must I be thanked on the telephone for calling someone, when the reason for my call is completely unknown at that point and for my benefit not theirs?

10. Education

There is something fascinating about schools. Like hospitals, they are closed institutions that all of us will probably have to be a part of for a period of our lives. On the few occasions that I have returned to my school in Manchester and walked down corridors that I walked down half a century ago, I find myself reverting emotionally and mentally to the boy I was then. Memories are triggered instantly by the elements of the school environment that are unchanged since the time I was there. And there are many despite the many improvements and alterations of the intervening decades.

It is strange to think that with the exception perhaps of one or two staff members who might have been pupils there all those years ago, there is no one there now that was there or knew me from the time I was part of the school's life. It is perhaps partly for this reason that I was persuaded to become a school governor twenty years ago. I am still a governor at the school two of my daughters attended. Even though they have now left the school I feel I want to continue to help to further the efforts of the school that served my girls so well in order to achieve the same for another generation of young women.

There are many frustrations in the world of education and I have sounded off frequently about many of them, as you will read.

My mother was a primary school teacher in London before and after World War Two and until she gave birth to me. And the profession of teaching has re-emerged within the Baker dynasty as my oldest daughter has now joined the ranks at a primary school near where we live.

I have always believed that those first years are crucial in the development of young people. That is when we learn not just how to read and write, but how to interact with each other in an unselfish and productive way. It is a time when we should learn that we are all different and celebrate that fact.
It is a time when we should allow those who are trained to do the job of teaching and let them get on with it.

27th November 2009

I was intrigued to read that Sir Ranulph Fiennes, one of that exotic breed who can genuinely describe themselves in their passports as an 'adventurer,' harbours an unsatisfied urge for revenge against the boys who bullied him at Eton.

It is a sobering thought to learn that a man who has run marathons in exotic places, who cut off his own necrotic fingertips with a Black & Decker saw in his garden shed, discovered lost cities, led any number of dangerous expeditions and been the oldest man to climb Everest is still haunted by the memory of being bullied 50 years ago.

A former politician, one of those accused by Fiennes, has strenuously denied that he ever 'laid a finger' on him, saying, 'It must have been someone else.'

You don't read many memoirs written by the bully. The bullied are slower to forget. I have very clear memories of being moved from my first school in Rochdale because of a group of boys who found my London accent 'posh.'

My parents moved to Lancashire from London shortly before I started school. My father was of the 'stand up to them and fight back' brigade. My mother was herself a teacher and perhaps understood better the effect of regular and systematic bullying on a small child.

The bullying of my and Sir Ranulph's generation was comparatively unsophisticated however (Do you like the way I bracket us together – Oakenrod School, Rochdale and Eton didn't have much in common, apart from the 'rod' bit I suppose).

It tended to be physical and verbal, just like today, but it terminated once you got to the safety of home. The stories that appear regularly in the media today tell of unremitting and mob persecution via the internet and mobile phones that drive isolated young people to seek to end the misery and their lives at the same time.

It is, for some reason, endemic in our society and it starts in childhood, despite the best efforts of the majority of parents and schools. As soon as any child says to a parent, 'Don't say anything, please,' then that parent should know the time has come to say and do something, however hard that is.

Schools have improved considerably over the last decade, but I still worry when any head teacher feels able to say 'There is no bullying in my school'.

9th February 2002

I come from the generation that was told rather forcibly that if someone bullied you, the only really effective response was to hit the bully back just as hard as he had hit you. My father had little sympathy when I returned home with a bleeding nose complaining that I had been targeted by the school thug. He believed that the Neanderthal responsible would move on to more compliant targets if I hit him back. Being in the real world of playground asphalt and tiled walls, I knew that any brief respect the school hard man might be tempted to have for me, would soon be forgotten as he systematically dismantled my face. It is a myth that all bullies are cowards. That only applies when they meet someone tougher than them. Most bullies have cased the joint before they start and know what they're dealing with. You are either made of the stuff that instinctively and immediately retaliates, or you are not. If you are then you don't think; you just act.

John Prescott is a case in point.

Someone threw an egg at him. He instinctively reacted and lashed out in the direction of the attack.

Fair enough, the right-minded would think. It would have flown in the face of natural justice to penalise old two Jags for his spontaneous reaction to aggression. But the media briefly bayed for his blood.

Fighting back is no longer acceptable apparently. It actually never was a good idea in the playground - as I discovered way back then because when I tried to do my father's bidding, I either got a more severe drubbing than would otherwise have come my way, or on the very rare occasions that I got the better of the aggressor, I invariably got into trouble myself, despite all my, "He started it, Miss," protestations.

But the "stand up for yourself" ethos has very definitely been replaced by the "submit, avoid or appease" approach. If someone threatens you with violence and demands your money, car or mobile phone, we are advised to avoid confrontation and give in to the thug's demands. And, of course, that advice is good. No car or phone is worth disfigurement or death. But however much sense this advice makes, if the adrenalin and sense of wrongness combine too powerfully, some people simply cannot instinctively do other than react to the sheer injustice of it all.

But today, retaliation is regarded with no less disfavour, it seems, than the aggression that provoked the retaliation. And the retaliator is more often than not easier to identify than the aggressor too, being by definition otherwise law-abiding. So Tony Martin languishes in prison for finally succumbing to the frustration and terror of being targeted by a succession of burglaries and threats.

A football player, Jamie Carragher, was pelted with coins. He picked one up and threw it back. Not a sensible thing to do, admittedly. If only because of the virtual impossibility of it hitting the original assailant. Being sent off from the field of play was, however, where the penalising of this retaliating victim should end. The calls in the media for stiffer penalties ring somewhat hollow and hypocritical when Governments worldwide, if they have the power and wherewithal, invariably respond with punitive and often disproportionate retaliation if they see themselves as having been injured in any way.

And they have time to think about it.

16th January 2009

The saying goes that 'Truth is stranger than fiction' and that has never been more true than it is today. At a time when thousands of people, whose jobs are useful and productive, are losing those jobs, as companies fight to balance their books by shedding staff, there seems to be no shortage of council employees nationwide who perform functions that are more demonstrably redundant in a struggling economy. The year 2009, it seems, is the year when a primary school in Sheffield has been banned from calling itself 'a school' because that word has 'negative connotations.' The good folk of Sheffield will, they believe, be more enthused by the notion of education if it is provided at a 'centre for learning.' Their secondary schools will benefit from the new improved image that is to be conveyed by calling them 'advanced learning centres.' The day that Bucks County Council adopts these ludicrous branding practices will be the day that I join the resistance.

It is not just the insanity of the decisions that these preposterous people make, but the fact that at a time when unemployment is growing and will sadly continue to grow, the people who make these kinds of decisions are seemingly secure in their jobs. Small wonder that according to the Princes trust, 10% of young people in Britain think that their lives are not worth living. What kind of world are we creating for them?

Last year a father of four in Cumbria was fined a fixed penalty of £110 when the lid of his wheelie bin was too full! Yes, it was discovered to be open by the heinous and shocking amount of 4 inches.

It is risible, but it is also a chilling symptom of the demise of common sense and the rise of a juggernaut bureaucracy that must be staffed by human beings. But they are human beings that neither you nor I know.

The only credible explanation for all this brain-numbing pointlessness is that national government is trying to get rid of its expensive local tier by allowing them to provoke an increasingly irritated populace to demand the dismantling of all local councils, like Tunbridge Wells that banned the word 'brainstorming' in case epileptics and the mentally unstable were offended. What about the offence caused to the rest of the population, and probably the very people they are trying to protect?

2nd October 2009

Schools all over Buckinghamshire will be either disappointed or relieved to learn that they are not at the forefront of the minds of OFSTED – the organisation set up to ensure that our children's education is being delivered effectively.

The much more important issue of baby-sitting is getting their full attention, it seems.

The national problem of people looking after each other's babies on a reciprocal basis has galvanised the mighty bureaucrats into action in the case of two detective constables from the Thames Valley Police in Aylesbury.

You'll never guess what they've been up to. They are best friends and, in order to get back to work, have been doing a 20 hour a week job share, so that while one works, the other looks after both their children, who are friends.

A perfect arrangement one would think – and one that enables mothers (who want to) to return to work as soon as possible, in line with current government policy. Many women would envy them such an obviously sensible arrangement.

Enter the OFSTED inspector, who having been alerted by a public-spirited nark to this flagrant abuse of regulations designed for quite another purpose, accused the pair of running "an illegal childminding business."

Looking after a friend's child constitutes a 'reward;' childminders 'for reward' need to be registered with OFSTED and to comply with regulations on educational targets and are subjected to regular inspections.

Even though they had had this happy arrangement in place for some time, clearly it was unthinkable that law enforcement officers should knowingly break the law. So, to avoid prosecution, DC Shepherd has now put her daughter into a private nursery at a cost of nearly £500 per month, half her salary, and has had to claim childcare benefits to cover the fees.

It may well be that the 2006 Childcare Act was so sloppily drafted as to provoke this clear absurdity. But are there really a sufficient number of officials, whose lack of common sense is matched only by their jobsworth adherence to subsection 2 paragraph 4, who are prepared to bring both OFSTED and the education system into disrepute by treating these two mothers so shamefully?

In the words of Harry Enfield, "OFSTED! NO!"

Babysitting circles all over Britain, be very afraid.

You're next for a visit by OFF ITS 'ED.

11th May 2007
Households across Britain are currently dangerous places. GCSEs, AS and A levels are imminent, and post-it notes festoon every domestic surface, bearing arcane information about the composition of the human skeleton or the causes of World War One. Teenagers teeter on the brink of meltdown, bringing back memories of my own rites of passage in the old talk-and-chalk days of education. I can remember that feeling of impending doom, as I realised that I should have paid more attention to the teachers who dragged us listlessly through the detail of Reform Acts of 1832 and the pluperfect optative of the Greek verb "to pillage."

Who can forget the rarefied atmosphere of the exam hall, with invigilators trying desperately not to look bored witless while ambling around checking that you hadn't tattooed the periodic table on the back of your hand or got a French dictionary hidden inside your wooden leg? Nowadays, of course, it would be the virtual reality nano-chip under the fingernail. Or the coughing major in the shrubbery outside the hall.

I am lost in admiration for the students today, as well as their teachers. It cannot have escaped the notice of anyone of my generation that the contemporary sixteen year old is expected to achieve standards in Maths and the Sciences, in particular, that are arguably equivalent to those that my lot studied at university. I ceased to be able to offer any help at all to any of my daughters in their Maths studies a good year or more before GCSEs. But then it does have to be said that my success in that subject was due solely to the fact that my Maths teacher bet me two and six that I would fail. With the benefit of decades of hindsight, I have realised that he was clearly a kind man dangling the bait in order to lure me to work harder rather than a poorly paid priest attempting to cash in on my struggle with calculus. I scraped a pass. Belated thanks, Father Hamilton!

The modern GCSE candidate sits exams a good month and a half earlier than I did, too. Ours were in July and we got the results in August, as I recall. So not only are today's examinees expected to know more, they are also expected to assimilate it half a term earlier.

I wish them all the best of luck.

16th May 2008

SATS testing has been under scrutiny in the media in the wake of the report of a House of Commons' committee in the week that pupils countrywide have been taking the tests. SATS (Standard Assessment Tests) are given to children at the end of years 2, 6 and 9. They are intended to show children's progress compared with other children born in the same month. They are a useful tool, it can be convincingly argued, for teachers and other education professionals to judge the efficacy of their teaching and the abilities of the children they teach.

The problem that the MPs have identified is that the results of these tests are now being fed into league tables that invite comparison between schools and give rise to parental dissatisfaction with schools that do not appear to them to be doing well.

High achieving, aspirational parents want high achieving, aspirational children and will move heaven and earth to get their children into schools that these league tables indicate to them will deliver for their children. The SATS results become important to schools not just for what they tell the school about their pupils' progress any more, but because the schools know they will struggle to attract quality pupils, or worse any pupils at all, if they are perceived to be less than successful. The fear expressed by the Commons' Committee and endorsed by teachers' professional bodies is that the teaching of the curriculum can be neglected in the quest to improve their position in the league tables.

There are so many ingredients that go into make a good school, many of which are incapable of measurement. Drilling students to satisfy the requirements of a testing regime is not one of them. Developing whatever raw material arrives at the school so that they reach their full potential is.

A school whose catchment area provides it with motivated, high achieving families with similar children finds league table success an easier prize than does a school in a less blessed area. But the latter school may well be going that extra mile for its children without reaping the league table benefit.

My four children are now nearly all through their schooling years and I have learned far more about the schools they have attended from getting involved and meeting their teachers than could ever be gleaned from the cold and almost meaningless information to be gleaned from a league table.

12th December 2008

In Buckinghamshire, we select children for secondary education by tests taken at the age of 11. These tests measure the level of a child's innate ability to process information, to "reason." Those whose ability is appropriate to what might be termed a more academic pace are selected to attend one of our Grammar Schools; those who would not thrive in that sector attend one of our Upper Schools.

If we were designing a system from scratch, it is arguable that we might not come up with this one; however, it is what we have and we are blessed in Wycombe with excellent schools of both types.

Two of my children attended a local Grammar School and two an Upper School. Their results at GCSE and A Levels were very similar. They all achieved their potential, but at a different pace. If, like some parents, who insist on using the words 'pass' and 'fail' to describe the results of the selection process, I had sent my daughters for 11+ coaching, they might all perhaps have squeezed into a Grammar School. They might then have struggled for seven years to keep up with contemporaries able to work at a faster pace.

Many middle class parents still have this obsession with demonstrating that they have clever kids to go with their nice houses and their smart cars. They complain (usually at the school gate to each other), if they consider that a school's 11+ 'success rate' is poor. I know of at least one parent who recently complained that a school's 11+ results should be better - for the simple reason that it was " a middle class school." This is no different to believing that because you are middle class your child should be able to run faster than a working class child.

And to promise rewards to a child if it "passes" – (the dreaded "P" word) to try to nudge a child up those few extra points only to struggle at a Grammar School– is, I believe, no less than cruelty. All schools are supposed to allocate a similar amount of time to familiarise children with the 11+ procedure – and if it were left at that, then the selection process would work to its best potential. However, many times some parents are told what the 11+ measures and its purpose – they still seem incapable of understanding.

3rd February 2006

Passion is a word much loved by the image-makers and the advertisers. It is also beloved by that modern candidate for Ko-Ko's "little list," the Mission Statement writer. The number of times I have encountered organisations that think their work is done when they've written the wretched thing and then fail signally to walk the mission talk!

You can always re-brand an image, apparently, if you convince the customer that you are passionate about your product. It is clearly easier to use your passion as a marketing tool if you are selling chocolate or fine art rather than corn plasters or plumbing. "Passionate about u-bends" doesn't really do it for many people.

But there are areas where that over-used word is entirely appropriate.

Education is undoubtedly one. I encountered an English teacher as a teenager who had both a passion for his subject and that extra essential; the need and ability to communicate that passion. My own children have developed keen interests in respectively Art, History and Mathematics simply because at an important point in their education they encountered, in a sea of very good teachers, the exceptional ones whose personal enthusiasm was so infectious that even the reluctant, timid and downright hostile are hard pressed to avoid learning. It is undoubtedly a god-given extra quality that cannot be taught or acquired; just as I, as an actor, have to reluctantly admit that I don't have the magnetic screen quality of Paul Newman, the stage and vocal presence of Paul Schofield or the personal charisma of, say, Jon Pertwee, who could walk into any room and everyone would look at him. Unlike most of us, he never had trouble getting a waiter's attention.

Charismatic teachers engage the interest of the student by being knowledgeable, of course, and passionately interested (and therefore interesting) themselves. Their styles may vary from the eccentric to the more conventional; their discipline may be effortless or hard won, but it is their passion that is the key.

I would like to mount a campaign (not another one, Colin?).

We are all too ready to whinge at schools for their failings; too rarely do we do what we ask the schools to do for our children – encourage and praise. Rather than complain about what we, rightly or wrongly, believe to be deficiencies, let's thank our children's schools for the excellent and passionate teachers. The information conveyed is the same, but the process much more pleasant for all concerned.

16th October 2009

Most people of my generation will have experienced quite forceful sanctions while they were at school, ranging from the pointless drudge of writing 'lines' or the painful administration of a strap or cane for repeat or major offences. However we may view that now in terms of the acceptability of inflicting pain on children, it is undeniable that behaviour in classrooms has not improved since corporal punishment became unacceptable. I recall having the small hairs on the side of my head twisted (not the most pleasant sensation), accompanied by a request as to whether I considered my conversation with my neighbour to be more important than the lesson the hair-twister was teaching. My reply, "Ah! Ah! No!" resulted in him stopping twisting and me stopping talking. Today, this otherwise excellent teacher would be prosecuted and would lose his job, along with those of his colleagues who adopted similar summary tactics.

Today, a teacher in Suffolk who forcibly removed a child from a class to prevent him from continuing to make racist remarks has been prosecuted for assaulting the child and, having been convicted, is awaiting sentence.

We only have the limited information available in a case where the complainant (the boy telling the racist jokes who refused to either stop or leave the class) is afforded anonymity but the teacher not. There is nothing to say whether other children supported either party. But whatever the detail denied us in this case, the fact is that a teacher described by his head as 'passionate and enthusiastic', with an exemplary record may lose his liberty and most likely his job because he tried to deal with a pupil who was preventing him from teaching the rest of the willing, well behaved children. It is almost a cliché but it is true – when I was at school, if you went home and said you had been punished for something – you got more of the same from your parents. There was discipline at home and respect for teachers who had similar expectations of children's behaviour at school.

Most teachers now fear the sound of parental footsteps down the corridor if they so much as look sideways at their little angels or have the temerity to give them low grades.

My daughter is currently training to be a teacher. I hope that by the time she qualifies, we have realised that "Every Teacher Matters" too!

16th April 2010

When I was watching Sport Relief last month, something struck me quite forcibly and I suspect I was not alone in finding it worthy of comment.

In between all the fund-raising entertainment are inserted film clips, showing many and varied examples of how the lives of those who live in the third world can be improved exponentially for minimal outlay. I am sure that sometimes we all find it almost too much to bear.

This year I found myself making the comparison between the attitudes to schooling displayed by those in Africa for whom it is a dreamed-of and unlikely blessing, and the recipients of free education for all in the UK. The pure and unalloyed glee on the faces of African children sitting in a crowded and rudimentary building equipped, if they are lucky, with no more than a few pencils and some paper upon which to write is difficult to reconcile with the demeanour of young people in what we like to call 'the civilised world.' It is also noticeable that young children who have to walk miles daily for food, water and, if they are lucky schooling, are much more likely to be doing so with a smile on their faces than their more privileged counterparts here. And not just a fleeting smile, but smiles that indicate a simple joyfulness that is enviable and infectious.

I know that I am oversimplifying and that the world inhabited by those children is vastly different to the world that we have constructed for our children. When you have nothing and are not bombarded with the confusing and distorting daily images of life that our children are exposed to, then life is simpler. When you live in the kind of poverty that third world children endure, being cool is irrelevant, as is the kind of shoes you wear or the fact that your parents don't take you to Disneyland. Civilisation brings with it a lot of baggage that perversely seems to inhibit civilised behaviour.

So my challenge to the electioneering politicians is simple. What can you do to put smiles back on the faces of young people? Real smiles. Smiles that come from a happiness that is more about who they are and what they can do than it is about what they have and what entertainment is offered to them.

I fear there will be no quick fix.

3rd June 2005

I was intrigued to read, last week, a quote from the deputy head of a local school on the continuing debate about Marlow Hill's arbitrary speed limits and the enforcement thereof.

He said that there are around three thousand pupils arriving or emerging daily from the three schools at the top of Marlow Hill and therefore any traffic-calming measures were always appreciated. He was, perhaps, being diplomatic in response to a query from the newspaper, because, in fact, the speed limits around that area seem to have no relation whatsoever to the presence of the pupils of any of those schools. The entrance to John Hampden School is, almost unbelievably, in a 70mph limit area. Any one from Wycombe High School or St Bernard's who walks down Marlow Hill is doing so yards from their schools in a 40mph limit.

Somewhat perversely, then, the only students actually protected by a 30mph limit are the ones at the bottom of the hill at Wycombe Abbey, who do not have a mass entrance or exodus every day, as Wycombe Abbey is a boarding school.

If one were to be mischievous, one might be tempted to suggest that young people attending a public school merit more protection than their state school contemporaries. Clearly that cannot be the case; but if the protection of schoolchildren is a contributory factor in the positioning policy of both speed limits and their enforcement, then perhaps someone from Bucks CC or the Thames Valley Partnership would care to explain the rationale for this bizarre anomaly.

It is undeniably nonsense to claim that road safety plays any part in the positioning of mobile speed detection devices at the bottom of Marlow Hill to catch cars who unwisely anticipate the upcoming 40mph sign. There is no pedestrian activity worthy of mention there and the only opening into the road is the rarely used one occupied sporadically by the police car containing the speed camera.

A system worth enforcing would be one where, whatever the speed limit around a school might be for the rest of the time, when children are arriving or leaving, flashing signs indicating a 20mph speed limit should operate; and that would be worth enforcing and would also attract the support of the vast majority of motorists who are otherwise unable to escape the conclusion that they are either the victims of bureaucratic incompetence or seen as cash gathering easy pickings.

8th August 2003

If you failed to see the first episode of "That'll Teach 'Em" on Channel 4 (9 p.m. Tuesday), then I urge you not to miss the next episodes. The programme makers have taken thirty Year 11 students, who have just finished their GCSE examinations, and transported them for several weeks into a 1950's school environment.

It is clearly not exactly the same experience as those of us who were educated then will remember. We weren't followed around by a camera crew, for instance, which might have induced even the bullies at my old school to desist from their hobby, at least while their activities were being transmitted to the world. Nor were most of my generation educated at mixed grammar boarding schools, alas!

But aside from those undoubtedly telling factors, the other elements of 1950's education, whilst undoubtedly heightened by the editing process, are familiar enough to those of us who endured and benefited from it; and you will find my generation equally divided between the "It was hell!" and the "…made me the man I am today!" brigades.

Many aspects of the now despised authoritarian regime resulted in an avoidance of most of the discipline problems that are endemic in society and schools today. It is, of course, clear that the splendid cast of teacher/actors in the programme will not be able to twist the small hairs above the children's ears while asking silkily, "I'm sorry Baker, were you labouring under the delusion that what you had to say to McGrath was more important or interesting than what I was saying to the class?"

Nor will they be able to propel pieces of chalk, while snapping "Pay attention, boy!" The law wouldn't allow it.

One cannot mourn the passing of violence perpetrated by grown men on small boys. But one can say that at the time we all completely accepted it; parents, teachers, children, ministers of the church and nuns alike. Especially the nuns, I hear from those educated in convents.

I know Andrew MacTavish, who is "playing" the headteacher and can attest that he is the gentlest, most courteous, witty and sympathetic of men and his reputation as a modern head teacher is unimpeachable. After retiring as head of John Hampden Grammar, he managed to control the savage, rebellious hordes of Wycombe High School girls during a recent brief sojourn as interregnum head. He did so with style and grace, earning the almost instant devotion of those 1300 plus girls. The good old "firm but fair" style works every time; and he did not see it as a weakness to be seen to want to get to know the girls and talk to them.

As his headship of the 1950's school is clearly intended to highlight the differences between then and now, it may be that we don't see that side of Andrew in the programme. But, my, he's a cracking actor! His face-thrusting tirade at the miscreant who failed to sing up in Music and was sent off for a cold shower was quite terrifying. And I'm sorry, but I loved seeing pupils standing when a teacher entered the room.

I also whooped with smugness when all those post GCSE 16-year-olds failed in droves to pass a 1950's 11+ exam. Of course! Hah! They don't teach long division any more. Or grammar. Or spelling. Or tables. And when the computers and calculators all die, where will all we be then, eh?

11. Light Relief

One of the many things that differentiates us from the beasts of the rest of sentient creation is a sense of humour. Without the ability to laugh at ourselves as well as others, we are indeed diminished, I believe. I fell downstairs recently and landed at the bottom ingloriously on my posterior. My instant reaction was to laugh. I am not entirely sure why. Perhaps it was because I could see myself through the eyes of the invisible spectator, who might be moved to mirth by this loss of dignity – and of course in this case it was only my dignity that was injured, so laughter was perhaps a natural response.

The ability not to take oneself too seriously is terribly important and humour is a great was to defuse a tricky situation sometimes. Many actors tell stories of how as children they managed to divert the attentions of the bullies by entertaining them. Make 'em laugh – and they may forget that they didn't like the cut of your jib a moment earlier.

Sometimes humour seems absent from a situation at the time. But recollection can be

7th April 2001

A company with which I have connections had employee problems lately. A member of staff was threatening legal action because, she claimed, the office in which she was working was suffering from a malady unknown to me before and called "sick building syndrome."

This affliction of the bricks and mortar meant that soon after arriving at work each day she felt ill at ease, uncomfortable, had headaches and feelings of nausea (not uncommon to much of the working population, particularly on a Monday morning, I would suggest). These unpleasant sensations decreased the longer and further she was away from her place of work. This phenomenon, lucrative to the lawyers of the afflicted, is another wondrous import from that beacon of civilisation across the Atlantic, where 4% of the worlds population produce 25% of the world's pollutants and whose President apparently wishes to make his mark as the first true global vandal of the 21st century by declining to join the rest of the world in reducing carbon dioxide emissions.

However, back to our reluctant worker.

The employee's attempts to gain financial recompense for this environmental malady were thwarted only by a timely move of the company concerned to a new building. The employee left - in search of another sick building, I surmise.

The shift in the balance of power between employer and employee was highlighted for me when I came across a document, dated 1852 and entitled "Office Staff Practices," found in a recently demolished building in Staffordshire.

It starts off by announcing - "clerical staff will now only have to be present from 7am to 6pm on weekdays." It then lays down terms of employment that would give the modern worker pause for thought.

"A stove is provided for the benefit of clerical staff. It is recommended that each employee brings in four pounds of coal each day, during cold weather. Clothing must be of a sober nature. Overshoes and topcoats may not be worn in the office but neck scarves and headwear may be worn in inclement weather.

No member of clerical staff may leave the room without permission from Mr. Rogers. Calls of nature are permitted and staff may use the garden below the second gate. This area must be kept in good order.

No talking is allowed during business hours. The craving of tobacco and alcohol is a human weakness and is forbidden to all staff. Now that the hours of business have been drastically reduced, the partaking of food is allowed between the hours of 11:30 and noon, but work will not, on any account, cease. Members of staff will provide their own pens. A sharpener is available on application to Mr. Rogers. All junior clerks will report to the senior clerk a half an hour before prayers and will remain after work to attend to the cleanliness of the office. Brushes, brooms, scrubbers and soap are provided by the owners, who expect a rise in the output of work as a result of these near-utopian conditions."

I would love to have been able to share the opinion of Mr. Rogers and his unnamed employers had one of their clerks requested recompense because the building in which he was working left him feeling debilitated and unwell. I suspect he would not have to worry any more about the state of the garden below the second gate.

We don't know we're born, do we?

14th March 2003

It's perhaps mischievous of me to suggest, at this particular point in time, that some Americans have only the vaguest notion that there is a great big world out there. When that fact is acknowledged, the detail can get quite hazy. I know of at least one local US friend who will take me to task, but I couldn't resist sharing the following cautionary tales.

An American called a travel agent inquiring about a package tour to Hawaii. After going over all the cost information, she asked, "Would it be cheaper to fly to California and then take the train to Hawaii?"

Another wanted to go to Capetown. The agent started to explain the details and options when she interrupted her with, "Look, I'm not trying to make you look stupid, but Capetown is in Massachusetts." The agent calmly explained, "Madam, Cape Cod is in Massachusetts, Capetown is in Africa." The would-be traveller's response was to hang up.

A man called, furious about his eagerly anticipated trip to Florida. He had been led to believe that he would have a room with an ocean view. The travel agent explained that that wasn't possible, as Orlando was in the middle of the state. His response? "Don't lie to me. I looked on the map and Florida is a very thin state."

A similar geographical naivety was demonstrated by the man who enquired whether he would be able to see England from Canada, as "They look so close to each other on the map."

One customer couldn't understand why her flight from Detroit left at 8:20 a.m. and got into Chicago at 8:33 a.m. The agent tried to explain that Michigan was an hour ahead of Illinois, but she could not understand the concept of time zones. Finally he gave up and told her that the plane went very fast, and she bought that!

"I want to go from Chicago to Hippopotamus, New York," a woman asked. The agent was at a loss for words. Finally, he said, "Are you sure that's the name of the town?" "Yes, what flights do you have?" replied the customer. After some searching, the agent came back with, "I'm sorry, ma'am, I've looked up every airport code in the country and can't find a Hippopotamus anywhere." The customer retorted, "Oh don't be silly. Everyone knows where it is. Check your map!" The agent scoured a map of the state of New York and finally offered, "You don't mean Buffalo, do you?" "That's it!" she replied, "I knew it was a big animal."

This might have been the woman who asked for an aisle seat so that her hair wouldn't get messed up by being near the window.

One businessman was enquiring about the detail of a trip to China. After a lengthy discussion about schedules, timings and accommodation, he was reminded that he needed a visa. "Oh no, I don't," he retorted, "I've travelled all over the world and have never had to have one of those. They accept American Express everywhere." A story beaten only by the woman who asked, "Do airlines put your physical description on your bag, so they know whose luggage belongs to whom? When I checked in, they put a tag on my luggage that said FAT and as I am a bit overweight...?" The agent explained that the city code for Fresno was FAT, and that the airline was just putting a destination tag on her luggage.

8th November 2002

A newspaper in Scotland has asked for nominations for the "Stella Award," which commemorates the truly elevating judgement in an American court that a young lady of that name should be awarded $2.9 million dollars after spilling a cup of scalding hot McDonald's coffee into her own lap. No, she wasn't nudged or jostled by an employee. Her chair didn't collapse. The handle didn't fall off her cup. She just spilled it. But apparently, the court in its staggering wisdom, decided that McDonalds shouldn't have made it so hot. The paper has asked newshounds to sniff out other examples of the judiciary's firm grasp of reality worldwide. There are some strong contenders.

One Carl Truman, in America again, was awarded $74,000 after his hand was crushed under a neighbour's car wheel. Fair enough, you may think, until you learn that he was trying to steal a hubcap at the time and the hapless driver was unaware of that fact.

A restaurant was deemed culpable in the eyes of a Philadelphia court (Oh wise judge!), when a young lady slipped and fell in a pool of spilled soft drink. This was despite the undisputed fact that the pool was there because the same young lady litigant had thrown it over her boyfriend a few seconds earlier. She pocketed $113,000.

A supermarket worker, who was sacked because she refused to remove an eyebrow ring while at work, has sued for $2 million on the grounds of religious discrimination. She is a member of the Church of Body Modification in Oregon and argued that her metallic adornment was no different from a Crucifix or Star of David worn by followers of Christianity or Judaism. A federal anti-discrimination commission ruled in her favour.

But there are decisions in this country that equally boggle. A deaf man in Lincolnshire won £7,000 in compensation after a hospital declined to employ him as a telephone operator and records clerk. A tribunal ruled that the hospital had not done enough to remove "the phone element" from the job. An open invitation, then, for those without functioning brains, to apply for the posts of tribunal adjudicators. Failure to be appointed could give rise to a successful action on the basis that not enough had been done to remove "the thinking element" from the job.

Fear of similarly opportunist litigation results in increasingly bizarre contortions to avoid legal responsibility for the next hitherto unprofitable incident. North-Eastern councillors have refused to support an area schools' carol singing competition for fear of distressing contestants who do not win. Scouts in Kent are obliged to get written consent from their parents before playing conkers – now classified a "dangerous sport." A church in Sussex has banned fresh fruit and vegetables from its Harvest Festival for fear of falling foul of Health and Safety regulations. After a child was stung by a wasp in a Cumbrian park, notices have been installed, warning that there may be wasps. One wonders what will happen when a child is injured by a falling warning notice.

I return to America for my final piece of evidence of a world going to perdition in a manually operated wheeled carrying device. This one is simply too wonderful to exclude.

A web site has been set up in the States offering leather-free collars, restraints, whips and harnesses for vegan sado-masochists.

More and more people are seeking cruelty free products apparently.

13th February 2004

Every organisation has to perform quite detailed risk assessment inspections these days in order to ensure that they are not sued for large sums of money when something foreseeable causes injury to their employees or visitors to their premises. This is a perfectly sensible practice and to be encouraged in workplaces and public areas that might otherwise not be terribly user-friendly in these days of ever tightening building and maintenance budgets.

Predictably however, like all things that start out sensibly, once something is the subject of legislation and control, those charged with the task of ensuring compliance start to look around for other areas in which they can exert their influence. Wearing a hard hat on a building site is eminently sensible, as is insisting that machines that can slice through steel are constructed in such a way that they are incapable of performing a similar function upon those who operate them.

Whenever I work on a theatrical production, or do any filming, a risk assessment is undertaken in perhaps more detail then is strictly necessary; but given the propensity for litigation at the drop of a steel rimmed hat, then one cannot, I suppose, really blame the production companies. I have been warned to be careful getting out of cars, in case I bang my head. On one occasion I was asked to sign a form acknowledging that I had been warned of precisely that possibility, even though I had managed to drive myself to the location without compromising the integrity of my cranium getting out of my own car.

But when Health and Safety Inspectors turn their (suitably safeguarded) gimlet eyes upon the training of the armed services and suggest that chlorine should be used to ensure that the water in an assault course tunnel used by marines is nice and clean when they struggle through with their backpacks and assault rifles – then what started out as being good defensive planning turns into a farce. They also apparently recommended that handrails should be provided to stop the trainees slipping on the muddy training slopes. The logical conclusion, if all other countries maintained a similar attitude, would be that conflict would become impossible, as none of the protagonists would be allowed to use any weaponry or engage in any activity that might inflict harm on themselves or others. And if I thought that were the case, then I would be all for it – bring on the risk assessors.

I was intrigued to read this week that the Home Office has invested £500,000 in reducing obesity among its police officers in London.

Overweight officers are being given Healthy Eating Cookbooks that contain exciting recipes for dishes like – wait for it – beans on toast. As a further part of the campaign, they will be offered the opportunity to strap on a false belly weighing one and a half stone, so that they can learn how they would look and feel if they were to put weight on.

This may or may not have been provoked by incidents like the one in Cumbria last year when a youth was ordered by magistrates to pay compensation of £100 to a police officer whom he had called "a fat b*****d." "I'm not fat, I'm stocky," the officer complained.

So at last there is a financial incentive to embrace portliness. Thomas the Tank Engine's old colleague the Fat Controller could have made a fortune.

2nd January 2004

I have discovered a programme called Grumpy Old Men on BBC2. It features my contemporaries, none of whom I would actually therefore characterise as "old," having a good moan! And I agree with practically everything they say.

So my New Year's resolution is to stop trying to accommodate the passage of the handcart which is hurtling on its way to the infernal regions with what is left of the world that I remember with fondness. In fact, let's all start shouting about the stranglehold on common sense that has been steadily applied by the establishment, the legislators, bureaucrats and corporate interests over the last decades.

We are letting the wrong people set the agenda for our lives. Whether you're a parent, a motorist, a shopper, a householder, bank account holder, a mortgagee or, like me, all of the above – you're being short-changed, disenfranchised and generally oppressed more than at any other time since we evolved into anything resembling a democracy. The trouble with creating a structure for the making and enforcing of rules is that once the juggernaut is rolling, it's hard to stop.

Bureaucrats will never say "Okay, we seem to have got it about right – let's go and do something useful like grow something or make something."

Middle England is rumbling. A section of the population that happens to enjoy killing small animals for pleasure has demonstrated how Middle England can rattle the ivory towers of the legislators and give them pause. If the same group of people combined with the rest of us to campaign for something worthwhile, then we really could stop them in their tracks.

How many people would like many far fewer TV channels and better programmes? How many would like banks with managers whose names you knew and whom you could call about your account when you needed to? Or a society that defended the householder against the burglar, supported the battered victim rather than the poor, deprived mugger? How many of you hanker for the days when discipline in the home and school was not a dirty word? You only had to listen to those 21st Century students who took part in the 50's education experiment for Channel 4's excellent "That'll Teach 'Em." With few exceptions, they agreed that they had appreciated the stricter environment and learned more.

We suffer the depredations of vigilante clampers who answer to no-one, it seems, and who can extract money from you to get your own car back, if you fail to spot the notice that seemingly empowers them, in effect, to steal your car. We have speed cameras that are there to raise revenue not to prevent accidents. And if you still aren't convinced of that, drive from Marlow to Stokenchurch along the B480 – a dangerous rat run which has claimed literally dozens of lives in the two decades I have known it. Where are the cameras? On the way out of Marlow, and downhill on the way out of Lane End - nowhere near a school, a hospital or any other pedestrian-intensive area, and both a short distance before signs increasing the speed limit. So what reason do you think they're there?

Let's keep reminding the new generation how it used to be and how it still could be. Let's be as grumpy as we can and defy political correctness, bureaucracy and user-unfriendly companies at every opportunity! Now that's what I call a New Year's Resolution!

26th Jan 2001

Regular readers will know that I like to keep you up to date with the effects on our lives of creeping political correctness and Euro-regulation mania. Recent offerings include the notion that snowmen (deep breath!), are not only sexist but reinforce white domination stereotypes. Dr. Tricia Cusack of Birmingham University has carried out a five year study into the cultural meanings of our frosty occasional friends and has come to the conclusion that they serve to strengthen the notion that women belong in the home and men belong in the public domain. Why otherwise would snowmen be built in gardens and public places? Just possibly because that is where the snow tends to be?

She points out that there is no coincidence in the fact that virgin white snow is used to create a male icon. I suggest that we could conduct a five minute study into the contribution that Dr. Cusack has made to the advancement of our species and come to the fairly unanimous conclusion that she really needs to phone a friend or return to the planet Zog, if they'll allow her back.

And the truly depressing part of this is that she probably received a generous EU grant to come up with this piece of frozen slush.

Perth and Kinroth Council in Scotland has issued an edict banning parents from making home videos of their children in school nativity plays. This apparently infringes the civil liberties of the wee bairns, by failing to give due consideration to their inalienable right to privacy. Until a full evaluation exercise can be carried out (presumably a five year study), an outright ban has been considered the safest policy. I think if the children have any barrack room lawtots in their midst, they might well argue that compulsory education is not exactly compatible with their freedom of choice and civil liberties either.

A new Handbook for Girl Guides, aimed at 14 to 25 year olds, suggests that Guides should discuss prostitution at their group meetings and petition their MP's to urge the legitimising of single sex marriages.

Even the Church of England has been tempted by institutional peer pressure to forsake the unfashionable high ground of tradition and go with the PC flow. A revisiting of the words of the marriage ceremony has produced the expression, "Let them be tender with each other's dreams" - and other clones of country and western ballads presumably? The new service book, Common Worship, has uprooted Compline, the long-standing if old-fashioned evening service, and replaced it with "Night Prayer – debriefing the day with God." And the story of the Last Supper, formerly containing the words, "In the same night as he was betrayed he took bread," is now unfolded by the far from evocative, "He had supper with friends" (One of whom, presumably, dissed him to the filth for forty quid).

It won't be long before the whole of Hamlet will be considered unacceptable in its present literary form and be reduced to "My old man's been done in, so shove off you mad slapper, I think I'll, like, top myself, you know what I mean?"

And if I even start to contemplate the state of mind of the Europoodles in Sunderland who prosecute a greengrocer for selling vegetables by the pound, then I shall be sorely tempted to join the poor benighted Dane.

15th April 2005

So there are elections in the offing which, depending on your levels of cynicism or eternal optimism, are either a waste of time or a great opportunity.

In Rome, the cardinals will be electing a Pope for a worldwide, third-millennium community that is ravaged by AIDS in Africa and in which women are finally, if slowly, being accorded the same employment and decision making opportunities as men. To save the lives of millions of the poorest people in the world, the Catholic Church must contemplate a sea-change in its attitudes to sexuality and the rights of the unborn. To address the issue of celibacy and the ordination of women the Catholic Church must shake away the cobwebs and take a good look around. Despite all the pronouncements about being able to devote oneself entirely to God, the requirement for priests to be celibate was, at least partly, a result of the church's desire to avoid the unpleasant possibility of having to evict from valuable properties the widows and children of deceased priests in order to house the incoming incumbent. This imperative was then justified after the event as being an issue of dogma, when in fact it had originated simply as a practical money-saving measure. An unmarried priest presented no problems.

And it flies in the face of reason to deprive the world of the services of a priesthood that is recruited from the "caring" sex as well as the traditionally less caring hunter/gatherers. But will those good and holy, but elderly and celibate, men seize the opportunity to save and enhance lives?

And in three weeks' time we will be choosing between the devil-we-know and the deep blue C, with mellow yellow in the wings.

Whatever happens, I just hope that even the most cynical and jaded electors vote, even if they feel compelled to vote for the one-issue independents. At least that sends a stronger message than absence. I would vote for the party that convinces us that it will work to gain the support of the other parties in bringing down greenhouse gases, halting global warming, pollution and waste. If ever a topic needed to be removed from the political debate, this is the one. If all three parties could be persuaded to present a united front in this one area, so vital to the future of our children, then it would remove the selfish-gene element from the election, because let's face it, if only one party promises to tackle the issue and restrict and control our consumption of fossil fuels, fertilisers and chemicals, then they are signing their political death warrant. Vested interests are too strong and can only be countered if our elected politicians seek unexplored territory – the moral high ground – together and set an example of co-operation to us all.

12th January 2007

I wonder whether there has been any net benefit to the public from the implementation of the Data Protection Act or the Freedom of Information Act. Every time they impinge on my life they seem to be a hurdle to be overcome rather than any kind of protection. Whenever officialdom has to be contacted from Baker Towers, the ladies who exclusively make up my immediate family always demand that I take up cudgels on their behalf. And that is how they see it – a battle and they know me for a tilter at windmills. I have learnt now to have the appropriate person standing beside me to authorise me to speak on their behalf. On a previous occasion, an insurance company refused to allow me to change the detail of a car policy because I was not "the insured", even though I paid the darned premium. Relying on the fact that I would inevitably be connected to someone quite different, I phoned straight back, identified myself by my daughter's obviously female name and effected the business satisfactorily. As long as you dance the ritual dance, everything is fine, because ultimately they are not interested in Data Protection at all, they are however very interested indeed in covering their ample corporate posteriors.

And as for Freedom of Information – first of all there is nothing "free" about it.

I tried to find out from Thames Valley Police this week the time at which they had been informed of a petrol spillage that caused several accidents locally earlier that day. A simple question with no possible sinister ramifications for them, one would have thought.

I was told I would have to write to Kidlington headquarters, that there would be a ten pound fee and, that if they were prepared to divulge this momentous information, I would hear back from them within 40 days. I imagine this tactic effectively reduces the number of queries they have to deal with.

One can't help remembering a time when you would have asked the local bobby who would have given you the answer five minutes later.

But we live now in world in which a department store manager can excitedly ask me for my autograph, being a "mad Doctor Who fan," one moment and then immediately ask me for corroborative ID in order to validate my store card. I thought he was joking…

He wasn't.

12. More Mundungus

Sometimes I just feel the need to sound off. I am lucky in that I am able to write about the things that make my blood boil and share them with an audience that I fully understand has exactly the same daily battles in their own lives. I do not pretend that I am unique in encountering the intransigence of monolithic institutions or in finding certain elements of public life appalling and shameful. I believe however that if we all stand up and shout about them often enough and loudly enough, eventually things will start to change.

Wouldn't it be nice?

31st October 2008

Ever since the first caveman got a cheap laugh, comedians have pushed the boundaries of taste into areas previously regarded as offensive or unacceptable. Humour has been used very effectively to challenge powerful individuals and oppressive regimes throughout history by brave writers and performers. However, there are occasions when comedians misunderstand or misuse the licence that audiences willingly give to entertainers. One such is Russell Brand.

I must acknowledge that he is not aiming his act at me, or indeed anyone I know over the age of twenty-five. However, his particular brand of humour and his proclaimed lifestyle is only tolerable (if unappetising) until he delivers his random obscenities on the radio at identifiable individuals who cannot respond. It is reported that he telephoned the elderly actor Andrew Sachs and left prurient macho ramblings about Andrew's grand-daughter on his answer machine.

Even Bernard Manning, whose humour was consistently racist, sexist and offensive, confined himself to performing to audiences who knew what was on offer and opted to go and listen to it. Brand and Jonathan Ross were broadcasting on Radio Two, hardly a niche channel for bar-room humour.

The programme was recorded, but still broadcast with all the offending schoolboy smut and cruel jibes intact. And for that, the BBC must take some blame. It may sadly be that Brand and Ross are paid so much money (the indecency of the amount of which is matched only by the content of their respective programmes), that the, by comparison, lowly-paid producers of their shows have little power to rein in their preening stars' excesses.

After seeing Russell Brand a couple of times, I realised that he was not for me. I have tolerated Ross despite his occasional forays into the humour of the lavatory wall, because he can also display an amiable quick-witted charm. But this sorry episode has ended my tolerance. I want to be able to watch television and listen to the radio with my family secure in the knowledge that the broadcasters value all of their audience.

Aside from the appalling discourtesy to the lady concerned and her grandfather and family, this whole sordid incident is also a clear case of bullying, something that as a nation we are trying to eliminate from both schools and workplaces. These two smug foul mouthed idiots have not helped that cause.

23rd October 1999

It is that insurance renewal time of year. Our car, house and life policies are all jostling for an injection of hard-earned Baker readies.

Being conservative by nature (or is that just bone-idle?), I have always tended to let existing arrangements continue. However, all those databases, that now carry the minutiae of all our lives, are connected to an apparently limitless supply of companies anxious to take our money.

Clearly, the insurance companies are in the forefront of this technology. I have been inundated with tempting glossy leaflets, offering variously to give me pens, vouchers to spend in High Street stores, tempting discounts and also to undercut my present Insurer's premium by "a guaranteed £35," in one case and by various "possible" larger amounts in other cases.

The fact that the last few weeks have seen the entertainment industry shamefully reluctant to trouble me for my services means that I am not disenchanted at the prospect of saving a bob or two on the premium. And I have the time available to telephone all those 0800 numbers for quotations. It has been interesting.

Every representative I have spoken to so far has recited, with varying degrees of animation - ranging from the automaton to the brittle and cheery, a little speech about our phone call being monitored for evidential purposes (well that suits me fine – they can't wriggle out of what they've promised later), and asking me if I want to receive details of their other wonderful financial products. That's less beguiling but it seems rude to snub them before we've even started our new and possibly enduring relationship, so, against all my natural inclinations, I agree to a forest of (I hope) renewable timber being shoved through my letterbox over the next few years.

Then the nitty-gritty. One company actually said that they couldn't offer me cover on my house because I am an actor! Whether that is because of the fear that fans will mob Baker Towers and topple them into the moat, or because we are perceived as being a feckless bunch who invite wildebeest into our parlours and never do the hoovering, I do not know. Another "direct" service, operated by a bank, announced with great pride that they had found the only Insurer who would quote for an actor's home.

This was a surprise to me, as four other companies had already happily quoted.

Knowing that failure to declare information can void insurance, I have also been scrupulous about admitting the claim we had for a minor flood caused by a freak storm in September 1998. One young lady then said that her company could not insure us as we lived in an area liable to flooding.

No, I replied, as a result of that incident when several billion gallons of rainwater fell on our bit of High Wycombe in a couple of hours, we have put land drains outside the French windows which unkindly admitted the mini torrent.

Sorry, if you live in a flood area, we can't insure you sir, she sang at me in that strange language, resembling English in content but not intonation, so beloved by the telephone sales species "Phonoroboticus irritandus."

But, to cut to the chase, I have found a company that considers actors no greater a risk for house insurance than other mortals and whose quote was 25% cheaper than my present insurer.

But it does strike me that there are companies out there whose advertising should say, "Only people we think will never claim should apply!"

22nd August 2008

As a child, when I returned home with a bloody nose at the hands of the school bully, my father's response was that all bullies were cowards and if you "stood up to them" they would soon learn their lesson. But as we all know, standing up to a bully actually meant that he could hit you for longer than he would have been able to do had you keeled over at the first onslaught. It is a myth that all bullies are cowards. That only applies when they meet an even nastier specimen than themselves. It is only in fiction that the meek inherit the earth. Most bullies have done their research. They often can't read much, but they can read the word 'victim' when it is tattooed across the foreheads of their prey. I did try to resist my eleven year old nemesis and ended up with a black eye as well as a bloody nose. Thanks Dad!

Fighting back is no longer advisable or recommended. It actually never was a good idea in the playground - as I discovered on the one occasion I resisted successfully and then got into trouble myself, despite all my, "He started it!" protestations.

But the 'Stand up and be counted' ethos has very definitely been replaced by 'Sit down and shut up.' In these drug-fuelled days of knife and gun crime, we are probably very sensibly advised to hand over all our portable electronic equipment and credit cards as non-confrontationally as possible. Too many decent people who try to protect their property are being left in pools of their own blood.

But however much sense this advice makes, some people simply cannot resist the adrenalin surge that comes with a sense of outrage and injustice.

But today, confronting the aggressor is regarded less favourably, it seems, than the thuggery that provoked the retaliation, as in the case of the One Railway employee who lost his job last year when he did what my dad had advised all those years ago and confronted a violent thug – and did so successfully. You get prosecuted if you succeed in stopping violent yobs and you get stabbed or shoved under a train (as happened to Linda Buchanan in Kent this week) if you don't.

Small wonder we all bury our noses in the paper when the drunk starts haranguing other passengers on the train. Shame on us.

17th March 2006

I cannot be alone in thinking it absurd to "Carry on Water Board" levels that we are facing hose-pipe bans and the looming spectre of stand-pipes in our "green and pleasant land" as early in the year as March. I give you England – a country renowned throughout the world for its climate that produces high rainfall, lush green meadows, occasional localised flooding when rivers burst their banks, and a very low demand for outdoor swimming pools. Who would have thought that an essential resource that has seemed not only omnipresent but excessive for centuries let alone decades should now be at risk.

Anyone who spent any time in countries that are blessed with hot dry climates will have marvelled at their seeming ability to have lawn sprinklers regularly busy during the early mornings. That's because they have husbanded their valuable water resources for generations.

However much the water boards protest that they are trying to stem the country-wide leaks that are costing the country a staggering three and a half billion litres a day, it doesn't seem enough.

In Bucks we live in the area served by Thames Water, the biggest water supplier and also the worst performer in the leak-loss tables, losing a massive 915 million litres a day. We are told, as if to reassure us, that the company is committed to cutting this waste of a precious natural resource to 725 million litres a day by 2009/10. I'm sorry? Am I missing something here? If the impending threat of standpipes is as serious are we being led to believe in the media, should we not as citizens be demanding slightly swifter and more effective action than this? Whatever level of manpower and resources has been committed to reducing the leaks by around 20% over four years should be multiplied by a factor of ten in order to reduce it to zero in half the time. Expensive? Yes, but over the long term much cheaper to the nation than the cost of the rationing, standpipes and the public health implications over a longer period.

If we do have to pay more in the short term for the luxury of good clean water in our homes in a globally warming world, then so be it. But let's not wait until the holes appear in the dyke wall before we stick our fingers in. Or to put it another way to the Water Authorities – "Get your fingers out!"

17th October 2008

There are many charity events asking for our support, but few that stir the nation with quite the same emotion as the British Legion's Poppy Day. On two occasions in the last few years, I have accompanied school trips to Ypres and the graveyards of the Somme. The sight of those white headstones disappearing almost into infinity could not fail to touch the flintiest of hearts. And then you read the details of the thousands of teenage boys who were slaughtered in order to gain a few yards that were promptly lost when thousands of Germans were slaughtered the following day. The "War to End All Wars" sadly did not live up to its name and whatever we may think of the justness or otherwise of any particular war, we still expect our young (and not so young) soldiers to go out and do their bit for Britain. British soldiers are still dying for us, although not in the obscene numbers that characterised the First and Second World Wars. There has only been one year since the foundation of the British Legion when a British serviceman has not been killed in active service of his or her country. Also, the scars of combat are still borne by many thousands of serving and ex-soldiers. The British Legion steps in where the very governments that sent those soldiers to do their duty all too often fail to show commensurate gratitude by properly supporting them on return to civilian life, either financially or physically.

The annual success of Poppy Day indicates that the British public knows the debt of gratitude we all owe to these people who to fight and perhaps die for the rest of us. In an increasingly selfish and fragmented Britain, the wearing of a Poppy at this time of year is as much a symbol of hope as were those real poppies that grew on the fields of carnage that inspired them. Next Saturday, 25th October, this year's appeal is being launched in the Chiltern Centre in Wycombe. I shall be working in Cardiff next week so cannot be there myself, but if you are around please go and show your support, and wear your poppy to demonstrate your support of both the fallen and the survivors, and to thank the British Legion for being there to support and help them and their families in our names.

24th October 2008

The credit card was trumpeted as the first step towards a cashless society. The advantage would be a reduction in opportunities for theft of money, apparently. Sadly, the reverse has proven to be the truth. The only difference is that the villains now remove our money from a safe distance, usually hidden behind several layers of computers.

I have experienced, on various occasions, the joy of being asked (usually in Manchester or Liverpool) to pay for my petrol before I fill the car, or to leave my credit card with a surly fellow who refuses to meet my eyes behind his plate glass window. Oh yes, complete stranger with the interpersonal skills of a dyspeptic warthog who does not trust me to pay for my petrol, I am certainly going to trust you with my credit card while I go and fill up my car!

And as, in this cashless society, I only have £10 in my pocket, instead of filling my tank I shall have to have a tenner's worth and hope the next petrol station is more user-friendly.

I note with horror that this lack of trust is spreading to our Buckinghamshire hostelries.

I took my family for Sunday lunch to a famous rural coaching inn near Beaconsfield that had been recently recommended to me. Because I only had cash with me, I had to pay for each drink and each course as it was ordered. If I had had a credit card, I could have put it behind the bar and paid for the lot at the end with it or in cash. As an alternative, apparently, I could have given them my car keys. This, fellow citizens, is not the world I ordered!

I am sure they have some reason to mistrust some of the British public, based on bitter experience when they have dispensed their food and drink and the sated customer has then done a runner.

But, I want to go to places where they trust me or have the wit to set up a system where their mistrust is less in your face.

And the paying at the end of a good meal (rather than piecemeal in advance) affords the added benefit to the staff of affording the opportunity to express one's gratitude both verbally and in other ways. But if you don't trust me…

13.   Election 2010

I love elections. I sit up all night watching the drama unfold as democracy grinds out its four/five yearly process and things change, or not, as they case may be – for the better and/or for the worse. It is a bit like the anticipation of the world cup. Every time we are bombarded to the point of overkill with analysis, discussions, debates and predictions. Each time there is the period of harsh reality at the end – the posy electoral period of uneasy calm and then the discovery that really everything is much the same but with different faces saying slightly different things with much the same effect.

Yes I am a tad cynical, I know. I shouldn't allow myself to get swept up in all the hype in the first place, I know.

We have the system we have – and when we look around the world at the many alternatives to the parliamentary democracy we enjoy in the UK, perhaps I shouldn't cavil. But we should always strive to get better, shouldn't we?

9th April 2010

A friend of mine is working for Esther's Rantzen's electoral campaign in Luton South, which set me thinking about the whole state of party politics in Britain and the current image of MPs. I can't help wishing that a few more high profile independents would stand in the forthcoming general election. Who can forget Martin Bell in his white suit, famously standing as an independent on an anti-corruption ticket in Neil Hamilton's supposedly safe Tory seat of Tatton and winning with an 11,000 majority - the first elected independent MP since 1951?

There is a prevalent feeling of 'a plague on their houses,' after a succession of scandals of varying severity over the last two administrations, culminating in the shameful cross party examples of piggy snouts in troughs via expenses' claims. It was the latter rampant freeloading that prompted the redoubtable Esther's foray into politics. Politicians really are going to have to go the extra mile to convince a wary electorate that they are not just talking the talk to get elected this time round – and it should be a very interesting election.

Our own MP is not standing, citing his disenchantment with the creeping domination of parliament by career politicians as the reason for forsaking his safe seat. I have heard nothing but praise for Paul Goodman during his nine years as our representative and have personal experience of his preparedness to work hard for his constituents. He further commands respect in his leaving. I agree with him that the people who represent us in Westminster should be men and women who have gained a wealth of experience and knowledge as a result of working in a huge variety of areas in private, corporate, professional and public life. What we have seen happening for some time now is the rise of the career politician, people who never wanted to be anything other than a politician and studied 'Politics' with that end in view. I would rather see dentists, doctors, teachers, plumbers, hairdressers, businessmen, accountants, developers, charity workers and, yes even lawyers who, after years of working in their respective professions or trades, feel they have something to offer society and can bring all their experience and skills to the table. In the absence of that – bring on the Independents, I say. No party allegiances – just a conscience and a will to make things better. Call me naïve, if you like!

23rd April 2010

I am chairing a hustings Q & A session at BCUC next Tuesday evening, when attendees will have the opportunity to find out more about Wycombe's parliamentary candidates. I am an admirer of the BBC's 'Question Time' and, in particular, David Dimbleby's light but sure touch in encouraging speakers to answer the question that was asked, rather than the one they would rather had been asked. I hope to follow his example and ask the candidates to talk about what they can offer the people of Wycombe. I am hoping too that there will the minimum of references to what they have been 'hearing on the doorstep' as they have been touring the constituency, as clearly these are always selected and edited to suit the agenda of the party the candidate is representing. They are also (dare I suggest?), incapable of substantiation. I am also hoping that precious time will not be wasted simply rubbishing the other parties' plans. In these situations, the party in power is an easy target because they have actually been doing stuff, unlike the opposition parties; but, we are where we are now and want to hear about the future, not what the other lot did wrong.

For the first time since I moved into this area, some thirty odd years ago, I have actually been canvassed by a candidate, rather than simply receive a mail drop. Some years we haven't even received the latter. I confess that Baker Towers is a little off the beaten track and, to be honest, I am not well disposed anyway to having to answer the door when I'm clearing the ash out from the fire or settling down to watch the football. However, the feeling that one's vote matters is encouraging.

And as a nation we do like to complain don't we? One year it's, 'Do you know not a single candidate bothered to knock on my door?' and another it's, 'He had the nerve to come banging on my door to ask for my vote just after I'd got the baby to sleep!'

On Tuesday, however, I shall be very keen to hear what the candidates themselves, rather than their parties, believe on a wide range of issues, including those that affect us locally - our NHS provision, school funding, immigration, housing and the noise from the M40 etc... Come and help give them a grilling.

30th April 2010

This is quite an interesting election. Not just because Gordon got caught doing what we all do and hope never to get caught doing – saying something casually derogatory about someone and being overheard. Cringe! Nor because Cameron's aids cajoled a father and his handicapped son to 'come and meet Mr Cameron' only to find themselves pressed into a photo opportunity. They're all at it. No surprise there.

The burning issue is the prospect of a hung parliament. The two major parties, who don't like the idea of their seesaw monopoly being taken away from them, don't like the prospect. Predictably, the Lib Dems and minority parties see an opportunity to turn their sizeable (albeit minority) votes into something that affords them more of a say in how in our country is run. All very reassuring. Self interest is alive and well, and heading towards Westminster.

On Tuesday, I was privileged to chair the hustings in Wycombe as the four main candidates here answered questions submitted by Wycombe residents. The hundred and fifty or so people attending contained many familiar faces on the local political scene, keen to support 'their' candidate and also many issue driven residents.

Gratifyingly, there was also a sizeable contingent of students from a local school. I started by asking for a show of hands by those undecided about where to put their precious crosses. Thirty or so hands were raised. At the end of the spirited and even (briefly) heated debate, I asked the same question and received a precisely similar response. I then asked if anyone had changed their mind during the evening and one hand was raised, by a young man who had learned that his previously favoured party wasn't 'left' enough for him.

You have to be made of tough stuff to stand up in front of a crowd, the majority of whom (and this applies to every candidate) actively don't want you and never will, and try to convince them to change their minds. I thought they mostly did a very good job indeed and, whatever made them decide to enter politics and whatever compassionate, idealistic, barking mad, predictable, core or fringe beliefs they have, at least they do have beliefs and are prepared to put their heads above the parapet in the sure knowledge that missiles will be on their way from all directions.

An interesting week ahead.

7th May 2010

Well, we have a new MP. What a night. Did you stay up until the wee small hours to see the drama unfold as all those Acting Returning Officers have their quadrennial moments of glory as thousands of us hang on their every word and a few of 'them' find themselves with a guaranteed income for a few years – or will it be less time before the next election, in this case? Isn't it strange, by the way, that in most cases the actual Returning Officer can't be bothered to turn up for the count and somebody else has to deputise for him or her, when the dramatic moment arrives?

Anyway, now the manifestos are all being quietly packed away along with many of the commitments therein. Just wait and see how long it takes to put the pledges into effect. Cynical? Me?

You will probably be aware that I am writing this column before the election results are known – in fact before the first non-postal vote has been cast. I am therefore anticipating the brave new world of post-election fever eagerly and with interest. Unlike many of you, I suspect, I think we leave it too long between elections I love struggling to stay awake to see whether the Swingometer or its 21st

Century equivalent is predicting a landslide or a hung Parliament. I love seeing the leaders avoiding appearing smug or defeated respectively as the scenario relentlessly unfolds over the night. I look forward to settling down with my glass of wine for a long night in as David and Jonathan – the Dimblebies without whom democracy could not happen – cope with the vagaries of outside broadcast glitches and the impossible optimism of the soon to be defeated.

It's much more exciting than the X-Factor, or Over the Rainbow, because we actually like some of those people and feel sorry for them when they ceremoniously hand in their red slippers. Let's face it; we don't have quite the same sympathy for unelected politicians when they disappear back to where they came from before they feigned an interest in the constituency that they will probably head out of when the dust settles.

Alright, yes I am cynical! But democracy is far too important to trust it to any of them for a whole five years. Let's have more elections. It's great theatre. That, of course, is why they have 'acting' returning officers.

14th May 2010

After the tumultuous political activity over the last few weeks, the dust of rhetoric and bombast is settling and the nation waits with varying degrees of expectation and hope to see what happens now that the last lot have been replaced by virtually all those people who aren't the last lot. If there were ever a time when consensus and cross-party co-operation were required– it is certainly now.

Take our national finances; two interesting figures appeared in the print media last week. The first was that our debt as a country is now over 850 billion pounds. To most of us who struggle to maintain a balanced family budget, that sounds like a chillingly terrifying - to the point of coma-inducing - level of borrowing. But, interestingly, in the 1950's in the aftermath of the war and the creation of the NHS, the level of government borrowing was apparently around triple what it is today in relation to Gross Domestic Product and we survived that. I was there!

The other fact that caught my eye appeared in the Sunday Times, which published its annual 'Rich List' recently. This informed us that the wealth of Britain's 1000 richest people rose by 30% last year, to a combined total of £334.5 billion pounds.

If just one thousand people have, tucked away in their piggy banks, a total sum equal to around 40% of what otherwise seems like our gargantuan national debt, then surely 60 odd million of us should be able to have a gradual whip round over the next few years and sort things out? And that's the challenge the electorate has laid down for the incoming coalition government.

In terms of that coalition, I looked up the words 'conservative' and 'liberal' in Collins' dictionary (NB Collins not Colin's – though it is both, in fact). I do realise that the capital 'C' and 'L' bring different connotations to those words, but it was an interesting exercise. The former is defined as, "favouring the preservation of established customs and values, and opposing change, moderate or cautious." On the other hand, 'liberal' is "having social and political views that favour progress and reform, generous in temperament or behaviour, tolerant of other people, using or existing in large quantities, lavish, not rigid, free." Hmmm.

Democrat? "Quite simple - a person who believes in democracy."

Let's wish them the best of luck.

28th May 2010

I do hope that, in jettisoning the expensive ID card plans of the outgoing government, the new lot don't get too carried away in the cause of privacy and human rights. The prime justification of the ID card reversal for me is the cost at a time when the country's coffers are a little on echo-y side. I am of the view that if you're doing nothing wrong you should not fear having to prove who you are; and if you are engaged in felonious or antisocial activities then anything that helps the authorities to identify you can only be a plus. But when the wherewithal is in short supply is probably not the best time to deprive our hospitals and schools of much-needed funds.

The privacy lobby may be well-intentioned in offering the comparison with totalitarian and oppressive governments in other areas of the world, but does that really compute here, I wonder? Would the British public ever allow any administration to use mere information to control an unwilling populace? I think not.

So, I remain in favour of CCTV cameras in places where the law-abiding, decent majority of the public can be protected by them and the criminal, the vandal and the thug can be identified and prosecuted or deterred from doing their nasty thing.

The modern new school emerging like a phoenix from the ashes at Cressex has very sensibly incorporated in its new food provision arrangements the means of quick and easy payment, via a thumb scanning system, which takes money from a prepaid account and has the added bonus of de-stigmatising poorer children who do not have to pay. All parents bar one have approved, indicating that most do not share the fear expressed by the human rights group Liberty, "When we were kids, finger-printing was for identifying criminal suspects in custody – not for the school lunch queue. Before schools rush to embrace biometric technology they should think about what this teaches our children about the value of their dignity and privacy."

Eh?

I struggle to understand how thumbprints differ from faces as a means of identifying someone. Would Liberty object to someone recognising a child's face and saying, 'Hello Egbert – I'll deduct the money from your account'? I sincerely hope not. So what are they asking for? That we all wear masks and veils so that no one knows who we are?

Am I missing something?

11th June 2010

I was heartened to read that our new MP, Steve Baker – no relation – chose my birthday this week to make his maiden speech in Parliament. While I was enjoying the banquet that my wife prepared to celebrate my continuing descent into senility, Steve was on his feet in the mother of all parliaments expatiating on a subject slightly too rarefied for your columnist to pass much comment. After giving a potted history of our town and its varied communities, he moved on to an analysis of the nation's financial problems, characterising over-consumption by consumers and the boom-and-bust cycle as being at least partially rooted in the ability of banks to meet demand by extending 'credit that is unbacked by real savings.' He is clearly a man on an economic mission.

But, in between the Wycombe bit and the quoting Richard Cobden on economics bit, were two sentences that all of his constituents, myself included, will hope to see expanded into similarly robust campaigning and action. Speaking warmly of our former MP Paul Goodman, he said, "Paul's top priority was Wycombe hospital and I have to say for the benefit of the *Bucks Free Press* that it will be my top campaigning priority. I mean that sincerely; no other issue compares to it, in terms of its ability to create anxiety and concern."

I suppose it is a tad pedantic of me to say that I hope he was saying it for the benefit of his constituents rather than just this paper, but I hope his campaign will be expanded to address not only the diminished and still diminishing hospital provision in Wycombe, but also the wider issue of general healthcare provision in the area. There are continuing rumblings about levels of access to our general medical practitioners, and doctors (it seems to me) are having to go through ever more hoops to provide a good and effective service to their patients. Just as we are hearing, and hopefully can believe, that the schools are to be handed back to the teachers and parents without the blight of theorising educationalists, targets and league tables, let us hope too that medical care can be wrenched back from the hands of bureaucrats, administrators and target-setters whose activities should play a very much smaller role in healthcare provision than is currently accorded to them. Wycombe deserves better.

14. 10 Years Ago

Is it really ten years since the names of Tony Martin, Damilola Taylor and Louise Woodward were in the headlines? As I scanned through the following selection of articles, I was astonished to discover how recent some of the events seemed in my memory, whilst having taken place a decade ago. Perhaps that is an inevitable result of my having achieved the age I have. Time compresses and the memory tries to accommodate all that information in the bits of the hard disk that are still capable of retaining it. Shame we can't defrag!

9th July 1999

Many television commercials have more money spent on them per second, and have higher production standards than the programmes that surround them. But... and here I feel a little bit like the boy who pointed out that the king was in the altogether... do you know anyone who has actually bought anything because of television advertising? Yes, I have responded to requests from the children for toys they have seen advertised on TV at Christmas time. But I cannot recall an occasion when I have independently thought either, "I must have one of them" or, "next time I get one of them – that's the brand I'll buy!"

Yet clearly it works for the advertisers. Otherwise they wouldn't do it. Certainly the sums of money involved in producing one advertisement and then buying airtime for it, would stretch the resources of most lottery winners.

Having seen the advertising output of other countries' television stations, I have always been very grateful that our commercials, in general, manage to avoid the hard-sell banality and tackiness that seems acceptable and commonplace elsewhere around the world. Many of the UK output are minor works of art. And, in general, you can't accuse the advertising agencies of unsubtle hard-sell tactics. Indeed, some are so niche-orientated or obscure that they defeat me. And I am a devotee of crosswords, conundrums and puzzles.

Many of the car advertisers create the most wonderful mini-masterpieces showing their unnaturally gleaming product racing through burning landscapes, earthquakes, along harbour walls and even upside down – none of which are qualities I require from a car. And, for the life of me, I cannot remember which manufacturer's vehicle was doing what!

And can anyone explain to me the intent behind the current offering in connection with a fizzy drink I have never heard of, and whose name, tellingly, even now escapes me. It features *Men Behaving Badly's* Neil Morrissey and seems to be exhorting us to trust his utterances in relation to the product because he's evidently a congenital liar. I am clearly missing the point but feel confident that I cannot be alone in this.

I suppose it could be a generational thing.

I drop everything at the moment to watch the wonderful pastiche of those Pearl and Dean generic adverts for local Indian Restaurants back in the 50's and 60's.

My children are amused by the scratchy soundtrack, jerky editing and wonderfully wooden performances but are nonetheless, inevitably, baffled by my whoops of recognition and nostalgic delight. I do remember the product in this case, though I will maintain a judicious silence on that subject here.

Occasionally the ad agencies get it spectacularly wrong.

"You're never alone with a Strand," was a campaign that I am free to mention because the association between the cigarette and loneliness of that trilby-wearing man, hunched in his tightly belted mackintosh, was so powerful that it lost even the sales that the brand had thitherto had, and it soon joined the ranks of the exotically named Olivier, Park Drive and Du Maurier in the ash can of history. I bet the copywriters kept quiet about their contribution to that particular campaign.

Perhaps someone could do a similar job for smoking as an activity and we would be spared the distressing sight of all those young people, girls in particular, who seem to be taking up smoking in increasing numbers. They have more hard information about the carcinogenic and life-shortening effects of smoking than my generation had and, against all logic, they apparently feel the price is worth paying.

13th January 2000

Before Christmas, Doctor Who was asked to officiate at the inauguration of a hi-tech public information system in the East Midlands. I accompanied the pensioned-off old Time Lord on the trip. My contact's husband was a farmer who raises Aberdeen Angus cattle in a traditional, rather than intensive way.

I returned home with a pack of various beef cuts. If I have ever tasted better, it is certainly not for a long time.

It made me think about what we, as consumers, have done to ourselves. And I really do believe that every one of us must share the blame for the fact that our demand for more, more, more coupled with cheaper, cheaper, cheaper has driven the quality of what we eat ever downwards along with the prices.

It's not the EEC, or Tony Blair, or the last Tory Government, it's not even the French. It's our fault. Every time we buy a cheaper foreign import, we bang another nail into the coffin of our own farming community. And, if that isn't sufficient motivation to change our ways, we are robbing ourselves of the opportunity to remember how good food used to taste when we were young.

I remember when chicken was an occasional treat on high days and holidays. Now it is as common on the table as the baked beans on toast of my youth. The demand is ever increasing. But our producers cannot compete with a world market which does not have to comply with our expensive animal welfare laws. Under GATT (General Agreement on Trade and Tariffs), we have no power to ban foreign imports for any reason other than our health and safety. Animal welfare isn't a factor.

As a nation, we are considerably more responsible and humane in our treatment of animals than can be said of most other countries of the world. We legislate to ensure that our pigs receive a fairly decent standard of life before they shuffle off to the great bacon-slicer and sausage machine in the sky. And few of us would argue that we should do otherwise.

Yet we - the very same people who compel our food-producers to treat their livestock decently - will buy the sausages that are a pound cheaper, without concerning ourselves about the life, and indeed death, of the pigs from other countries, whose care, if such a word is appropriate, would be totally unacceptable in the UK. When it comes to our wallets, we pop on those handy blinkers, and buy the foreign import.

The culture of price-cutting wars exists only because the supermarkets have every reason to believe that that is what we want. The moment we demand quality and higher standards, they'll oblige us. Chickens reared intensively, that have been chucked into boiling water and mechanically plucked after a short life fed on growth hormones and other unnatural feedstuffs, simply don't taste as good as chickens that have been allowed to develop and feed naturally.

And if you don't believe me, just try an organically-reared chicken from a good butcher, even though it can cost up three or four times as much as the £3.99 one in the supermarket.

If you agree that the improvement in taste and texture is considerable, maybe we should all go back to succulent chicken once a month instead of an indifferent one every week?

And I am not being just jingoistic or even protectionist when I say that means buying British and buying organic.

We should take pride in being the world leaders in standards of animal husbandry.

25th July 1997

The buying and selling of a home is allegedly as stressful as redundancy, divorce or the loss of a loved one. I can see why. Whenever I have been engaged in the wretched business, I am always on the wrong side of the equation. As a seller I have always dealt with a purchaser whose initial reluctance to purchase is replaced by a ferocious series of exacting demands as to fixtures and speed of completion. As a purchaser, whenever I eventually have found the house I do want, I am invariably one of half a dozen prospective and eager purchasers, the other five of whom are hurrying towards their solicitors' offices at the very moment I am viewing, with suitcases full of gold ingots and bearer bonds, anxious to pay a premium for the property. All I can deduce is that either a lot of porkies are told or there is a phalanx of perverts driven demented by losing at Monopoly, who satisfy their frustration by getting tied up, for a short while, in housing chains.

For several months, my brother and I have been attempting to sell the home which my elderly mother has recently vacated to go into a sheltered home. Her continued stay in this genteel abode is dependant on our being able to invest the proceeds of the sale of her house.

Particulars are drawn up; viewers view. Some of them are not interested and rude, some mildly so and make ridiculously low speculative offers - and some appear very keen. The first eager purchaser got as far as exchange of contracts and then did the equivalent of patting his pockets and saying, "Oh dear, I've come out without any money! Good lord, is that the time?"

Two weeks wasted there. Then, along came two prospective purchasers simultaneously.

They both understandably opened negotiations significantly under the asking price. The Estate Agent initially refused to broker an auction process on the basis that it was gazumping. I took the view that gazumping entailed going back on a previous commitment to sell as a result of a subsequent increased offer and strenuously insisted that the first person to offer the actual asking price would have a deal; otherwise we would only consider the highest bidder. I thought that fair. The offers nudged upward until party A indicated that his latest offer was final and he needed to know that day. It was sufficiently close to the asking price to accept.

Solicitors started to solicit. Ten days later, our erstwhile eager beaver purchaser turned, overnight, into, "Who was that masked man?" Personal problems, apparently. Right. Deep breath. Well, at least couple B will be now be overjoyed to learn the glad tidings. No such thing. They were so miffed at our choosing the other party for a difference of only a few measly hundred quid, that they were no longer interested, thank you very much (toss curls, exit stage right).

I am totally at a loss to explain the mental processes of the great unwashed British Public sometimes. When, after months of searching, I finally found the house in which we currently live, I was so desperate to get it I offered the asking price instantly. Had I been pipped by another who then backed out, I would have leaped at the chance to get back into the frame.

So who are these people who sort of want a house, but not enough to ignore their wounded feelings at a temporary setback? And what on earth is wrong with attempting to get as much as I can for any house, let alone one that is being sold to secure a ninety year old's future?

Meanwhile friends insist on telling you, "Do you know, we sold our house while the estate agent was still putting up the For Sale sign!"

April 28th 2000

We do pride ourselves, in these little islands perched precariously on the edge of Europe, that we somehow epitomise that which is best about democracy. We are free to say pretty much what we like, to think pretty much what we like and, indeed, do pretty much what we like, provided in all cases that our exercise of that freedom does not impinge upon the collective or individual freedom of others to do likewise, within the framework of our legal system.

We have recently learned that a man, living alone in an isolated spot and already the victim of several burglaries, defended his property against three intruders by discharging a weapon in their direction as they climbed the stairs of his home late at night, with intent to rob. One of the criminals was a sixteen year old boy with a large number of previous convictions. He was killed. In many countries that also claim to be democratic (and it could be argued in this context that they have a greater claim to that description), that would have been the end of the matter. The other two would-be burglars would have been arrested and charged. The householder would have received the sympathy of society for being placed in the position where he had to take such radical action to defend his property, and suffer the trauma of killing another human being, albeit a burglar.

In democratic Britain, Tony Martin has received precisely the same life sentence as the Yorkshire Ripper, Rose West and terrorists who have planted bombs that have maimed and killed, at random, people attending church services in Northern Ireland.

I would risk large sums of money on a bet, that any poll conducted on the subject would unequivocally urge the immediate liberation of Mr. Martin. Some, I suspect, would advocate that he be awarded a medal.

Yes, he had illegal possession of a pump action shotgun, which he used to defend his home. He had broken the law in that respect. But he would have received precisely the same mandatory life sentence if the weapon he had used had been legally held, so that is not really an issue.

Had he not been able to defend himself, it might very easily have been Mr. Martin's funeral we were regretting rather than his incarceration.

Together with almost everyone except burglars and politicians (a revealing common-interest group), I earnestly hope that common sense will prevail and Mr. Martin will be restored to the community and given the protection that our under-funded police forces have been unable to provide in rural areas.

This case might provide just the spur that will persuade our political masters that there might be votes in better, higher profile community policing.

I recently heard the story of a local thief who escaped justice because of an evidential blunder, despite having been caught red-handed. He now regularly passes by the premises of the frustrated victim making those gestures, beloved by the Neanderthal when driving cars, indicating his contempt for them and total lack of repentance or gratitude for a lucky escape from justice.

You only have to watch those police documentaries showing a car thief driving with reckless disregard for human life before crashing into some innocent traveller. They usually incur a ban and a few weeks community service.

When thieves and thugs use the system to plunder and rape society, and the law-abiding are penalised in a draconian fashion for defending their property, then I would suggest that we need to re-examine our claim to being a democratic and just society.

23rd September 2000

In case you think that every week I toddle down to Gomm Road and set the fingers flying on an ink stained BFP keyboard to fill this column, I should disabuse you.

For an innocent columnist like myself, visiting the mother ship is a rather daunting experience. All those reporters in trench coats, roll-ups dangling from their mouths, chucking their hats on the desk shouting, "Hold the front page;" the bellowed imprecations floating through the peeling door that bears the legend 'Charles Mann;' the sobbing cub reporter who has just had her big exposé spiked (the one about the councillor with the concrete ball factory); the photographer banging his head against the wall trying to think of a new way to capture on celluloid the presentation of a charity cheque.

And there's the editor's suite with the Rottweilers slavering outside the door and the symbolic blood-stained thesaurus hanging from a hook.

No, I prefer the comparative calm of Baker Towers. I used to fax the sacred text, but now that the 20th century has penetrated to Wycombe Marsh, my column is teleported in byte-sized chunks and then reconstituted via the wonders of e-mail. In order to accelerate this miraculous process, I succumbed to the lure of BT's new digital all-ringing, all-enhancing Home Highway. It has provided me with high speed digital access to the internet. And I cannot deny that it has enabled me to reduce the time spent online sending and downloading information.

But... and there's always a 'but,' isn't there?

Six days ago my phone went dead. I quickly established that all my neighbours were similarly incommunicado. They, however, were reconnected the following day, because they were good old-fashioned steam operated analogue phone users. Your state of the *ark* digital columnist however is still unable to make or receive any calls.

Until very recently a call to 151 about a telephone fault would connect you to a real person and a fairly local one at that. The new, wait for it – yes – computerised system you access by pressing buttons and navigating a multiple option maze. You eventually get the chance, if you really must, to speak to a human being.

That person will be many hundreds of miles away from you and will not know the area, or its engineers. It was surely not all that long ago that the engineer himself would call you back and tell you what the problem was and that he would have you properly connected before you could say GPO.

That was before digitalisation. All my neighbours have fully working phones because they are analogue. The engineers understand them.

My nice new version is pretty tricky, apparently, and only a handful of Telecom engineers are able to do the business. I have frequently gazed in wonder at those BT wizards sitting in a hole in the ground, surrounded by what seems like an explosion in a multicoloured spaghetti factory, and giving every impression of knitting it with confidence. So if those geniuses can't cope with digital, can you imagine how complicated it must be? And now I have got an echo on my mobile phone, so I can hear myself as I complain bitterly to BT.

Anyway, if this is not a white stripe down the edge of the page it is because I posted these words and they got there in time.

9th March 2001

There is an apocalyptic feel to Britain at the moment.

We have seen a young boy, Damilola Taylor, stabbed to death on his way home from school; babies and toddlers tortured by the very people that the rest of the us would expect to love and care for them; a rail accident in Selby, tragically breaking the world record for high speed train crashes with a combined impact speed of 140 miles an hour. Terrorists have detonated a bomb outside the BBC to remind us - as if a reminder were necessary - that the Irish situation is abiding evidence of the effects of the irresistible force meeting the immovable object. A policewoman in Oldham was knocked down and then, allegedly, deliberately run over, when investigating a stolen car. In Ipswich, unthinkably, a woman in her nineties has been raped. An already decimated farm industry, having barely recovered from the destructive long-term effects of BSE, is now reeling yet again under the onslaught of an outbreak of Foot and Mouth disease. To many, it seems unthinkably grotesque to slaughter thousands of healthy animals in order to stem the spread of this highly contagious disease, whose worst effects are economically devastating rather than fatal to the stricken animals. Etched on our memories for some time will be the images of those interminable rivers of fire and smoke pierced by the forlorn legs of the prematurely slain cattle stretching up through the flames and smoke as a memorial to the sheer pointlessness of their particular lives. One can only begin to imagine the frustration and impotence of an industry that has already been battered by more than its fair share of disasters, both naturally and politically generated.

It should be no surprise that many people are questioning the way that we have, as a nation, allowed ourselves to become dependent upon the rest of the world for our food and thrown away our former self sufficiency. And once again, the rest of Europe is looking accusingly across the channel at an aggrieved country that willy-nilly seems incapable of escaping the fickle finger of fate. We know that we are a law-abiding nation; that we generally scrupulously follow and enforce the rules that other European nations seem to casually disregard. Yet it seems that each time the music stops it is only Britain that hasn't got a chair to sit on. I suspect no-one would take a second glance if the Bible's four horsemen were seen galloping round Handy Cross.

So my children came home from school last Friday to find newly attached signs at the end of the all the footpaths leading to our home telling us that to prevent the spread of Foot and Mouth the footpath was closed. Transgressors could be liable to a fine of up to £5,000. It is, of course, an acknowledged administrative ploy to do something unpalatable on a Friday afternoon and leg it to the safety of the weekend to avoid the subsequent flak. After an uncertain couple of days, on Monday it took several few phone calls to establish that as public footpaths constitute the only access my home, we could use them. The intention, apparently, is to keep the countryside free of those who do not need to be there, rather than maroon those who do. But the signs don't say that.

Mind you, at the moment, who wants to go out anyway?

28th August 1999

Most people who own fax machines will have experienced the irritation of finding that they have been sent material from companies who are trying to sell something or want something from them - usually money.

Unsolicited letters and fliers through the post are bad enough, but it is the work of seconds to file them in the bin under "R" for rubbish. But a fax is printed on my machine, using my paper. I bought a fax machine for my convenience, not in order to increase the profits of companies with whom I have no relationship and whose products interest me not a jot.

Today's consumption of my resources styled itself a "National Lottery Poll." If I wished to contribute towards the debate as to whether the Lottery ought to be profit free, I could fax my opinion to a company called 21st Century Fax Ltd. It all sounds fairly inoffensive on the surface. After all, most people agree that the profits of the lottery should be given to good causes.

But then you read the small print. Calls cost £1 a minute at all times. The fax takes one or two minutes to return. So, at best, I am being asked to pay £2 for the privilege of enabling someone else to charge a third party for conducting a poll. At worst, no one gives a toot about the results of the poll; they are however quite keen to invest pence sending me a fax urging me to spend pounds by sending them one back. And presumably, enough people rush to their faxes to take part in what they apparently believe is a state of the art manifestation of the democratic process to enable the perpetrators of this neat little earner to clean up. If so, I despair for us.

And the polls all seem to be carefully chosen to provoke "outraged from Halifax" to leap to his bally fax and right a palpable wrong. Recent subjects include Duty Free, GM Foods and Keep the Pound.

Cynical readers will not be staggering back in amazement to learn that 97% of people who don't know a scam when they see one registered their vote to keep Duty Free, 90% consider GM food unsafe and 90% want to keep the pound. Although I have no personal interest in duty free shopping when I am travelling, the other issues are ones whose conclusions I would heartily endorse. They are all issues specially selected to attract strong reactions.

I would love to know how many people so generously confirm what we already know, thereby lining the pockets of these alleged pollsters.

At least the good news letter that I also received this week from a well know digest publisher, offers me the possibility of holidays or untold wealth if I purchase a book from them. They tell me that I, Mr. C. Baker, of High Wycombe, have been lucky enough to be carefully selected from thousands of other less fortunate residents for special attention because I satisfy their rigorous selection procedure, and if my special key bears the same number as the key to their top prize (oh joy unconfined it does, it does!)...

It seems I have somehow become a personal favourite of all the people who work for their company. Indeed, the managing director would like to invite me round for tea and cakes, were he not quite so busy counting his money and laughing a lot.

But, despite the reams of bait for the gullible, if you do actually want the book – then why not?

23rd August 2002

Whilst, as a Wanderers' supporter, I welcome the return of Lawries' lads to their new playing surface at Adams Park, marking the beginning of the new season of football, this pleasure also marks the end of a spectacular summer of sport.

The sequence of World Cup, Wimbledon, the Commonwealth Games and then the European Games has been a rare feast for those of us who love to see the best in the world competing against one another.

I spent the first half of my life living in and around Manchester and was delighted to witness the spectacular success of that city in organising the Commonwealth Games. I have long been impatient at what seems to be the prevailing view in the dominant South-East of England that any international activity should be London-centred.

I cannot see, for instance, how anyone can disagree that Birmingham, being placed close to the geographical centre of the country, is the ideal place for a national sports' stadium. I attended an event at the NEC recently. Close to the intersection of four major arterial motorways, it is the ideal place for any mass entertainment venue. But, despite all logic and reasoned argument to the contrary, the benighted citizens of Wembley are going to be obliged to tolerate the construction (and use by millions) of a national stadium squeezed into the bottom right hand corner of the country, with demonstrably inferior access and greater impact on the local community. One can only wonder at the insanity of it all.

But Manchester's organisational excellence and warm hospitality (which surprised only those who don't know the people of that City), proved that the London factor is not essential in order to organise and attract spectators to international events. Indeed, one could suggest that it would be hard to imagine attendance figures in London that would rival the amazing support given to the Games in Manchester. Hopefully, other regional centres will now benefit in the future from this discovery of a fact already known to the residents of other large cities around the UK.

The fact that all these events occurred during the Queen's Jubilee made the year all the more special. In fact, the Windsor Touring Cavalcade was doing quite well in terms of improving its image and getting "out there" among us common folk, until the rather sad moment when Her Majesty failed to do what the nation was willing her to do as plucky, seriously ill, six-year-old Kirsty Howard handed her the symbolic baton at the opening ceremony of the Commonwealth Games. She received it politely enough, with a smile, but formally. Had she felt able to bend down, take the little girl's hand and speak to her, or even (however unlikely) give her a hug, the monarchy would have been safe for another generation and the tumbrels wheeled back into frustrated republicans' secret hidey holes. It is, I suppose, given their history of aristocratic repressed emotion, unlikely that such a thought might occur spontaneously, but her advisers let her down terribly, by failing to point out how much the monarchy might have benefited from such a willingness to show overt affection for a plucky little six-year-old, who was breathing only because she was carrying with her an oxygen tank.

Better to do a good thing for a dubious motive than not to do it all.

7th March 1997

I have spent the last few days coming to terms with something that many readers will have faced themselves and will therefore, I imagine, understand my mixed feelings.

At the age of 90, my mother has had to move out of the home in which she has lived alone for nigh on 20 years and into a retirement home. She has been a widow for thirty years and had moved down to Wales in her 70's to be near my older brother, whom she probably correctly saw as the more reliable son to have around the corner than her second born - the jobbing actor who might easily get snapped up by Stephen Spielberg and disappear for months on end (Ah well, I can dream can't I?).

As a result of my mother's touching faith in my employability, I have only had to deal with my guilt at being a hundred and fifty miles away, while my poor brother has had to cope with all the many and increasing problems that arise when the elderly struggle to come to terms with the fact that their bodies are no longer able to fulfil the requirements of a still-active mind and then, latterly, when the still-active mind slowly loses its ability to process and store the continuing flood of incoming information. It is, it has to be said, an uncomfortable and uncertain future that may lie ahead of many us if we fail to succumb to an earlier return to sender.

The fact that this fiercely independent woman had managed so remarkably well for so long might easily have tempted us to suppose that it could go on for ever. But a series of falls and memory lapses - some trivial but others, connected with gas fires and sell-by dates, potentially more lethal - convinced us that the moving finger was writing and had to be read and acted upon. We were incredibly lucky to find, within a few hundred yards of my mother's house, a charitable trust that owned two large and inter-connected houses, one of which was a nursing home and the other containing rooms of varying sizes into which the elderly residents could bring their own furniture and effects.

My mother was persuaded that it might be sensible to get her name on the waiting list of this rightly very popular retirement home. Despite her reluctance to consider herself as a candidate for a place full of what she disingenuously refers to as old dears (being in their seventies and eighties), this ultimately pragmatic nonagenarian consented.

When a place became available there were enough concerned and influential neighbours to advocate the undoubted advisability of the move. Thank goodness. My brother and I, of course, being still her little boys, despite both being in our fifties, would not alone have carried sufficient weight to persuade her.

But despite the certain knowledge that my mother's future and continuing safety depended on the move, it was a strange and fraught day that I spent in Cardiff this week. Reducing the contents of a three-bedroom house to one room is hard enough, and becomes doubly poignant when the bric-à-brac and impedimenta of a life are subjected to the scrutiny that is necessary when deciding what is essential for the well being of a lady in what must be seen as her final years.

To her great credit, some would say, my mother has resolutely refused to succumb to the beguiling temptation of allowing the ethereal tranquilliser of television to work its magic on a tired brain. She makes no concessions to the medium which has afforded me a living and believes that most of what can be seen on television is rubbish nowadays, a view which she has held for some fifty or so years to my certain knowledge. The truth is rather that she has always been a doer not a watcher. She enjoys books and, despite cataracts, reads a lot. But most of her life has been her home. Tidying, making tea, going to the shops, and generally busying herself in the business of simply being a householder. She now has to face an existence where most things will be done for her in order to ensure her safety and health. It is going to be very hard. It was hard on her sons too, to witness the unspoken acceptance of the irrevocable reversal of roles by the woman who bore us and controlled our formative years.

14th February 1997

The tragic death of nine-month-old Matthew Eappen in Boston Children's Hospital this week has resulted in an 18 year old English au pair girl from Cheshire facing a charge of murder in the American Courts.

At the moment the facts of the case are known only to those involved and it would be wrong to make any assumptions at all about Louise Woodward's guilt or innocence based on the information available in the media.

The case does however highlight an alarming tendency in the so-called civilised world to put the welfare of children second to the personal ambitions of the parents. Parents are less inclined to sacrifice income or leisure time in the cause of rearing their children. And I am not talking about those who need two incomes to drag themselves above the poverty line.

We rightly expect those to whom we entrust our children as teachers, childminders, or nurses to satisfy fairly rigorous requirements. We train them, examine them, interview them, screen them and take up references. However, the very same people who have these high expectations for the professional qualifications of those who have temporary custody of their children can also display an apparently cavalier disregard for those standards when they allow into their homes, to care for babies, young girls who have little or no experience of life outside of full-time general education and their own families. More often than not an au pair has no desire to pursue a career as a nanny, but is simply taking advantage of the need of others for affordable childcare to get away from home, meet people and have fun. And whilst these are in themselves innocent enough ambitions, they are not necessarily those that most people would regard as appropriate qualifications for a child carer.

These girls then suddenly find themselves with sole custody and responsibility for infants who can only communicate their needs by crying...

Anyone who has ever been a parent, or indeed has spent any time with a child, who has screamed inconsolably and unceasingly for what can seem like hours on end, will understand that sensation of teetering on the brink of unthinkable urges. Very occasionally and tragically, parents sometimes cross over that line of self-control that separates the unimaginable from the actuality and a baby is harmed. Nature, alas, equips people differently. The law of this country rightly treats these cases very carefully and allows for the variable post-natal states of mothers in particular. But if the natural parents of a baby are capable of almost unbearable stresses in dealing with the unstoppable screaming of their very own and loved offspring, how in the name of all that is reasonable can we expect a teenager who is little more than a child herself to be better than we are in that situation?

The fact that the vast majority of au pairs are female is a result of the false assumption that there is some genetic imperative in the female to care for babies and more than that - that because they are girls, they also instinctively know *how* to care for babies.

I know many people who have allowed young girls they barely know to baby sit for them, in return for an hourly rate considerably lower than that which they pay their cleaners. The miracle is that there are not more incidents when parents have cause to regret their casual attitude to the well-being of the babies they undoubtedly would die to protect.

I was accused of being harsh when, some years ago, I dispensed with the services of a nanny who had lied to us about events that had taken place in our home whilst we were away. Even though it did not involve our children, it seemed to me, and still does, that absolute trust must be the basis of a relationship between parent and nanny or au pair. But I do now acknowledge my mistake in putting a teenager in the position of having to exercise more self-control than I would perhaps have been capable of at her age. Our only other reluctant foray into the world of au pairs was one summer when an indolent but inoffensive girl from the Czech Republic lay on our sofa for a few weeks complaining of the heat and spooning peanut butter into her mouth directly from the jar. We have never tried again.

18th February 2000

Over the last year, the A.A. has conducted a detailed investigation into the way in which we co-exist with our cars in this country, as compared with our European neighbours.

I was not surprised to learn that we spend more time than other Europeans commuting in our cars and travel less by bus, tram, metro and bike. Nor was I surprised to learn that we pay the highest price for our petrol, as well as shelling out more in motor taxation. And, of course, our cars cost considerably more in the first place.

These statistics do not sit easily with the information that only Denmark has invested less than the UK in transport infrastructure, and only Poland had worse congestion. We are seemingly the nation with the most congested roads in Western Europe, and have fewer miles of motorway than the other countries in relation to density of population and land area. And fewer kilometres too, for those of you who are metrically inclined!

When we add those depressing statistics to the knowledge that UK investment in transport and roads has been at around a half of average European levels for 25 years, I think we have every reason to feel less than enchanted by the huff and puff about "Transport Policies" that emanates from certain ministers with more than their fair share of chauffeurs, Jaguars and privileged parking.

Twenty-five years ago, the total raised in road taxation - some £12 billion - was also roughly the total amount spent on our roads and transport. Today, only a sum equal to ONE SIXTH of the revenue extracted from the motorist is ploughed back into roads or transport.

If you need evidence of the great transport rip-off, you only have to negotiate the pot-holes along the average ill-maintained city street, or attempt to park where there is only highly priced and woefully inadequate provision, or try to make an accurate assessment of how long any journey might take - or indeed look for any form of public transport that goes where you want to go at the time you want to go there.

And neither party of government can wriggle out of the blame for this, despite all their sanctimonious tut-tutting when in opposition.

And they all do it - witness the local party political puppet who wrote to this paper with a knee-jerk "knock the other lot rather than address your own deficiencies" response to my recent plea for BOTH major parties to be honest about the cost of providing decent education and health services and not just grub around for our votes by short-sighted promises of low taxes.

As I drive around Wycombe, I see signs telling me how many motorists have been prosecuted for speeding. There are none telling me how many car thieves have been caught. Or how many vandals who regularly torch cars and dump them on the common where I live have been brought to justice. Or how many radios ripped from cars in our car parks have been recovered. Or how many traffic delays have been eased.

The motorist is treated appallingly in this country and if tolls are introduced, as threatened, on roads that our taxes have already paid for several times over, without there being a decent alternative public transport system in place, then the politicians will see a lot of hitherto well-behaved worms doing defiant wheelies over all their majorities.

Suggested headlines?

No transport of delight.
For whom the toll smells.
Enough to drive you mad.
Milking the car nation.
Money for old roads.
Traffic jam.
All roads lead to groan.

15. It's "*Would have*" not "*Would of*"!

Yes, you already know that I am obsessed in a mild way with words. They are after all the tools we use to bridge that otherwise vast chasm that would lie between us all as human beings. Were we not able to communicate accurately our thoughts and desires to each other, we would have made much progress from the days of the club, the loin cloth and the cave.. Some of course would maintain that we have not done so anyway, even with the benefit of verbal communication.

I view words in much the same way as a builder views his materials. Put them together in the wrong way – and the building falls down sooner or later. As an actor and occasional writer, words are my bricks. And they are bricks that can be put together in many wonderful and mind bending ways. Just think of Jane Austen, Shakespeare, Dickens and Harold Pinter, for starters. All using the same language, and all doing it such very different and inspiring ways.

19th March 2010

A good friend has berated me for writing in this column 'different to' instead of 'different from'. As one who regularly criticises the verbal infelicities of others, I confess that I was mortified to have been identified as a preposition abuser. Before apologising to the nation, I decided to double check. To my surprise, and slight relief, I learned that I may not be entirely without justification in using this form. One of the greatest published authorities on the English Language, H.W. Fowler says: "That 'different' can only be followed by 'from' and not by 'to' is a superstition." But I must concede that most other publications opt for 'from' as the preferred form, whilst acknowledging that 'to' is just about acceptable and in most circumstances preferable to the even less-favoured 'than.'

I can sense some people reading this and thinking 'Who the heck cares? As long as we understand each other, then why should it matter? Language is constantly changing, so let's just go with the flow."

They have a point, of course; but do we really want to end up with everyone writing in text speak, or 'txt spk'? Am I just being an old linguistic Luddite, when I shudder on receiving a text inviting me to join someone for a drink after the show – "C U @ pub l8r 2nite?"

My only consolation in this case is that this form of communication will die out instantly when more sophisticated voice recognition software is available for phones in the very near future. To be fair, it is not just laziness that drives this mangled brief-speak, it is the fact that it reduces messages in size and therefore cost. I am not a great user of text myself, preferring the e-mail, but in both cases I cannot bring myself to do other than laboriously type the whole thing about with my far from flying forefinger. In that way, I am different FROM my children, who use their mobile phones with the same speed and casual dexterity as those demonstrators employed in shops to sell wonder kitchen utensils that can skin a grape, fillet a haddock or cut a coconut into thin strips in microseconds. Then, when you get it home it takes you weeks to learn how to peel a potato with it at half the speed that you could before you were bamboozled into buying the wretched thing.

14th July 2006

Most television stations, like most newspapers, manage to remain solvent as a result of advertising revenue. Advertising must work for the advertiser, as well as the broadcaster and publisher, otherwise they wouldn't spend those countless billions making expensive commercials, many of which cost more to make than feature films, were cost measured solely by on-screen time.

Having seen the advertising output of other countries' television stations, I am very grateful that our commercials, in general, manage to avoid the hard-sell tackiness that seems commonplace elsewhere around the world. By comparison, the UK offerings are minor works of art. Indeed, some of ours are so arty or obscure that it's hard to identify the product. Car manufacturers create the most wonderful mini-masterpieces showing their unnaturally gleaming product racing through burning landscapes, earthquakes, along harbour walls and even upside down – none of which are qualities I require from a car. But, for the life of me, I cannot remember which manufacturer's vehicle was doing what! Are there really people out there who intended to buy one kind of car but change their minds because another car turned itself into a huge robot and danced around a frozen lake for thirty seconds? "Very handy that, when negotiating Handy Cross in the rush hour – I'll get one of them!"

I was recently discussing the advert where young man is introduced to his gorgeous potential flatmates in their penthouse overlooking a football stadium. You know the one? I quoted the line about the brewer that doesn't do flatmates, but if they did they would be the best flatmates in the world. Apparently, I quoted the wrong brewer. So that advert was wasted on me; I'm still not sure which it is now. And even if I were able to remember, I would choose my beer on the basis of which one I had tried and liked before, and was available in the pub I was in at the time.

Maybe adverts work for people with greater product and brand identification retention than I have. But I haven't met anyone who will admit to that being the case.

Indeed, I am hard-pressed to think of a product that I have ever bought, as a direct result of an advertisement, which I would not otherwise have bought. Although I would check a local paper to discover local suppliers of something I already wanted.

But then I would say that, wouldn't I?

13th January 1998

The status of the little cluster of islands that makes up The United Kingdom has arguably waned over the last century. We can no longer credibly claim to be a major power in the way that we were a hundred or more years ago. And, indeed, there is probably a lot to be said for that. We no longer have to face the prospect of living with the moral consequences of our ancestors' fairly arrogant and not always entirely benevolent treatment of those distant countries that formed part of the British Empire.

Some would argue that we still have a role as a major player in the financial markets of the world and remain a focal point, if nothing else, for the countries that formerly belonged to the Empire and Commonwealth.

But I believe that the strongest influence of the British Isles today is probably as a result of our language. It is undoubtedly still the language understood and used by more people in the world than any other, a fact borne out by the gratifying revelation that the number of people that learn English in China exceeds the total population the United States.

All the more reason, therefore, why we should have a clear understanding of what exactly it is that we want our language to do for us. Of course, it must evolve, and only the mentally constipated would really wish to stem the natural evolution of what is effectively an independent life form. I have therefore no quarrel with linguistic changes which occur as a result of the desire to express the new ideas and aspirations of successive generations. Hence the evolution of the word "wicked" to convey something quite other than its original meaning, is I believe not a cause for concern. However I am concerned when words lose their meaning because of the laziness or ignorance of those that use them, and our broadcasters are not entirely without blame in this area.

I was once taking part in a radio version of "Titus Andronicus," Shakespeare's tasteful piece about serial murder and cannibalism. There was some dispute on the studio floor about the pronunciation of a Roman name, so I was asked by the director to telephone the Pronunciation Department for guidance (yes - there really is a Pronunciation Department at the BBC!). I dialled the number and a voice at the other end answered in best North London telephonese with artificial and cheery swooping cadences,

"Hello ProNOUNciation Department, can I help you?"

"It doesn't matter", I replied.

We sorted it out for ourselves.

I suppose, therefore, that I shouldn't be too surprised when newsreaders on all channels consistently muddle up, for instance, the words "de-fuse" and "diffuse." If I had a bottle of Spanish Red for every time I have been informed that bombs have been spread all over the place, rather than rendered harmless, I would be permanently incapable of writing this column, which, of course, some might regard as a cause for celebration.

I would much rather have the deliberate hijackings of words to describe new ideas and feelings than the casual erosion of our language through laziness or ignorance. So, much as we may mourn the passing of the word "gay" in its former sense, it is an unavoidable consequence of an evolving language that it should change; and interestingly, the state of light hearted, innocent joy conveyed by that word in the 20's and 30's is probably not one which has any place in our pre-millennial world.

A more worrying trend is the proliferation of jargon in the business and communications industries. "To continue linear progression as a physical, interactive and viable entity as opposed to terminating the integral functionality of elective and autonomic vital and cognitive systems" is not an improvement on "To be or not to be..."

23rd April 2004

A friend of mine is a former English teacher who has had occasion to mark GCSE papers in the past. Knowing of my keen interest in the joys to be had from the use of our versatile and rich language, he recently shared with me a collection of metaphors that he had collected over the years from English essays. I append some of them, so that you may benefit from the writers' creative and literary genius.

His thoughts tumbled in his head, making and breaking alliances like underpants in a tumble dryer.

She caught your eye like one of those pointy hook latches that used to dangle from doors and would fly up whenever you banged the door open again.

The little boat gently drifted across the pond exactly the way a bowling ball wouldn't.

Her hair glistened in the rain like nose hair after a sneeze.

Her eyes were like two brown circles with big black dots in the centre.

Her vocabulary was as bad as, like, whatever.

He was as tall as a six-foot-three-inch tree.

Long separated by cruel fate, the star-crossed lovers raced across the grassy field toward each other like two freight trains, one having left York at 6:36 p.m. travelling at 55mph, the other from Peterborough at 4:19 p.m. at a speed of 35mph.

John and Mary had never met. They were like two hummingbirds who had also never met.

The door had been forced, as forced as the dialogue during the interview portion of Family Fortunes.

The plan was simple, like my brother Phil. But unlike Phil, this plan just might work.

The young fighter had a hungry look, the kind you get from not eating for a while.

He was as lame as a duck. Not the metaphorical lame duck either, but a real duck that was actually lame. Maybe from stepping on a land mine or something.

She had a deep, throaty, genuine laugh, like that sound a dog makes just before it throws up.

It came down the stairs looking very much like something no one had ever seen before.

The knife was as sharp as the tone used by Glenda Jackson, MP, in her first several points of parliamentary procedure made to Robin Cook, MP, Leader of the House of Commons, in the House Judiciary Committee hearings on the suspension of Keith Vaz, MP.

The ballerina rose gracefully en pointe and extended one slender leg behind her, like a dog at a lamppost.

The revelation that his marriage of 30 years had disintegrated because of his wife's infidelity came as a rude shock, like a surcharge at a formerly surcharge-free cash-point.

The dandelion swayed in the gentle breeze like an oscillating electric fan set on medium.

It was a working class tradition, like fathers chasing kids around with their power tools.

He was deeply in love. When she spoke, he thought he heard bells, as if she were a dustcart reversing.

She was as easy as the Daily Star crossword.

She grew on him like she was a colony of E Coli and he was room-temperature British beef.

She walked into my office like a centipede with 98 missing legs.

Her voice had that tense, grating quality, like a first-generation thermal paper fax machine that needed a band tightened.

It hurt the way your tongue hurts after you accidentally staple it to the wall.

Who says creative writing is a dying art?

16. Dicing with Death Wearing a Safety Helmet

Political correctness and Jobsworths. Need I say more?

4th June 2004

I regularly share with readers the mind-numbingly ludicrous excesses of the directives issued in the name of "political correctness." I do so in part to provoke humour as much as outrage, but am rapidly coming to the conclusion that such gentle protests are failing to make any impression on that tiny handful of people who seem to inhabit a completely different planet to the rest of us. Very, very occasionally I meet someone who defends the mandates of the politburo of profound pointlessness. But they only serve to highlight the fact that the majority of the sane British population are getting grazed chins on a daily basis as they trudge around slack-jawed at the endless stream of irredeemable tosh that emanates from people who have without question been promoted to levels that way exceed their modest thinking ability, and who seem immune to the protests of their saner fellow citizens. What started out as a laudable attempt to highlight and curb institutionalised prejudice and unfair practices where they existed has evolved into something that is as obsessive and socially constipating as the McCarthy-ite anti-communist witch hunts of half a century ago.

I will continue to rail against the worse excesses and will encourage you, dear sane reader, to refuse to have your life constrained by them. I would encourage our legislators and courts to do what they can to stop litigation being employed as a means of lining the pockets of the increasing number of greedy opportunists who find a way of nailing employers, neighbours, teachers, policemen, etc. for a bob or two because they called them a twerp, which as everyone knows could be taken to mean that they come from Antwerp in Belgium and carries the implication that Belgians are unintelligent. For the record – I have just made that up – but you can bet your Euro MP's monthly allowance that someone would have believed it and acted accordingly, had I not owned up to my deception.

So this week's examples of the continuing erosion of common sense?

BBC presenters have been encouraged to abandon the use of the expression "taking the Mickey" in case it offends its Irish audience, despite the fact that the expression emanates from cockney rhyming slang (Mickey Bliss). That omnipresent fear of litigation has resulted in children at a primary school being banned from bringing in sun cream in case it gets in other children's eyes. A 19th century painting of a monkey playing a violin in a public gallery in Barnsley has been removed for fear of offending animal rights groups. In Felixstowe the Environment Agency has erected signs the whole length of the sea wall bearing the useful message that falling off the wall could be dangerous. A governor of a school in Surrey has resigned in disgust because schools were instructed to train teachers how to spot symptoms of "the bends" in case their delicate infant charges contracted the decompression sickness suffered by deep sea divers whilst at the local municipal pool. And the outgoing acting director general of the BBC marked his brief tenure in that post by issuing an edict that one in fifty characters in BBC dramas and quiz shows must be disabled. Trainee teachers have been told to avoid the word "brainstorming" for fear of offending pupils with epilepsy. Instead they are being advised to use "word storm" or "thought shower."

What about weather forecasters' and bath manufacturers' sensibilities then?

Twerps!

6th June 2008

In my self-appointed role as scourge of the jobsworth and the politically correct, I update you on the latest excesses of those grey people that inhabit some bleak parallel universe. Not that my denunciation will have much effect until we man the barricades of reason and pull down their ivory towers – how's that for a mixed metaphor?

West Cross near Swansea boasts a 150 year old monkey puzzle tree – at the moment. A local council spokesman said: "Safety experts have likened the fallen tree foliage to discarded syringe needles and warn they pose a probable risk of serious injury to children." I had a monkey puzzle in my garden as a child and regularly came into contact with its needles, which bore more resemblance to blunt pencils than needles. It is once again the pernicious fear of litigation that prompts these bureaucrats to sniff out infinitesimal risks and pull out the sledgehammer of stupidity to deal them.

A fire brigade in Hampshire has been told to stop taking its fire awareness demonstration around schools. It involved setting fire to a chip pan to show how easy it was to do – and how dangerous the result. It seems even the fire brigade can't be trusted to do that safely.

But are we surprised when the police in Kent have refused to break up illegal raves, despite repeated requests from Shoreham residents, for 'health and safety' reasons. It is apparently too dark in the woods at night (now that has worrying implications for future policing, given the tendency of the ungodly to ply their criminal activities under cover of darkness). The other reason? Breaking up parties is dangerous because, "the ravers might drive home drunk."

But we live in a country that is offering A level examinations in Popular Culture and Communication – a subject that includes exploring the relationship between cinema-going and dating and poses such searching questions as "Is skateboarding better than polo?"

Am I being cynical, or could that be an attempt to offer schools the chance to move up the dreaded league tables by taking on subjects that students will seize avidly, irrespective of their ultimate usefulness, at the expense of, say, history and science which demand a little more intellectual rigour and application?

In January Gordon Brown promised to fight the culture that removes hanging baskets from the streets and stops children joining the Scouts or Guides. Erm? What happened, Gordon?

12th May 2006

There was a letter in a broadsheet this week signed by leading figures in local government. They were requesting that more decisions should be made locally rather than nationally. "Well they would, wouldn't they?" as Mandy Rice Davies once notoriously said. The heartfelt plea was probably at least partially provoked by the clear intention of this government to disempower the county councils whose activities have not always accorded with the national grand plan.

Here are a few examples of the work of local councils.

A man in Staffordshire, who spent £1500 of his own taxed income cleaning up and re-turfing a piece of council land behind his home that for 30 years had been an dumping ground for rubbish, has been ordered to restore it to its original state or face prosecution.

A retired squadron leader lollipop man on the Isle of Man, who temporarily deserted his post to help a group of children who were struggling to cross a junction a few yards away, has been sacked for misconduct.

A 73-year-old pensioner was not allowed to board a bus carrying a tin of emulsion. Under Health and Safety Regulations paint is classed a "hazardous substance" and must be carried in two containers (e.g. a tin and a box or bag).

That local authority and its driver saved many lives that day.

Bristol County Council recently planted 100 yew trees near a children's play area. A risk assessment has now revealed that the leaves are poisonous and even though they taste unappealing enough to deter any child from consuming a fraction of the amount required to affect their health, they are now all to be dug up again.

In Somerset, a life guard and her husband (ironically enough a health and safety officer) were not allowed to take their three children swimming in the municipal baths because council rules required every child to be accompanied by an adult.

And the NHS Trusts don't want to be left out of the act. Nurses in Cornwall have been ordered to keep a record of chocolates, flowers and other gifts they receive from grateful patients. They have to fill in a form itemising the details of the donor and the value of the gift. The results will be analysed to measure patient satisfaction.

And anyway we are not patients, but clients, apparently.

Our patience has clearly run out!

12th March 2010

We are all just voices crying in the wilderness, it seems. That is all of us except the extra-terrestrials who are now living among us. They must be shape shifting alien invaders because no human being could be responsible for the stories I am about to share with you.

A businessman was travelling with his pregnant wife on a BA flight from Gatwick. He was sitting in the middle seat with his wife on one side and a twelve year old boy, travelling alone, on the other side. Apparently, BA will not allow male passengers to sit next to children 'they don't know.' He was told that the plane would not take off unless he moved. He reluctantly complied but is now quite rightly suing BA and has promised to donate any subsequent damages awarded to the NSPCC. We should cheer him to the rafters in his fight against the invading alien robots, who are also to be found among the management of the Royal Mail, or Insania, or whatever it is now called.

A postman in Southport has been sacked because he signed for a parcel on behalf of a frail old lady when a delivery van's arrival coincided with his turning up with her post. He knew her well and was aware that she would be unable to easily get to the deliverer's depot to collect it. He delivered it to her later in his own time. Understandably, the aforesaid FOL telephoned the sorting office to commend his public spirited thoughtfulness to his managers. Being alien invaders bent on the destruction of humanity, they commenced disciplinary proceedings against the good postie, who has now lost his job and is predictably suffering from stress. One of his colleagues in Southport, with a twenty-five year unblemished record, was also dismissed. He had left his van unlocked while he delivered letters at a remote farmhouse at the end of a long single track lane.

The local MP, Dr Pugh, says, "It would be quite easy to leap to the conclusion that there is an underlying strategy to find reasons to shed experienced staff, so as to cut costs, replace permanent staff with casual or reduce pension liabilities."

No, no, Dr Pugh. That is unthinkable. No responsible employer, with human employees would do that.

It is the beginnings of an alien invasion. They are coming to get us and we must resist.

30th March 2001

My brother married a girl from the Welsh valleys; my mother has lived in South Wales for twenty years. For the first time in my life I wouldn't mind being Welsh – and I am sure the feeling will pass quite quickly, so please don't worry.

I wish I were Welsh for one reason only - so that I could make it quite clear that to take any umbrage at Ann Robinson's remarks about our Celtic neighbours is further evidence of a PC world gone mad. The racism that developed in Britain, largely unchecked over several decades, and which was predominately directed against our Afro-Caribbean and Asian fellow citizens, was clearly intolerable and in some cases even evil. It needed to be rooted out of society and seen for the cancer that it is. However the knife that was used to excise this pustule is flashing around all too randomly now and has sadly created a climate in which every casual utterance is dissected with, it seems, the express intention of extracting offence where none reasonably exists. There is a world of difference between the nasty and unfunny racism that Bernard Manning used to employ to entertain a similarly Neanderthal audience at the expense of an understandably sensitive immigrant population, and Anne Robinson's comments about the Welsh in BBC 2's Room 101.

If you haven't seen it, the programme invites high profile contributors to assign to the aforementioned room things, ideas, people and activities that they abominate. The programme is hosted by the comedian Paul Merton. It is intended to be humorous.

Jeffrey Archer, TV Chefs, Cheese Footballs and Opera have been recent guests' tongue-in-cheek and idiosyncratic pet hates for despatch to the room immortalised by George Orwell in 1984 (the book, not the year!).

Having read the outpouring of righteous indignation from the Tafia, west of the Severn, after the first airing of Anne Robinson's contribution, I watched the programme in order to judge for myself. The formidable and entertaining diva of dismissal, known for her deadpan insults and humiliation of the contestants in The Weakest Link, offered the Welsh for inclusion on the basis that they irritated her, because they were better than us in many areas including sport and singing. Hardly the most hurtful of jibes! Her parting shot, clearly intended to be humorous, was, "What are they for?"

I find it absolutely incredible that Huw Edwards, the newsreader, whom I had previously, and clearly erroneously, assumed to be a balanced individual by nature of his job, saw fit to demand that the BBC should not repeat the programme on the basis that Anne Robinson's remarks were offensive to all Welsh people, including himself. Thank goodness that the Beeb had the artistic courage to stand up to the PC thought-police and insist that the Welsh needed no more protection than any of the other groups or individuals lampooned in this light hearted programme.

The whole question of genuine racial discrimination is damaged by incidents like this, and the recent case of the Asian police officer who, having successfully appealed against a failure to win promotion to superintendent, was offered prioritised status in subsequent promotion rounds. He is now suing again, for racial discrimination, as having now been promoted on that basis, he has been professionally damaged by the loss of respect of his peers.

Beam me up, Scotty. Sorry! I mean "Englishy!"

9th June 2000

The Nanny State is taking over.

I have always found policemen to be a pretty decent bunch of people, doing a difficult job as well as they can, given inadequate staffing levels and the bureaucratic stranglehold endured by all public institutions. The police are in the front line and frequently have to carry the can for society's ills and successive governments' deficiencies (miners' strikes, football hooliganism, council tax riots et al.).

However, recent cases highlighted in the media will not serve to maintain the public support that any nation's police must clearly have in order to continue to provide an effective service.

The motoring issue is thorny enough without adding to it the absurdities highlighted recently. Indeed, it has always been my opinion that it may be unhelpful to have the same force to both police traffic and combat crime. Disgruntlement is inevitable, when two policemen in a high-tech expensive vehicle stop a motorist because a tail light is out, if that same motorist's car had recently been broken into and the crime didn't merit the attendance of a single officer. Of course, the two incidents are separate; roads have to be policed and resources to fight crime are stretched beyond the limit. But human nature being what it is, I would suggest that a long hard look at the service being provided to the majority of citizens, who are essentially law-abiding by any sane definition of those words, is long overdue.

The cases that highlight this for me are those where drivers have been stopped and fined for respectively sipping from a water bottle while stopped at traffic lights and eating a chocolate bar while driving down the M3. The latter was fined £20, which was later cancelled after a public outcry. The former is refusing to pay her £20 on the spot fine, thereby risking a fine of £1000 and four points on her licence. I applaud her stance.

Both of these incidents took place in Hampshire. This begs the question whether there has been some sort of policy edict from above on the subject. If so, one fervently hopes it has been misunderstood by over-zealous officers.

Otherwise, we all face substantial penalties for offences we can only guess at.

I have always marvelled that smoking while driving is acceptable. If drinking water at traffic lights is evidence of lack of control of a vehicle, then how about holding in one hand a burning tube of tobacco, which can be dropped with dire consequences at any time and which sends an irritant into the lungs of the driver. Also, if talking on a hands-free phone is unacceptable – what about talking to your passengers and/or listening to the radio? What difference is there?

The most dangerous thing that I have ever done while driving was involuntary, but truly scary. Whilst in the outside lane of a motorway travelling at 70 mph, I succumbed to a sudden fit of sneezing. I must have sneezed a dozen times. Have you ever tried to keep your eyes open while sneezing? It's impossible. I managed to maintain my line and distance from other vehicles, but I would much rather have done so while eating a chocolate or talking on the phone.

The case on the front page of this paper last week is quite another matter. If everyone routinely chucked their refuse and fag ends out of their car windows, we would be knee-deep in garbage.

The £25 fine meted out was milder than the inconsiderate driver deserved.

13th May 2005

You'll like this one, dear, sane reader. A young lady friend took some children into a pub in Marlow for lunch. One of the children wanted a baked potato with cold baked beans. A simple enough request, you would have thought. However, my friend was told that Health and Safety Regulations (sigh!) meant that they were unable to serve cold baked beans, but could only offer hot baked beans – which the child did not like. My friend, who patently has a lot more patience than I would have done in similar circumstances, gently enquired whether it might be possible, having heated the baked beans, to pop them in the fridge for a while. Not being there, I am not sure whether the waiter had to check through the Health and Safety Baked Bean Temperature Control Inspectorate Regulations, but he agreed.

As is implicit in the actual name of this food, the beans are actually cooked already, so the litigation-busting effect of heating them up is lost on me. Maybe a reader who has their finger on the pulse (and beans are pulses, aren't they?) could explain this nonsense to me.

The same friend returned to her home recently to find that some young men had encamped in her garden in order to drink and smoke and generally enjoy what her herbaceous borders had to offer. When she asked them what they were doing there and requested that they leave, they simply stared at her without speaking and carried on doing what they were doing before climbing back over fence a little while later. Meanwhile she had telephoned the police, who asked her if the intruders into her garden had damaged any property in gaining access. They hadn't. They had simply climbed over her sturdy six-foot fence. As there was no damage, the police were unable to help. Trespass is a civil matter and unless there is damage or threatening behaviour, the police are powerless to act to protect a young woman, living alone, from the random incursion of louts who know the law well enough to know what they can do with impunity.

My friend, who is now contemplating moving house as a result of this unwelcome and newly discovered vulnerability, asked the police if it would be okay to run barbed wire along the top of her fence. And, as you have probably already guessed, no it isn't. An uninvited intruder, it seems, has more rights than the citizen in their own home.

If anybody in local or national government is reading this column, will they please do something, anything, to tip the see-saw back in the direction of the citizen and away from the thug, the criminal and the sociopath who are currently using every loophole in our inadequate criminal legislation to cock an insolent snook at the rest of us?

1st July 2005

When those party leaflets drop through the letterbox before an election, none of them say "When elected we propose to chop down all the fruit trees along your road in case someone slips on the fruit and sues us." But that is what the Council in Havering in East London plans to do at a cost of £150,000 of its council taxpayers' money.

And the reason that they don't do tell us of their intended legally defensive initiatives, is because they have a pretty shrewd idea that we will decline to vote for them on the grounds that they are clearly potty. Nor, for similar reasons, do they say, "Your vote will guarantee that we site our speed cameras in places that will really irritate you all because they are demonstrably about revenue-gathering rather than accident prevention. Furthermore when you draw this to our attention we will refuse to let you know the conviction rate (or Income Stream as we call it). Who do you think you are? You've had your say and in five years you can have another go, but we won't tell you then, either!"

I am sure that prospective Sussex Councillors promised any number of things but somehow contrived to omit to promise to ban the use of egg boxes in handicraft and art "in order to reduce the (non-existent) risk of salmonella poisoning." A Lewes School has been reluctantly compelled to follow this inane ruling from the Mad Hatter and March Hare whom the good folk of Lewes have clearly elected as their local representatives and who have underlined their credentials as comedy bureaucrats by banning the use of toilet rolls, for similar health reasons. I am surprised they allow us to bring our nasty germ-ridden children into their schools!

I would urge one of our universities to commission immediately a research study into the effects on thitherto sensible and public-spirited citizens of the post-elective euphoria that induces the delusional imperative to create and enforce unnecessary and ludicrous regulations.

Perhaps they could start by examining the decision of the British Board of Film Classification to prevent the under 12's from viewing the recent Doctor Who episode in which a Dalek is kept in chains and maltreated, on the basis that it encourages children to see violence as an acceptable means of resolving disputes.

Dalek: "Exterminate, exterminate!"
Bureaucrat: "No, conciliate, arbitrate ... AAAARGH!"
The rest of us (trying hard not to smirk): "Oh dear!"

24th March 2006

I would rather live in a world where some people might be offended, scared, fall over and hurt themselves or do something really stupid than a world where those things were impossible or criminalized.

When I read that officers in the metropolitan police have been told not to use the word 'suicide,' in case it offends, I know the touchy-feely strategists have lost the plot. Apparently, the deceased would rather be styled "victims of self-harm." Though how the functionary incapable of joined-up thinking came up with that notion, it is hard to fathom. "Self-harm bombers today killed twenty people"? Mind you, 'suicide bomber' is itself a little euphemistic. They are really murder bombers. To call them anything else implies that their own demise was their primary purpose and those who were blown to pieces around them were merely an unfortunate side effect.

Other recent delights include a six year old girl in Hampshire being banned from wearing a watch at school, 'in case the metal winder injures another pupil when she puts her hand up to answer a question;' Welsh drama teachers being advised to cut the love scenes from school productions of Romeo and Juliet and substitute 'hugs of friendship' (yuk) for the kiss between the dying lovers; and a church in the West Midlands that had to pay £75 for planning permission to erect an cross in its grounds, because according to their contorted logic, a cross outside a church constitutes advertising.

Last year the NHS spent a quarter of a million pounds warning pensioners of the dangers of ill-fitting slippers, and the Arts Council spent £77,000 sending a team of artists to the North Pole to make a snowman. Meanwhile, Micklefield library may close due to lack of funds.

And this week I learned, from that "insider" beloved of newspapers, that writers for the new series of Doctor Who are instructed not to allow Daleks (or indeed any other alien monsters) to massacre humans, for fear of copycat crimes. You can just see those implacable aliens drifting aimlessly around in space wondering what to do with their extermination devices, until by chance they hit upon an old Dr Who video. Terrorism, viruses, religion and "people chanting" are banned. And there is a perplexing edict not to give a surname to a dead child. A child with just a first name is okay to bump off in a story, apparently.

Work that one out if you can!

25th July 2003

I was diverted this week by the story of the circus performer who has been obliged to wear a safety helmet while plying his trade of tight rope walking. It appears that, as ever, nanny UK is following European directives to the letter and therefore Goussein Khamdoulaev will now perform his death defying somersaults on the high wire, fifty feet above the gasps of the crowd, wearing a hard hat. The Moscow State Circus acrobats, contortionists and jugglers are also regarded as at risk of cranial injury if performing without hard hats and may be asked to don them. The managers of the Circus point out, with some justification, that this Brussels-inspired diktat may actually tend to increase rather than reduce the risk of injury; it will clearly provide the potential to affect, however minimally, the intrepid performer's weight distribution and the therefore his balance; it also restricts peripheral vision and could even slip down and restrict it even further. This is yet another example of the prevalent disinclination to allow common sense to be applied in the application of regulations that may have been designed to be beneficial in the broader scheme of things, but that signally fail to acknowledge that one size does not fit all. The notion that the performers in a circus (traditionally places in which the apparent dicing with death and danger are, as it were the main attraction), should be compelled to adopt the safety procedures and apparel designed to protect workers in industries where that is not the prime object – is quite simply ludicrous.

One is led to believe that in France and Germany there is a popular healthy contempt for the minutiae of European directives that affect the day to day life of citizens. Anyone who has spent any time in either of those countries will have witnessed abundant evidence of their less constipated view of the detail of EEC bureaucracy. This contempt is apparently matched by a corresponding disinclination on the part of the authorities to overzealously enforce them. And in this attempt to hold back the tide of petty officialdom and reduce governmental interference in matters more properly left to the individual, our European neighbours seem to me to have got it right.

If high wire artists have to wear hard hats, why not clowns? They hurl themselves around fairly ferociously and are prone to chuck buckets around, drive collapsing cars and routinely belabour each other around the head. As for the guy who sticks his head in the lion's mouth... Alright, I know that's not allowed any more, but it does conjure up a beguiling image. And what, I would love to know, are the Health and Safety regulations for knife throwers? The spectacle of a cleaver-wielding stalwart hurling cutlery at a young lady encased in full body armour fails to have the same potential for excitement as the more traditional method.

How long will it be before hard hats will be compulsory for riders of carousels at funfairs? Or football players? Or anyone who has to go up stairs? Why not compel audiences at rock concerts to wear ear plugs? (Actually, that's not a bad idea!)

It is just as well that public execution is not still practised in the UK. We would doubtless be treated to the sight of the condemned being asked to don a hard hat before mounting the scaffold to join the similarly adorned executioners and priest.

30th October 2009

I have thought of a way to save the country a shed load of money. It would only take the time necessary to draft and enact legislation severely restricting the ability to claim financial recompense for the footling incidents and accidents that are currently manna from heaven to lawyers and the litigious.

Last year, a company selling ice cream directly to the public instructed its staff not to put toppings on customers' ice creams 'in case they slipped over them if they dripped off.' Customers now receive their ice cream and the topping in separate containers and must combine the two themselves. Drips are then the legal responsibility of the customer, not the vendor. Multiply this by thousands of other companies selling to, or dealing with, the public and the scale of the defensive behaviour dictated by fear of litigation becomes apparent. Less than a generation ago, if we hurt ourselves doing something fairly normal, we shrugged and dealt with it ourselves. Now the instant reaction for many is to rub their hands together with glee and seek one of those compensation lawyers who advertise their ambulance chasing wares on morning television.

Clearly flagrant and gross breaches, or cavalier disregard of sensible safety practices are, and should be seen as, reprehensible and should be punished. On the other hand, councils should not have to spend our money putting up signs along the sea wall at holiday resorts warning us that falling ten feet and more onto a beach can hurt, or into the sea can cause drowning. But I have seen such signs – as have you, probably. And they are of course basically just proclaiming 'Don't blame me if you're a moron,' rather than demonstrating excessive anxiety about our well-being.

Stick 'May contain nuts' on anything that might be considered edible and you're safe. And let's stick it on bags of nuts as well – just in case some hot-shot lawyer can convince a court that his befuddled client thought cashews were sneeze remedies.

The BBC is clearly concerned about public safety for eggs sitting on walls and arachnophobes too. A CBeebies show recently had all the king's horses and men making Humpty 'happy again' and Miss Muffet made friends with the spider. The Brothers Grimm wouldn't stand a chance now, would they?

Jack and Jill went up the hill to form a focus group to discuss safe water collection, no doubt.

20th October 2006

I keep thinking we will turn back from the lemming-like march towards the insanity evidenced by a tiny handful of the politically correct who have a disproportionate ability to affect our lives.

The revulsion that most of us feel for their agenda seems to stir them not a jot. The late Joe Orton wrote a very funny play called Loot, in which a citizen challenges the official who has invaded his house to produce a search warrant. The official replies that he doesn't need one because he is not a policeman, he is an official of the water board and they don't need warrants. As the state feels able to play a steadily greater role in the minutiae of our lives, that scenario seems less and less fantastic or funny.

Last month a Northamptonshire nursery owner was, after a fourteen-month legal process, finally cleared of assaulting a two-year-old child in her care.

Her crime? She forcibly prevented the toddler from hitting a baby over the head with a brick and made the child sit on a "naughty chair." A visiting inspector reported her despite the child's mother protesting that she herself used similar sanctions and completely approved of the nursery owners methods and trusted her. Thank goodness most magistrates are made of the same stuff as the rest of us and went so far as to reprimand, for an inappropriate intervention, the school inspector who precipitated the year long process.

Somewhere between the harsh discipline of Charles Dickens' Dotheboys Hall and the absurd "no touch" attitude, prescribed by a handful of bureaucrats, lies a happy medium that will restore a sane world in which children understand that they are not allowed to do whatever they like and dispose of the notion that two year olds mustn't have their behaviour restricted just for the convenience of adults.

We already are allowing a few perverted individuals' crimes to circumscribe the behaviour of 99.99% of the population. The end result is a populace uncomfortably aware of the consequences should they venture to assist lost or frightened children. Casual affection, sympathy or congratulatory hugs from adults to minors are now seen as possible triggers for prosecutions and the overprotective intention of the zealots who see evil in everything will leave as their legacy a sterile loveless society within a few generations, unless we all resist their debilitating grip on our lives.

17. Your Call is Important to Us

Hot on the heels of political correctness and the jobsworth mentality comes the Biggest misnomer in commercial life – customer service.

How many times have we all had to deal with a voice on a phone that trots out the anodyne phrases about their desire to help us and their wish to do so as efficiently as possible, before subjecting us to an obstacle course of multilayered option alternatives, untrained 'advisers', supervisors who are the offspring of bull mastiffs trained to deter dissent and an endless ability to conveniently lose all previous evidence of telephone calls and correspondence.

Read on and share my compulsion to Rage against the Machine.

2nd April 2010

Here's a new way to extract money from the consumer. The problem with our otherwise perfectly functioning oven was that the spring mechanism that closed the door wasn't doing its job, so as much hot air escaped into the kitchen as busied itself cooking our food. Being loath to spend money unnecessarily, I put a turn button into the wooden frame adjacent to the oven to keep it closed, which has served its purpose for a while. But as we are having our kitchen updated, we decided to rectify the deficiency. The service engineer declared that we needed a new door, costing a hundred and thirty five pounds. Gulp. It was only when I checked the cost of a new oven of comparable standard that I decided to bite the bullet and have a new door fitted. Total cost with two call-outs – just under two hundred and thirty pounds. Double gulp. Shrug. Move on. That is, until I emptied the remnants of the old door and the hinge assembly out of the box the engineer had chucked them in. It became clear that we had paid for a whole new door and assembly, when all that was defective was a small part of the hinge assembly, which a quick search on the internet revealed is available for the princely sum of forty seven pounds.

So I contacted the service department to ask why I couldn't just buy the hinge assembly that came with the sparkling but unnecessary new door.

After a great deal of debate over several calls, which I confess became a little heated although polite on my part, it transpired that in the years since I purchased my oven, they have changed the fitting detail of the hinges. So the new hinges will fit my old oven, but not my old door. And, of course, they no longer manufacture the old hinges. The difference is merely in the attachment to the door. Game over!

This tactic of manipulating consumers into buying more than they need or want is not restricted to one manufacturer. Car owners will know that it is often impossible to get the bit you actually need to mend your broken headlight, say. You have to get the whole darned thing. The waste occasioned by such policies in an age when we are all rightly concerned about conserving our dwindling resources is phenomenal and tragic.

9th July 2010

Please would someone form a militant group to defend the rights of the consumer? Enough is enough. Do you remember how we really did believe (d'oh!) that the age of the computer and the internet would simplify all our transactions and dealings with service providers?

This week I wasted a measurable fraction of my life trying, on behalf of my daughter, to make sense out of the labyrinthine payment-dodging manoeuvres of the Student Loan Company, who have given her different – and that is *radically* different – advice and information each time she has phoned them over the last year in connection with the funding and grant for a course which she has now finished and which still has not been resolved. A third party might marvel at the adroitness with which they dismiss the advice given by other employees of the same company and moreover blame the applicant for failing to supply information they have never asked for. But the applicant experiences only frustration and rage. The same rage and frustration was felt by a friend who has tried unsuccessfully to have a telephone line and internet re-connected at a home she and her husband moved into in May. Like my daughter, my friend - a calm and gentle woman not known for her excesses of fury, told me that she hated what the telephone company had turned her into as she has spent tens of pounds phoning them on her mobile only to be referred by engineering to customer support, who in turn referred her to the new customers department, whence she was referred to faults, etc., etc. Each time involved a new selection of multiple option button pressing. Each time she had to experience the embarrassment of asking the resident of some distant country (who is presumably cheaper than their equivalent here) to repeat what they were saying several times as she could not understand their heavily accented English. On several occasions, after hanging on for fifteen or more minutes, she was cut off. When she gave up and cancelled the order and went to another provider, suddenly company number one is interested, deluging her with plaintive, 'Why have you left us?' messages.

We're all sick of call centres, of multiple choices that never offer one that fits your requirement, of companies that make it impossible for us to speak to someone who can actually solve our problems.

13th December 2002

Manufacturers are no longer prepared to back their own judgement when marketing new goods. They want to see the colour of our money before they even make them now. My first whiff of this new sales strategy came in the summer when a catalogue appeared in my mail one day from one of the London museums. Atypically, I succumbed to a spot of impulse buying and, having failed on several attempts to make the order via the Internet, I rang the telephone order line and requested three tempting goodies from the brochure. Days later, I received separate letters informing me that the three items were currently not in stock. An imminent birthday prompted a telephone call to enquire how they could be out of stock when I had only received the new catalogue on the day I made the order. It soon dawned on me that the glossy brochure was simply a means of assessing the demand for goods that would then be imported according to subsequent orders. The final part of the order arrived some three months after it was made.

Then there is digital radio, which has been advertised heavily and tantalisingly on the wireless and television for some time. As a lover of radio, I was keen to experience the new stations available only on digital and also (as a sports lover) to get Radio 5 Live without the attendant variable reception on Medium Wave. Then began the frustration. A stand-alone digital radio was not to be had "even for ready money." I have been waiting for months to get one and finally heard that the local shop at which I ordered one has finally, this week, had a delivery.

BT is currently trumpeting its broadband service for access to the Internet. You'll love it, they tell us. It's so much faster. So reliable. Eminently desirable. But I can't get it. That is, until enough people in my area crawl on their knees through fire, broken glass and scorpions to beg for the service, when they just might incur the expense of upgrading the local exchange. As I said before, they want to see the colour of your money first. This is the same company that disconnected my Internet service when I neglected to inform them that my credit card details had changed recently. Having incurred the expense of lugging my computer into the repairer to discover the cause of my sudden inability to get online, I finally discovered the true cause and gave BT my new card details. Service restored, I was amazingly diverted to discover that after disconnecting me they had sent me an e-mail telling me why!

I belong to the generation that found it unsurprising that a local shop (that was not part of a chain) stocked the goods that you wanted. And if they didn't, then as you were a customer, they would get it for you. The world in which we live now does not regard the requirements of individuals as significant. If I had a pound for every time I've been told that there is "no demand" for something that I would buy a dozen of if the store had any, then I would be less concerned at the prospect of having to fund four daughters through university education, now that the generation that benefited from state-funded tertiary education may see fit to deny that privilege to its children.

5th November 2004

To accurately reflect the recent frustration that I felt when trying to put credit on to my wife's pay-as-you-go-mad phone, I would really have to fill this entire column with capitalised, bold "**A**" s ending with "**RGH.**"

On behalf of all of you who have had similar experiences but no means of venting your spleen, I will share the sad tale, bearing in mind that I know that my sorry tale will inevitably pale compared with the similarly mind-snapping sagas of others.

It happens to be Vodafone, in my case; but I suspect that all providers are as guilty of the same arms-length treatment, euphemistically called customer care. The little handbook I received with the new sim card suggested that I could add money for time (and time is money, you know) by paying for it under my own existing monthly-billable contract. Just ring this 08000 number! I did. I negotiated my way through endless multiple options, none of which were specific to my particular requirement. After 20 minutes, a completely incomprehensible lady on a distant continent said something I could not understand, and said it many times. Eventually, I gathered that her computer was down and that I would have to hang up and phone again. I asked to speak to a supervisor. Her computer was down too; and any way she couldn't transfer calls. I pointed out that were I to let her off the hook so easily and ring again, I might well wait twenty minutes only to get her again while her computer was still down. I also asked her why she had answered the phone, if she knew she couldn't help me; the eighth time she replied, I deduced that she had no control over the people who put calls through nor could she contact them. When I said I was going to take my custom elsewhere, she thanked me for calling Vodafone. I returned to the booklet to try a different means of paying for talk time. It encouraged me to use the Internet. I logged on to the site. I needed to set up an account and passwords. I went through the procedure and was sent a unique password to the mobile that I had then to input into the web site, which rejected the password that I had correctly and faithfully reproduced three times and then told me that I couldn't apply again for 24 hours. Great!

But there was a help line number. I rang it.

You're ahead of me, aren't you?

Multiple options. I then waited, ten minutes this time, before a brisk (and, mercifully, this time comprehensible) recorded female voice asked me to call back as they were very busy at the moment and – of course – with no sense of corporate irony that I could detect, thanked me for calling Vodafone, before severing the connection.

Then I went to a Vodafone outlet with cash in hand – but their computers were "down."

You never had that trouble with two tin cans and a piece of string.

I saw and greatly enjoyed an excellent production of The Little Shop of Horrors mounted by WYSPAS in Wycombe this week, featuring an engaging flesh-eating plant, Audrey.

I would love to add to its diet the sociopaths who devised multiple choice phone systems and who locate call centres in distant lands.

How else can we get rid of them? Any bright ideas?

2nd May 2003

Wouldn't it be nice to think that the fairly substantial increase in our Council Tax demands is going to be translated into a superior delivery of many of the local services that have been starved of funding latterly?

Maybe our local police stations in Wycombe and Marlow will be manned for longer hours. Maybe, even, when we dial 999, we will get through to someone who is familiar with the local area? A businessman friend of mine who lives locally was working late one evening recently and went to investigate the sound of breaking glass. An intruder had broken into the premises and was in the process of helping himself to items that he seemed to feel were in need of summary release into his custody. My friend and a colleague happened upon him while he was helping himself and pursued the burglar, when he legged it through the window in the direction of the local pub. They eventually discovered the miscreant hiding in an empty upper room of the pub and detained him there while they dialled 999.

The operator asked them where they were calling from and was given the name of the village. "Where's that?" enquired the operator. "Wycombe!" came the urgent reply. "Where?" she persisted, giving every sign of having only vaguely heard that such a place as Wycombe might exist. When my friend suggested that this unnecessarily protracted conversation was unhelpful as they were somewhat busy restraining an intruder, he was asked if the burglar was being violent. It would have been interesting to know what extra steps she might have taken had the answer been, "Yes, he is belabouring us both with an iron bar while I speak."

All my informant wanted was to have a police presence at the spot ASAP. It took almost ten minutes of giving a wealth of detail, including eventually the postcode, before my friend had the satisfaction of hearing a promise of immediate assistance. He had wanted to be put in touch with a local officer at a local station. But that is not what happens any more. Apparently, according to one of the officers who eventually turned up, a 999 call made in the Thames Valley could conceivably be answered by an operator in Solihull or Doncaster, who for very understandable reasons would have scant knowledge of the local geography of Wycombe. It is a trifle perplexing that the (let us say) Doncaster operator should wish to get information from the complainant rather than simply pass the caller on to someone local who might instantly be familiar with their own patch and be able to snap into appropriate action. But the answer probably is that there simply isn't anyone manning a phone out of hours in a local police building. And that is why I join my friend in hoping that this is one of the things that might change as a result of the greatly increased revenue we are providing for local services.

Within ten minutes of the call, a police car arrived; then another, then another, then another. The fifth was a van complete with dog handler. A total of ten officers. Very impressive, in fact. No complaints there. But can we have our manned local stations back too, please?

The days when the local bobby was as familiar a community figure as the milkman, postman and clergyman must, I suppose, remain a memory and a dream. But dreams can sometimes come true…

13th December 2003

I can only imagine that the people who decide to save the cost of paying British workers a fairly low wage by paying foreign workers even less do not themselves use the services displaced by their decisions. I am referring specifically to call centres, those stress-inducing creations whose sole purpose seems to be to minimise contact with the paying public, by provoking the fainted-hearted to disappear into a morass of multiple options before simply giving up.

My daughter asked me to help her phone her bank a week or so ago. She was with me, but didn't feel confident that she could pick her way through the telephonic maze. I got within a hair's breadth of reaching an actual living, breathing human being but fell at the last hurdle. Having negotiated half a dozen multiple choices, I reached a final one that asked me if I was calling on behalf of myself or another person.

A simple enough question but as it turned out one that was a trap for the unwary. I honestly opted for the latter option; even though my daughter was there with me, she wasn't answering the questions. A voice whose owner I could have cheerfully strangled (slowly!), then informed me somewhat triumphantly, I thought, that the Data Protection Act would not allow them to give account information to third parties. I was then summarily disconnected. We had to ring up again and go through the same labyrinthine process to reach the point where, with consummate cunning, I answered in the negative to the trick question that led to the trapdoor of disconnection. I handed the phone to my daughter when a non-recorded human voice came on the line (probably rudely awakened from his masterly inactivity by the unwelcome occurrence of a call actually getting through to him).

This week I wanted to make a small alteration to the detail of my internet delivery package. I phoned the help line number printed on the paperwork that came when I signed up a mere two months ago. It was, of course, already out of date information. A recorded announcement gave me another number. I dialled it and found myself disturbing the peace somewhere on the Indian subcontinent. The charming lady on the other end and I had the devil's own job understanding each other. She eventually decided that I needed "Customer Services". Another number. I dialled that and spoke to another charming young lady who may have been in the same room as my first young lady, or indeed may have been on another part of the same sub-continent, but who had precisely the same problem understanding my unfamiliar tones as I did hers. She couldn't help me and referred me to Internet Sales. My new telephonist sounded suspiciously like the first one I spoke to, but gave no sign of recognising my dulcet tones.

To cut a long story short, I spoke to four different ladies in Asia before a helpful gentleman with a Geordie accent sorted out my small problem in a minute flat. Now that was an accent I was familiar with, thanks to Kevin Shearer and Co.

The entire process, however, took more than thirty minutes of the precious time that I have left on this planet.

Don't get me started on banks. Do you remember when they used to have phone numbers in the directory for your branch?

Yes, so do I.

Sigh!

26th September 2003

I was brought up in the generation that was expected to sit in silence when a teacher addressed it, or to stand up when one entered the classroom. We did not dye our hair at the age of nine. We wore a school uniform. Even the most rebellious were rarely tempted to deviate too far from acceptable behaviour; the few that did were on the receiving end of summary and swift retribution. When they went home to complain, they received an extra dose of remedial encouragement from their parents. And the end result was, undeniably, a more pleasant land in which to walk abroad.

We didn't see this as an infringement of our civil liberties, but as confirmation that we lived in a world where mutual respect was the rule rather than the exception.

Wherever you look now, there is abundant evidence that the current, and some would have it more enlightened, methods of child-raising are quite simply not working. The very generation that was brought up in a world where the clip round the ear (metaphorical or actual) seemed to produce a calmer, less aggressive society is, for reasons that I am unable to fathom, now predisposed to confront a policeman or teacher that raises an eyebrow (let alone a hand) at a child. I do not advocate battery of children as a means of turning them into passive and pliable servants; but a firmer, more consistent attitude to what is acceptable behaviour in the school, the street and, more importantly, the home might just haul us back from the brink of chaos.

When I was a child, there were no "no-go areas" and there was a lot more and worse poverty. Teenage children did not gather in community parks to drink, bellow profanities and leave broken glass and rubbish for local inhabitants to routinely clear up every morning. If you want to see evidence of that just visit, say, the playground between Aylesbury Road and Wellington Road in Princes Risborough one evening – or take your children to play on the swings the following morning. And they're not deprived; many thousands were spent building a skateboard area that they don't use now. Residents report that local police, whose station overlooks the park, are reluctant to move them on, on the basis that they can see what they're up to there.

On holiday, many of our young people appear to be incapable of showing any self-restraint whatsoever – a fact that the media parade before us has alleged entertainment in endless series dedicated to that very subject.

If you sit in a traffic jam for more than a few moments, someone will hurl an empty coffee cup or other rubbish out onto the grass verge before too long. And walk down any British High Street at any time of day and you will be treated to youths bellowing expletives at each other.

Unless we are all prepared to make it quite clear that we find this unacceptable, it will get worse. And bad behaviour is certainly not restricted to those whom some might see as deprived. In fact, the contrary is true. Most of those who seem intent on proving Margaret Thatcher's bleak declaration that there was "no such thing as society," have been given many more advantages than the well-behaved "socially deprived" of the post-war generation ever had. And some of them play in the Premiership.

20th July 2001

A few weeks ago I shared with you the saga of my rejection as a suitable person to attest to the identity of a fellow citizen on a passport application. Apparently being an actor, a columnist on this newspaper and an upright citizen are not in themselves evidence of my reliability in the difficult business of knowing who someone else is. I was unacceptable, I was told, as I did not have a degree. A degree, it seems, confers upon the recipient not just a rather fetching black gown and a hat upon which you can mix cement, but also the unique gift of trustworthiness and honesty. I was irritated to find that my profession is regarded a shadowy sub-class of non-people in the eyes of the bureaucrats.

As often happens, if one pigeon gets you, you can bet your last crash helmet that another one will be along soon.

This week the Baker tribe decided to break the habit of my children's lifetimes and go abroad for a short holiday.

Therefore passports were needed.

The instructions that accompany a passport application form leave the applicant in no doubt that the smallest error will result in the documentation returning to sender once it has spent a few weeks ambling around the system. And failure to contain your signature entirely within the boundaries of a little brown box is the most heinous offence of all. A way of ensuring that such an official regurgitation doesn't blight your holiday plans is to take the completed paperwork to the Post Office and have the forms checked. I developed writer's cramp filling in our address more than twenty times, checked the appropriate boxes and trotted my neat handiwork around to my solicitor so that he could attest to our collective identities.

Then off to Consignia, as we must now call the Post Office. In my book, if you consign something you are sending it off to some unspecified and unwelcome fate. "Post Office" has a familiar solid feel about it. "Consignia" sounds like the name of a waste disposal unit.

Of the four forms presented, three were rejected. My otherwise learned and able solicitor, with the seasoned pragmatism of his profession, had simply crossed out minor errors on two forms and put the post code in the wrong box on another. Before computerisation – which is of course there for our benefit – that would have been acceptable. Not now. How many trees have fallen to supply the forms rejected to satisfy the microchip?

Three new forms. More writer's cramp. More witnessing by my solicitor.

Back to Consign-it-here.

A different face behind the counter. The forms are scrutinised again. Slowly, carefully.

Then the knife thrust. "The person countersigning hasn't put in his qualifications." "But he's a solicitor." "Yes, but what are his qualifications? It doesn't say whether he has a degree. He may have just have worked his way up from the bottom."

I resisted the urge to comment on the staggering implication that this would have disqualified such a common upstart from credibility in the eyes of the righteous.

I registered incredulity. "He's a solicitor. An officer of the Supreme Court. You don't work your way up to that. You pass exams."

She went off to check. She returned.

"Apparently, we can accept that," she said in the grudging tones of one who clearly felt standards were slipping.

The Luddites had a point.

23rd March 2001

Last week, a neighbour asked me to sign a passport application form for her son, whom I have known for fifteen years. I did so and countersigned his photograph as required.

She returned the following day because, having made a mistake and put my Christian name in the wrong box I had then crossed it out, initialled it and corrected the error.

My friend had availed herself of the services of the Post Office who can check application forms for accuracy before they are sent off to the Passport Office. The counter clerk insisted that the form should be filled in without alterations, initialled or otherwise. A little finicky, after all in every other legal document I have ever encountered alterations are acceptable if initialled by the parties concerned. But okay, if that's the way it has to be – back to square one.

So I filled in the form once again, carefully and neatly. I contrived again to squeeze my signature into the box indicated. Apparently, if the pen strays outside the parameters of the box, the application will also be rejected. That's computerisation for you. It's all supposed to be streamlined via the wizardry of the microchip in order to benefit the customer. The computer doesn't like things that don't fit in a little box, byte or bit. So, I reduced my admittedly somewhat flamboyant signature to a fraction of its usual size and crammed it into the inadequate space. I was grateful that my name has only ten letters. Presumably anyone called Persephone Featherstonehaugh-Pamplemousse, who habitually signs things using their full name is debarred from attesting to the identity of British citizens, unless they proficient at tiny writing.

The following day, my neighbour returned with the chastening news that the same post office employee had scrutinised the application again and rejected it again. The witness, she explained, has to be a professional person.

Well acting is a profession; he is a professional actor.

No, it has to be a doctor, MP, solicitor or clergyman.

But he is actually a very recognisable actor, quite well known in fact.

Well they might accept him if he has a degree.

People with degrees are better equipped, apparently, to know whether other people look like their photographs and vice versa. They are clearly a better class of citizen too. And even though MPs don't necessarily all have degrees, they are also trustworthy folk by virtue of having been elected to public office.

So you could get Jeffrey Archer to sign your passport application, or Neil Hamilton, or indeed Jonathan Aitken, with or without degrees. Dr. Shipman could sign your passport application form. But an actor! Sir Anthony Hopkins would not be considered by the passport office sufficiently reliable to verify the identity of another (unless he had a degree of course).

So my neighbour went off in search of an upright member of society who may turn out to know her son less well than I did, but whose profession alone might qualify them to fill in a form testifying to the identity of another human being.

So all you shopkeepers, farmers, nurses, chair makers, footballers, motor engineers, dustmen and actors - don't get ideas above your station. You are neither intelligent nor reliable enough to attest to the identity of your friends, according to the Home Office.

Unless, of course, you have a degree!

28th May 2004

Many people have said to me lately that there is little point in continuing to argue against the planned relocation of maternity and other services from Wycombe Hospital to Stoke Mandeville, on the basis that it is already a done deal. I am not sure whether those people are realists or cynics, but only the most blinkered or thick-skinned bureaucrat could make such a radical and dangerous decision hard on the heels of an expensive upgrading of the very facilities that are now mooted to be unceremoniously dumped.

On the basis, then, that someone somewhere might be moved to think again in the face of the very real risk that lives may be lost as a result of that extra forty or more minutes that it would take an expectant mother to travel to Stoke Mandeville, I am moved to share with you a tragic series of events that occurred in Bishop Auckland a couple of weeks ago. The circumstances are chillingly similar to those that pertain locally. The Bishop Auckland hospital was built a mere two years ago and opened with a special care baby unit and consultant-led maternity services. Within a few months the local health authority declared their intention to downgrade the services to "midwife-led" maternity services, with no obstetricians present or immediately available, leaving mothers that might be considered to be at risk to travel to Darlington, some twelve miles away. A petition bearing 10,000 signatures did not deter those concerned from carrying through their plan.

Andrea Harrison was admitted to the hospital just two days after the maternity unit with the downgraded services re-opened. Her baby showed an increased heart rate, was put on a monitor for an hour and then the decision was made to transfer Mrs Harrison to Darlington. No ambulances were available, so Mr Harrison was advised to drive his wife there as quickly as possible. When they arrived, a caesarean section was too late to save the life of the Harrisons' daughter, Olivia. Clearly the situation in this case was complicated by the unavailability of an ambulance, but that is something that could also very easily occur in Wycombe. Whatever the cause of the baby's sad death, Olivia was living when she left Bishop Auckland. Had the same facilities and expertise that were available in Darlington been available there, Olivia might well have survived her birth and now been at home with her two older brothers and her parents.

A family in High Wycombe might be called upon to pay a similar price for the savings made by reducing services to patients here.

The absence of suitable medical provision in an area will always play a part in the lack of survival of some people. But to take away excellent healthcare that already exists is a very different matter. This tragedy in Bishop Auckland occurred two days after services were reduced. In the event that a Buckinghamshire family suffers a similar heart-rending bereavement, we will doubtless hear the same platitudes being issued by the representatives of our local health trust

- "bookings for the midwife led unit are proving very popular with local women" ... "still have full confidence in the unit" ... "deepest sympathy" ... "always looking for ways to improve our service."

Words, just words.

Let us, please, all do what we can to prevent those words being heard in the wake of a similar tragedy for a local family.

9th October 2009

If I still had my TARDIS I might be tempted to pop forward a few years and see if there is still any kind of hospital care or accommodation in Wycombe, which surely is a town large enough to justify having a hospital that offers all but the most specialised medical care.

Already maternity and paediatric services have been despatched to Stoke Mandeville, as of 19th October. As a result, given the nature of the road from Wycombe to Aylesbury, I know of several people who are considering having their babies in Oxford, which, although some ten miles further away, may be more reliably accessible in an emergency.

Now we hear the bosses of the NHS Trust are considering chopping off the top four floors of the existing hospital because, they say, they are 'mixed-sex and a fire risk' (presumably the latter is not perceived as a result of the former).

How an earth is a mixed-sex ward constructed any differently to a single-sex ward to the extent that changing its use demands demolition? I can't imagine that the top floors were mixed-sex in 1969. That 'innovation' came in much later when the Thatcher government introduced mixed-sexed wards to reduce the number of beds in the NHS. Hundreds of wards were closed to save money and those beds have never been replaced. And Tony Blair failed to deliver on his promise made before both the 1997 and 2001 elections to end the practice of male and female patients being forced to share a ward. How chopping the top four floors of a hospital that is already unable to offer single-sex wards has the potential to increase the possibility of it happening defeats me.

It is also reported that the NHS Trust want patients treated in the community instead of hospital, which they say will 'cut overall demand.' Does this sound familiar? The words 'Care in the

Community' were used to describe the initiative that enabled the closure of scores of psychiatric and other institutions in the eighties (as well as all those wards) and we all know what kind of care the ejected patients received thereafter and the effect on the wider community. And, of course, it will cut overall demand! As the old joke goes - "My dog won't eat meat!"

"Why won't your dog eat meat?"

"Because we don't give him any!"

5th October 2007

If you are a parent, teacher or governor at one of our local faith schools, then I have bad news for you.

A local Church of England primary school recently suffered the loss of most of the lead from its roof at the hands of thieves, who cared a lot more about their drinking and drug money than they did about local children. Schools buy into an insurance package through Bucks County Council, so if the felonious morons were capable of anything resembling thought, they may have thought that the school would be able to claim under that policy. So did the head and governors of the school. However, it seems that, for reasons obscure at the moment, Bucks County Council changed the level of cover for "Voluntary Aided Schools," which are the Church of England Schools and Catholic Schools in the area. Now, the cover the local authority provides for these schools is only for the ten percent share of building works for which the school governors bear financial responsibility. The 90% share that should be provided from funds provided by government or the local authority is now not covered by insurance and those bodies are not falling over each other to offer funds to this small village school. It appears that the balance, which is a significant sum, must come either from the school's budget or from the capital funds that are available to every school each year for necessary building works and improvements. So, no improvements to that school this year. Several thousand pounds, which should be spent on providing facilities for primary school children, will now be spent repairing the damage caused by miserable, furtive scavengers who care not a jot for anything beyond their immediate need for cash.

You will be amazed, or perhaps not, to know that this parlous situation has existed for a couple of years, but most of the affected schools know absolutely nothing about it. Although one school in Oxfordshire, inundated during the recent floods around Oxford, found that they were similarly uninsured for the bulk of the damage they suffered.

One can only wonder why Bucks County Council and the relevant religious educational authorities that control the schools have allowed this happen.

Perhaps someone from those bodies will finally share their thoughts on this imponderable with the schools that they are mandated to protect – and do something about it.

30th May 2008

I first realised that the banking system wasn't philanthropic thirty odd years ago when, after years of my being in credit, my bank bounced a cheque, citing "insufficient funds." My salary had not cleared and the sum due to my local off-licence would have plunged me into the heady realms of a three pound overdraft. I fired off a letter pointing out that for years the bank had had the benefit of all my spare cash and that I found it fairly rich (sic) that they begrudged me a little bit of theirs for a couple of days.

I have learned since that banks understand large overdrafts much better than tiny little ones. In fact, they like the big ones very much indeed and get disappointed when I make the occasional foray into credit and promptly try to encourage me back into indebtedness.

My big grouch is not with my bank in particular, but all banks. The age of instantaneous worldwide communication doesn't seem to have nudged the monolithic banking system into even the 20th Century yet. I received a cheque (check?) from America this week. When I tried to pay it in I was informed that it would probably take six weeks to clear. "Surely you mean six days?" I enquired politely. They didn't. The actual piece of paper I handed to the teller would, apparently, have to be returned via snail mail to the New England bank upon which it was drawn. This process was typically taking around six weeks.

There was something in the manner of the teller that indicated to me that she was aware of the complete ludicrousness of the situation.

She didn't actually shrug in shared hopeless bewilderment, but the acknowledgement of common incomprehension was unmistakable. I couldn't do other but take her advice and refer back to the drawer of the 'check' to ask them to remit the funds electronically which, even then, would take three or four days, as in the UK.

Where the money goes between leaving the drawer's account instantaneously and arriving at the payee's much later is, of course, quite clearly a place where the banks can use it to make money for them. If they were only to admit that and shift it instantaneously, as is clearly possible, then we might all accept any slight extra cost to recompense them for forgoing that hidden income.

21st September 2007

Have you noticed that large companies very often make it nigh on impossible to contact them directly? Telephone listings for individual stores or bank branches are now as rare as blue police boxes.

You phone a call centre where someone to whom you have never spoken before (and will never be able to speak to again) goes through well-practised conciliatory avoidance techniques.

I have been experiencing this ulcer-inducing phenomenon in my repeated attempts to get Ikea to replace a zip-less cushion cover that was part of a corner sofa purchased two weeks ago. Having already negotiated the replacement of the damaged sofa that was delivered initially (they had to replace the whole thing rather than the third that was damaged), three attempts to replace a cushion cover have thus far failed.

The first took me back to the store to find that the promise that it would be there waiting for me was not one that had been communicated to anyone but me.

Each time, I speak to a different really friendly young lady in Leeds. Or at least I think she's different. It may be that it's the same one who changes her name for every caller to enable her to take you through your odyssey of frustration again and again like a dreadful consumer *Groundhog Day*.

The latest northern lass expressed horror and outrage at the litany of errors and failures that I recounted to her for the umpteenth time. I was beginning to feel like the poor old king who "only wanted a little bit of butter with his bread". She promised that a named, and therefore seemingly important, colleague would get back to me within "twelve working hours". Four days later, I decided that unless those employed by the Swedish retail giant only work three hours a day I needed to take more drastic action and write to head office. It worked with British Gas, when I wrote to the CEO of Centrica.

But could I find their corporate address? Or a phone number that wasn't to the same customer call centre that had disarmingly and repeatedly raised and dashed fresh expectations? Eventually Google offered a glimmer of a possibility via another frustrated consumer's blog and I have written more in anger than in hope.

I fear there are many similar stories for many similar companies.

And we used to build furniture in Wycombe, you know. Sigh!

18. Wycombe Man

My articles over the last decade and a half have been written in a High Wycombe newspaper, the Bucks Free Press, for mainly a High Wycombe readership, although since the advent of the Bucks Free press online service, there is a gratifying response from further afield. I even have readers in America and Australia whop write in with their feedback on some of my fulminations and ramblings.

But obviously, sometimes I need to comment on matters that are more local and parochial. I have lived where I do now for longer than I have lived anywhere in my life before, I realised recently. I was quite surprised. One tends to think of childhood homes as being those we inhabit for the longest time. Perhaps that is just a trick of memory as childhood seems endless when one is living it, but is, in fact, a small fraction of a normal life span.

My children have all lived in those we live in now for the whole of their lives. It is quite strange to think that there may (and probably will) be another home that they will occupy for even longer.

Anyway I am now undeniably – a Wycombe man.

19th Jan 2001

Readers will notice a sudden absence of dwarves in the neighbourhood. Yes, I shouted "Oh no there isn't!" for the last time this winter on Sunday night, when the pantomime completed its sixty-first performance at the Swan. And for once, thanks to the flu jab and several tons of vitamins, I had survived the obligatory merry, seasonal bacterial nasties, with my voice intact and actually able to shout my denial of the existence of the all-too-visible ghost at my elbow.

On behalf of the splendid group of actors and entertainers involved this year, I would like to thank all of you who came to see us, and enjoyed it enough to tell your friends about it. This is clearly the case, as Snow White and the Seven Dwarves proved to be the most successful panto since the Swan opened, breaking the previous record set by Cinderella five years ago.

It is very gratifying to see our flagship local theatre going from strength to strength. I know there will always be people who regard theatre as a luxury that they can do without and complain that the money could be better spent in other ways.

It might just seem a persuasive argument, until you question what it is that we are all here for. If it is simply to be born, eat, sleep, work and shuffle off into oblivion, then maybe they are right. But the "Why spend money on the Arts?" argument crumbles when we examine the things in our history of which we are most proud. These are, almost without exception, the architecture, art, literature and drama of past centuries.

Shakespeare, Dickens, Sir Christopher Wren, John Constable and more recently Sir Paul McCartney have left a legacy that will be remembered and valued long after the detail of contemporary political and commercial life has faded. And the reason is that spiritual and artistic experiences and creations that lift the human spirit make at least a little sense out of the apparent inconsequentiality of the rest of our lives. Alongside our various religious beliefs, with which they are inextricably linked, the "Arts" are as much a food for the spirit of humanity as bread and water are food for the body.

All this may sound a little over the top in the context of pantomime, but with the advent of television and home electronic entertainment, panto is often the only live experience that some families have of the performing arts. If I had a tenner for every person who expressed surprise and joy at their first experience of live entertainment after seeing a panto, I would not be a millionaire exactly, but I would be able to buy you all a large drink!

At a time when town centres are fighting the centrifugal commercial force (and punitive parking restrictions) that propel shoppers to the out-of-town stores, a theatre can be the vital, beating heart that keeps a town alive at night.

We are so lucky to have ours — and I cannot praise highly enough the dedicated and talented staff, backstage and front of house, who have, in most cases, been there since the theatre opened — always an indication of a well-run enterprise.

Let's hope our Swan, like the royal bird, is a protected species. To ensure that it is, take a look at what it has to offer — there's something for everyone in its programme of shows! See you there.

19th May 2006

If you have spare time and would like to contribute to your local community, there are few more rewarding or challenging ways of doing just that than by becoming a school governor. I was cajoled by the then headteacher of my children's local primary school to offer myself as parent governor fifteen years ago and I am still a governor of that school, even though my children have all moved on. It seemed a waste of all that acquired knowledge to do otherwise. And I had grown fond of the school, its staff and my fellow governors.

Whilst the job is not for the faint hearted, like all acquired skills, the more you put in the more you get out. It takes a while to learn the ropes, but after a couple of meetings and the benefit of the excellent training sessions offered by Bucks County Council, you would soon find, whatever your previous experience or skills, that you were contributing and helping the school.

And I am addressing these words to you, dear reader, because I know that Bucks CC is looking for people to offer their services as governors.

The days when only retired local worthies became school governors are long gone. Governors come from a variety of backgrounds, have different and varied experience and can be any age. And whilst it is quite useful if at least some governors have accountancy or budgetary skills, legal or business knowledge or educational backgrounds, the only real requirement is common sense and the desire to offer constructive assistance to head teachers in providing what is essentially the most important job in the world. One generation of good parenting and good education would undoubtedly reap dividends. Wanting to help and to be a critical friend is the prime requirement.

If you feel that you might be the kind of person who could give some time to help our schools, then the Governor Support team at County Hall in Aylesbury would love to hear from you. And on a separate matter – if you feel in need of a good bike ride and would like to help support your favourite charity, there is still time to take part in Rotary's Pedal Push on Sunday! I shall be on the Rye all day to see the riders off on their sponsored ride – come and join us. Get on your bike, put your crash helmet on and join us.

19th February 2010

Wycombe apparently has the fourth highest level of empty shops of any town in the South of England. The three bigger retail losers are Guildford, Southampton and Bracknell – in that order, the latter having a 19.3% empty shop rate. This is very clearly a sign of the times in terms of the disposable income of the majority of shoppers and their comparative reluctance to part with the cash they do have. However, as always in times of change it can flag up an opportunity to rethink our town centres. The multinationals and supermarkets are building more of their out-of-town shopping malls and driving the smaller shops and family concerns out of business; there is also the growth of internet shopping. And yes, those mammoth concerns have their corporate toes in the door there too, as a result of their ability to undercut smaller traders with bulk purchasing. But, this also offers the opportunity, via the internet, for small niche traders, whose speciality shops foundered perhaps because the catchment area of their high street shop was insufficient to enable them to pay the ever soaring commercial rents and earn a living too. Now, via the Internet, they can offer their special or unique products to a far wider customer base than before. And here they have an advantage over the hyperdupermegamarkets. Anyone who has seen a favourite product disappear off the shelves because "There is no demand sir," will know what I mean. The fact that I am demanding, pleading, cajoling, threatening to buy my coffee/bread/breakfast cereal elsewhere, counts for naught against the demands of the great god 'Volume'.

And we have called this fate upon ourselves by demanding ever cheaper products, thereby squeezing out the grocers, fishmongers, butchers and hardware shops of our childhood memories. And there is no turning back the clock alas.

But as a random afterthought, do you ever as I do sometimes, walk along a town centre street and look up at the façades of the houses and imagine what preceded the superimposition of the glazed commercial shop fronts that obliterated some lovely regency and Victorian house fronts?

So, maybe let's buy via the internet and from the out-of-town supermarkets and who knows, a decade or so from now we might see town centres to their former, residential glory? The night clubs etc. would have to move elsewhere too, of course. Just a thought.

5th May 2000

Every year there are more signs, hoardings and notices in our towns and villages. Some are informative, some helpful, some entertaining and some are frankly none of those things.

For instance, as you leave Wycombe on the A40 westwards and pass the junction with Bellfield Road, there is a large green Highways sign indicating that at the next junction (with Desborough Avenue), the road straight ahead goes to Oxford and a turning to the left goes to Cressex and the M40. A sensible stranger wishing to remain on the A40 would therefore opt for the outside lane in order to go straight ahead. Right?

Wrong!

A moment later, when our careful visiting motorist has already committed himself to that lane, white arrows painted on the road indicate that the lane in which he is driving is for the exclusive use of those wishing to turn right into The Pastures, a direction not considered worthy of inclusion on the enormous sign back down the road. Any subsequent attempt to edge back into the left hand lane is inevitably greeted with the characteristic cheery and affable acceptance of such activities by the average motorist, whose gestures can be interpreted as "Want to pull back in front of me again old chap? Of course, no problem! Take your time. Oh look, the lights have changed to red and I've missed them. Never mind. Happy to oblige! Bye! Drive carefully now!"

And all concerned watch a flock of Gloucester Old Spots fly serenely overhead in formation towards Adams Park.

Obviously residents learn quickly and painfully that the signage is idiosyncratic and unhelpful. But road signs are surely intended for people using the road for the first time, for strangers. It may well be that one sign is the province of the Dept. of Transport and the road marking that of the County Council, but could the second on the scene not have thought to liaise with the first? (Oh there go some Vietnamese Pot-bellied over Castlefield!)

Earlier this year, a rash of lovely new Public Footpath signs appeared on the common on which I live. This sounds like a good thing. Sadly they were, almost without exception, distributed fairly arbitrarily by the subcontractors employed to do the job, sending countless backpackers off into a thitherto unexplored bracken limbo, whence they probably never returned.

All over Wycombe there are notices telling us that "in the last three months, 1367 motorists have been caught speeding in this area." These signs have been up for some considerable time, but the number has never changed.

Well, clearly our authorities wouldn't knowingly spend our money to broadcast false information, so does this mean that there is a running quota; that as past speeders fall out of the beginning of the three month period, only precisely that number are then stopped and prosecuted, in order to ensure the continuing accuracy of the signs?

The only alternative explanation is that the information is load of old tosh, that was only true on the day it was put up? Surely not.

I am particularly fond of a sign that I came upon some years ago. It was wooden, carefully painted green and about two feet square. Its surface area was taken up completely by the following message, meticulously lettered in gold – "Do not affix any notices to this board."

Of course, had the board not been there in the first place then the affixing of anything at all would have been problematical.

But I'm sure the committee that dreamed up that particular piece of inspired nonsense had its reasons.

21st March 2008

A friend of mine who travels to London regularly at weekends, being more environmentally friendly than I am able to be (given my working hours and the times of last trains), always uses the train. She parks her car in the top car park at the station in Wycombe, the only one available to her at the time she leaves, as the lower car park is always full very early in the day.

The Saturday before last, when she returned at 7:30 p.m., she found that the gate to the top car park was locked, offering the prospect of leaving the station by the main entrance, turning right up Crendon St., right again into Totteridge Road, then via a narrow and lonely lane into the upper car park. Being a lady on her own, and as it was a rainy night, she did not fancy this and spoke to the staff on duty to this effect. She was told that the gate had been closed for security reasons, as children 'had been playing in the top car park and making a nuisance of themselves on the platform.' She enquired as to their concern for her security and the health and safety implications to her, a customer of Chiltern Railways, of which she said she had always been a great supporter.

She tells me that there were four members of staff congregated around the front of the station, one of whom she persuaded to come and unlock the gate to allow her access to her car without the long walk round in the rain and dark.

She was shown a sign informing the public that the gate would be closed after 2pm on Fridays and Saturdays, which seemed a stark acknowledgement that Chiltern Railways had thrown in the towel and were prepared to lock customers out in order to manage the unruly behaviour of a few children. Leaving aside the simple tactic of using staff to secure the station, surely for instance the installation of a camera to alert staff to any trouble would quickly resolve the situation and enable the fare-paying passengers (who also pay a healthy sum to park at the station) to access their cars on their return to Wycombe. Given the resurgence of our town predicted in the wake of Eden's opening, it would seem in the interests of both the town and the railway to ensure that the station is safe, convenient and attractive for customers. Locking out passengers is not the solution. And the prospect becomes even more unsatisfactory when one brings into the equation the disabled, parents with pushchairs and the elderly. Clearly there is a sufficient number of them to justify the recent removal of the cross barriers on the slope up to Platform 3 in order to provide easier access for prams, pushchairs and wheelchairs.

Once again the bad behaviour of a minority is to be allowed to adversely affect the lives of the majority of law-abiding, paying customers and it is unacceptable.

23rd June 2000

If the sun really does shine on the righteous, then those who gathered in Higginson Park on Sunday for the Marlow Millennium Musical must have led exemplary lives.

The organisers had made contingency plans for every eventuality – flood, deluge, gales, plagues of locusts and Armageddon. The one possibility that never occurred to them, of course, was that it would be the most perfect, hot sunny day. Fortunately, the fear of a seasonal downpour had resulted in the children who were performing being under cover, otherwise there would undoubtedly have been some cases of junior sunburn and heat stroke.

The audience, comprising mainly parents of the performers and representatives of the many local bodies who had supported the event, were free to bask by the river in what the realist inside me suggests might be our only perfect summer day.

The event matched the surroundings and weather.

We are lucky in this area to have an abundance of talent upon which to draw. I am always delighted to see children being encouraged and empowered to become involved in the performing arts. I hasten to add that this is not because I would like to think that they would be tempted to enter the ridiculous profession which I joined in an era when, even then, it was not an awfully good idea. Now it has become even harder, if that is possible, for any but the tiniest handful to make a living, let alone achieve anything more significant than that.

But I do believe that it is impossible to overstate the range of benefits that can be derived from early exposure to the satisfaction to be had and the liberation to be found in theatre, music, dance and all other forms of artistic expression. How better, for instance, to understand the feelings, pains, beliefs of others than to put yourself in their place? How better to help the less extrovert to become more confident than to enable them to do so as part of a team of their peers exploring ideas together in order to put on an entertainment for others? I do hope that drama as a curriculum item will never be jettisoned to make room for the core subjects, because I believe it can, when used well, inform and enhance all the other subjects.

In Marlow on Sunday there were two performances, utilising the talents of over five hundred children from 13 local first and middle schools, with additional musical contributions from Great Marlow and Sir William Borlase's Schools. The Primary children were performing New Millennium Heroes written by our prolific and talented local composer Sheila Wilson. In the ten years since her first musical *Hosanna Rock!* (written for Sandygates and St. Peter's Schools) it has become the nation's most frequently performed Christmas Musical. I would venture to suggest that one very strong reason for this is that she writes thumping good tunes – catchy, upbeat and fun for children to sing.

And it was the best possible use of Millennium Lottery funds that I have seen to date. Marlow Councillor Priscilla Stallard who first took up the idea, Marlow District Council, Wycombe District Council and the Millennium Commission should all be congratulated for seeing the merit of a project that has the potential to inspire the children who are the inheritors of the next age to be the heroes of that age by learning the lessons of the past and embracing peace.

It was a delightful afternoon. Let's hope the musical's message gets through.

2nd July 2010

Earlier this week a ten-year-old boy, Steven Holland, put a bucket in his grandfather's garden in Hughenden Avenue, High Wycombe, so that passers-by could donate to a charity set up by the boy's older brother, Rob, before he died in 2007 of a rare form of cancer, Desmoplastic Small Round Cell Tumour. Steven will also be climbing Snowdon along with around forty other people in September to raise funds for the charity, Rob's ARTTT, which is funding a three year research programme at the Royal Marsden Hospital in Surrey. This is a familiar way of enabling the surviving to make a little sense out of the sad loss of a loved one. In their names, we do what we can to ensure that fewer other families suffer similar bereavements.

There were about ten pounds in the bucket, mostly donated in small amounts by children on their way to school, when it was stolen. This was a sad enough event in itself; even sadder is the fact that most of us are probably not surprised to learn that there are enough people prepared to steal a child's charity collection to make the act almost predictable. How we have arrived at a point in our society where such formerly unthinkable behaviour has evolved from being rare to commonplace is something many of us struggle to understand. There are very few people for whom help is not available, if they ask for it. It is, of course, inarguable that the main thing that has changed in a generation is the availability and widespread use of drugs that have the effect of dehumanising abusers to the point where the thought of depriving cancer research of funding does not deter them from an act like this.

Fortunately, the other thing that is also just as predictable is that when we hear such a sad story, it galvanises us into action. The

Rotary Club of High Wycombe at their lunchtime meeting this week responded to this depressing event (the theft, not the lunch) by emptying their pockets into a more secure bucket and raised £175 for the charity. I suspect that the Rotary Club will not be alone in responding so instantly and generously. Let us hope that young Steven's memories as he climbs Snowdon will be of the generosity of the people of Wycombe rather than the sad degeneracy of one person.

28th August 2009

It is important to look beneath headlines. A headline is an attention grabber, designed to make people buy papers or read the item concerned. So headlines saying '1,000 CCTV cameras to solve just one crime, Met Police admits' can, out of context, distort our understanding of what CCTV is designed to do and what it actually does. First of all, it has to be said that a CCTV camera is no more than a dedicated, full time witness of whatever it is pointing at. If something unlawful happens within its field of vision, it will be recorded. A human being has to access that information either at the time, if they happening to be physically monitoring that particular camera out of the hundreds they are responsible for, or later if requested by the police or another agency. The latter takes time; and very often the time to check through hundreds of tapes is not available for understaffed police forces, as a colleague of mine discovered when his parked car was damaged at Cressex recently. The report this week that has been characterised as the Met saying that CCTV doesn't work well enough is in fact not criticising CCTV itself, but suggesting that better training and better use of CCTV might produce better results. It refers to 'untrained officers ... downloading and viewing CCTV images in their hunt for evidence,' and goes on to say that cameras were effective in crime-fighting if the images and information from them are used properly. Moreover, none of the 1984 'Big Brother' media paranoia ever takes account of the deterrent or public reassurance effects of CCTV. The ideal scenario for CCTV would be that it deterred all criminals from committing crime because of the certainty that they would be found out. Fewer arrests could be a result of less crime. And if the prospect of CCTV-monitored streets means that decent citizens who might otherwise avoid city streets at certain times of day feel able to go out again – that too is a desirable, but unquantifiable outcome.

The people who complain about there being too many cameras also complain when there isn't a camera pointed at their car, or their house when something untoward happens. CCTV helps find lost children, helps protect police and emergency services from unjust accusations from the public, and each camera costs a lot less than a pair of eyes on policeman on the beat.

27th March 1998

The story I am about to tell you is perhaps not one which will shock the nation or generate front page headlines in the tabloids. It is a very ordinary and local story, versions of which, I am sure could be told in every town, village and hamlet in the land.

It concerns a couple whose young son was killed on his way to school at Wheeler End many years ago and whom they mourned throughout their lives. They used to regularly walk the mile or two from their home on Wheeler End Common to the Church at Cadmore End, where their son was buried, in order to tend his grave and decorate it with flowers. They continued to do this into old age and because the walk became less brisk with their advancing years, they often wished that somewhere along the route there was a handy bench upon which they could rest.

Accordingly, when they died, they left a bequest to provide a seat for future generations at the point midway between Wheeler End Common and Cadmore Common. This would not only provide comfort for fellow residents and strangers alike, but it would also serve as a memorial to Fred and Gladys and their long-deceased but much-loved son.

In August 1997 the bench was placed by the boundary stone between the two parishes. Three weeks later it was no longer there and was eventually discovered some distance away, where it had been flung into some bushes.

It transpired that the original fixing of the bench had not been to Council requirements, so the bench was recovered and stored in the garage of the Chairman of the Parish Council until conditions were suitable to install the bench, with "substantial fixings to the ground within a hard surfaced pad which would prevent vegetation growing up through the seat."

A local builder made an excellent job of complying with the requirements of the Council and, on March 15th, the bench was firmly fixed to a concrete base sunk into the verge of the lane, facing over the common. A brass plate commemorating the deceased couple was attached to the cross timber at the back. I noticed its return with some pleasure on that day.

Forty-eight hours later, the plaque had been ripped off and the slats in the back of the seat had been smashed and splintered out. One can only assume that a couple renowned for their good works and simple life had no personal enemies who might wish to desecrate their memory in this way. So clearly the act was simply mindless vandalism.

Now any vandalism is beyond my comprehension, but I suppose I can just about understand that there are some people who might be moved by envy and spite, say, to kick in the headlights of a Rolls Royce. It is still a stupid and mindless act and achieves nothing; but it might be seen for a split second to have a logic to the perpetrator.

But I cannot begin to come to grips with the desire to smash something which the very thug who is venting his incomprehensible spleen could himself use to sit on. There was no exclusivity about the bench. It was there for everyone. And some brain-dead piece of sub-humanity felt the urge to trash it.

One of the things I hate about that kind of action is the feelings of vengeance that rise in my own bosom. They are disproportionate, of course, and run along the lines of "Floggin' is too good for 'em," and "Strangle them with their own entrails!"

I suppose it is the sheer helplessness that the rest of us feel when confronted with actions which have no connection to any of the criteria which motivate the rest of us.

29th January 2010

I'm not sure whether another voice crying in the wilderness of potholes is going to achieve anything to improve the parlous state of our roads, which were bad enough before the 'big freeze' and are now approaching the level of disrepair associated with what we are pleased to call 'third-world countries' for no logical reason.

I now completely avoid Cressex Road and take a detour to avoid the succession of suspension-wrecking craters. But the one that got me and dented my wheel sufficiently badly to break its seal with my tyre was along the B482 from Stokenchurch, just before it reaches Lane End. There is a trench there that neatly captured the nearside tyre of this unwary motorist and ejected it with both the inner and outer rims of my wheel bent backwards. One would be tempted to think that whoever is in charge of dealing with these potholes had shares in a tyre company, such is the lack of any warning or protection for the motorist. We can accept that it is probably asking too much that all the yawning craters should be fixed as swiftly as we might like. But, there is a yellow arrow in front of my nemesis, designed presumably to inform the repair crew that this is indeed the one they need to fill in, although if they don't spot that for themselves they'll need to change the tyre on the vehicle that brings them there. Whoever painted that yellow arrow could equally well have surrounded the chasm with some cones to alert the vehicular lemmings that are going to be caught in its gaping maw until it is repaired. When I took my car to get the wheel and tyre fixed, the mechanic asked me which of the many Wycombe potholes had caused the damage. I started to tell him and he interrupted me, "Oh I know the one, I had to fix my sister's car a couple of days ago because she got caught by that one."

I think if, as may well happen, someone's suspension gets banjaxed by the Lane End open cast mine on Finings Road, I would advise them to check up on the law on 'nonfeasance' whereby, as I recall, failure to repair (say) uneven flagstones within a reasonable time after having been notified of same renders a council liable in damages if someone injures themselves as a result of that failure.

21st May 2004

A few years ago my wife was castigated by a friend for telling a bishop that she (my wife) lived in High Wycombe. Her innocent admission took place at a confirmation ceremony, which my wife was attending as a sponsor for our friend's teenage son. During the service the Bishop had politely asked my wife where she lived. Seemingly these events are somewhat less formal than they used be and offer the opportunity for polite conversation. The truthful answer "High Wycombe" was clearly audible around the school chapel to the apparent dismay of our friend. To be fair, her subsequent berating of my wife was semi-humorous; inasmuch as she was aware of the pettiness of her reaction but nonetheless complained, "Couldn't you have said you lived in Marlow or Henley, dear, rather than – pause for effect – High Wycombe?"

Whilst Wycombe may not benefit from a swiftly flowing river banked by lush meadows or boast Nash terraces, Roman baths or broad tree-lined esplanades, it has much to commend it. I have been to Grimsby and to Billingham in Teesside; believe me, High Wycombe is okay!

My answer to any dismissive reactions to our town is, "How many other towns do you know that weigh their mayor in and out of office to ensure that during his term of office he hasn't been getting fat at the expense of the citizens?" This charming and idiosyncratic custom dates back to mediaeval times when Wycombe was in the vanguard of democratic thinking. In those days it was more than possible for holders of high (or even medium or low) office to feather their nests substantially during their tenure, thereby extending their wealth and consequently their girth. Checking on the extent of the latter, publicly in the High Street, on leaving office was rather a neat way to encourage a proper resistance to temptation.

Nowadays, I suppose, one could argue that the tradition is more helpful to the mayor than it is to the citizens. After all, a mayor may be called upon to attend three or more official public functions a day during his year in office. At each function food will be offered. The toll that could be inflicted on the health of a civic dignitary of hosting and attending all those banquets, lunches, dinners and cocktail parties could be considerable. What started out therefore as a means of protecting the interests of the public at large is now more likely to prevent the mayor from becoming publicly large. The weighing-in ceremony is therefore perhaps a means of focussing the mind of the poor chain-bearing consumer of endless mass catering on the unwelcome consequences of extending his personal rather than municipal corporation.

Many years ago, I accepted a wager from a friend that he could lose more weight than me within a specified time frame. It occurred to me that I could lose a significant amount quite quickly if I were to drink several pints of water immediately before our weigh-in, wearing shorts and a t-shirt. This simple ruse resulted in some minor temporary discomfort and a donation to my charity three months later.

The mayor of course has the opportunity to adopt that strategy or secrete about his capacious ceremonial robes the odd piece of lead piping or house brick.

I am sure that Councillor Tony Green, however, resisted the temptation to improve the chances of his being cheered out of office by employing such chicanery.

2nd March 2001

I was delighted this week to see evidence of the good natured community spirit of the people of Wycombe. There was a blur of pancakes and frying pans up and down the High Street on Shrove Tuesday, when all manner of unlikely teams competed in a light-hearted but spirited way for the Great Pancake Race Trophy. The race was the first of what it is hoped will be an annual event to raise awareness and much needed funds for Wycombe Mobility, the charity that works to help the disabled shopper to gain access to the shopping and other attractions of our town centre. Many local traders and organisations fielded teams of three runners each in the relay race along the High Street to the Guildhall. Teams from Biffa, Sainsbury's, Chiltern Shopping Centre and Wilkinsons competed strenuously against representatives of the Hobgoblin Pub, Wycombe Leisure, St. Augustine's and Wycombe Parish Church, which was represented by three nimble vicars who were only narrowly beaten to the semi-finals by three uniformed members of the Thames Valley Constabulary, who demonstrated remarkable dexterity, holding their helmets on with one hand while tossing pancakes as they ran along the cobbles of the High Street. I blighted the chances of our giant toppling football team by telling an interviewer from Radio 1170 that I thought that the three lads from Wycombe Wanderers would raise the trophy. I was so convinced of their effortless form in the first leg that I predicted that their win in the pancake tossing would be an omen of their impending success in the FA Cup, first against Leicester and then bring 'em all on for the semis!

I was impressed by the nonchalance, if not the wisdom, of the first runner for Radio 1170 who decided to run with a fag in his hand. Whilst it didn't give out exactly the right health or lifestyle message to the youngsters in the large crowd who turned up to watch the inaugural Pancake Derby, the fact that their team came last reinforced the message that health and cigarettes are not fellow travellers – or indeed sprinters.

The three members of the constabulary made it to the final and should be congratulated on their good humour and sportsmanship, which endeared them to the crowd. They were, however, beaten in the final by the spirited team from Argos. The young lady who ran the first leg took off like ferret on roller skates and her early lead was never pegged back by the police.

I was delighted to present them with their trophy and look forward to watching the event next year, when I am sure many more teams will want to have some fun in the freezing cold in aid of such a good cause.

As I left I saw the three vicars team returning to St Mary's and an eddy of wind raised the black cloak of their departing captain sufficiently high to reveal the running shoes beneath. It was good to know that they did not put all their faith in the almighty.

It is only left for me now to decide on my strategy for Lent. Last year I eschewed alcohol, except on Sundays. This year maybe biscuits, sweets and chocolate.

But as luck would have it, I did the big shop yesterday and the cupboard is crammed with precisely the things I would have to forego! Decisions, decisions!

4th April 2008

Well, the build-up to the opening of Eden (as Adam and Eve must have also recalled) was pretty intense and feverish. I did not attend, as my recollection of such occasions, as a member of the public, has not encouraged me to think that I would find the experience an uplifting one. If I have a phobia, it is ochlophobia, a pathological aversion to crowds. But I was diverted to read, in the Letters page, complaints about "scantily clad young women" dancing around our streets. Anyone who has been in Wycombe town centre when the pubs and clubs are in full weekend swing, will be used to the sight of inadequately-dressed young females cavorting in the streets, most of whom have less to celebrate and far too much to show than the troupe of impressively costumed dancers whose exotic images graced the pages of this paper.

Personally, the advent of Eden has not been entirely welcome, but for different reasons than most. I have four daughters who have descended upon the vastly improved retail opportunities and environment offered by Eden with the same zeal as paparazzi who had discovered that Britney Spears was visiting the place with her friend, Prince Harry (Note to BFP photographer – this is a joke – it is not real – honest!).

The downside is not just financial, but physical. Because I was with them on the first trip, I was faced with the choice of standing outside "Very Skimpy Clothes R Us," as is the common practice of fathers since shopping-time immemorial, and freezing to death, or actually going into one of these shrines of young fashion and feeling like a Morris Dancer in a Biker's Pub.

And that was the one thing about Eden that I had failed to anticipate. A large section of it is open to the elements, and that was particularly relevant on my first visit as the weather was far from pleasant and I had thought I was going to be undercover. But now I know that, it will no longer be a problem.

The majority of the shops are, understandably, aimed at the market that spends the most money on clothes – young people and women. The shopping environment is infinitely superior to that Wycombe has provided hereunto and I have no doubt that once parking problems have been sorted out, then Eden will prove an enduring asset for our town.

19. Acting Up

It is quite sobering to realise that I have earned my living as an actor for forty years at the time of writing. I am under no illusion that I have been other than very lucky. This profession has always been an insecure one that is subject to the caprice and whim of producers and casting directors and the fickle nature of fashion.

When I started out in my career that was almost uniquely true of my profession and associated creative industries. Now there is no such thing as job security anywhere, and certainly no such thing as a job for life. The acting profession has joined the mainstream – or is it the other way round, I wonder.

What is it like to be an actor? One swings from anxiety that there will never be another job to anxiety that one isn't up to the job that one has. We live on our nerves, but the rewards, once the panic and anxiety are quelled and we survive yet another first night, are great. I am not talking financially necessarily here, more about the sense of achievement. The satisfaction derives considerably from the effect one's work has on others.

7th June 2002

If there is any truth in that old saw about the sun shining on the righteous, then our sovereign, and the millions who turned out in London to celebrate her jubilee with her are just about as righteous as they come. Given the fact that the weather collapsed into Noah-galvanising inundations the following day, for once the British weather had a sense of occasion, if not generosity.

Any thoughts I may have had of joining in any jollities were dispelled, when I was smitten by one of those bugs that only afflicts actors when they have a week off. My seven days respite from being a 1942 squadron leader were marked by the surrender of my larynx to a nasty army of bacteria drinking one of those techno-drinks that keep up your energy and bearing razor blades.

"So you want to swallow, do you, you idle actor? Take that!"

So we were not among the stalwarts who slept on the metropolitan flagstones in order to get a glimpse of our Queen in the Golden Coach or the nice new Bentley. Instead, I retired to my bed, trying to drown the malevolent bacteria in hot lemon, honey and whisky. The bacteria seemed to thrive on it.

I dozed intermittently, propped up by more pillows than her Majesty has ever dreamed of, even in a marrowfat moment (lying down was not an option, the razor blade bearers punish you if you cough while lying down and try to force your windpipe out through your ears). In between the spasmodic bouts of suffering (I wouldn't want you to think I was enjoying myself now!), I was able to watch the Buck House Pop Bash and marvel at the predictable ineptitude and crassness of most of the celebrities who turn up to fill in while Eric Clapton (the man is a God!) gets his guitars plugged in and S Club 7 count each other.

Why, oh why, can someone please tell me, do comedians still feel obliged to try to be a little bit cheeky to the Royals and then do a "Whoops, have I gone too far?" routine, when they have clearly (a) not been slightly funny (b) ignored the evidence of their own senses when previous celebs have been similarly naff and (c) reinforced the Royals' already jaundiced view of what we, their subjects, find entertaining? If ever there were a case for a right royal jubilee clip round the ear...

Edna Everage, who referred to the Queen as the "jubilee girl," was arguably the only one who could actually truly get away with such lèse majesté!

But, in between the sporadic embarrassment, the music was actually great stuff. That brave husk of a Beach Boy, Brian Wilson, made a rare and greatly appreciated appearance reminding us of his towering creative genius, in the company of those other wonders of 20th Century popular music, the great Eric, Sir Paul, Stevie Winwood, Ray Davies, Phil Collins who seemed to be drumming for everyone, Queen's Brian Way, who did the same with his guitar and riffed a great national Anthem from the roof of the Palace... they were all there.

And the vision of the night - Ozzie Osbourne, legendary biter of bats' heads, object of generation of parental despair, who rocked like a good 'un and then offered humble, and clearly sincere, rock star congratulations to the greatest act of them all (my words not his).

16th May 2003

The customer is always right; five simple words that express a very sound business philosophy, despite being demonstrably untrue as a statement of fact.

Sadly, it is a philosophy that is, in many areas, falling into disuse. When a service provider demonstrates their willingness to go that extra mile for their customers, it is a welcome surprise rather than an everyday occurrence.

Some of it is our fault. The cheapness of goods in the supermarket has lured us to forsake the smaller local shops. The goods are cheap because they are bought in large quantities; large quantities therefore have to be sold. If not enough people buy an item then it disappears off the shelves forever. "There's no demand," actually means there is not enough demand for them to get it just for you and the insufficient numbers who actually do want the item.

It is a principle that many in my profession would do well to take on board. I am constantly surprised by fellow performers who will criticise an audience for failing to roll around the aisles in mirth at the hilarity of their performance. I remember once introducing my wife backstage to a TV presenter who appeared with me in panto a few years ago. His first words to her were "You were a terrible audience," which aside from being quite simply rude, demonstrated a complete failure to appreciate the relationship between audience and actors. My wife, who was an actress before opting for the much harder job of child and animal husbandry (wifery?), shares my distaste for audience-bashing. They pay for their seats and owe us nothing. If they choose to sit in stony silence while we cast our (clearly resistible) pearls before them, then that is their privilege, however much we may wish it were otherwise. It is admittedly frequently perplexing that something that made an audience almost expire with laughter one night evinces no reaction at all the next, but simultaneously it is one of the exciting things about theatre. Every show is different. The audience is an integral part of the experience but, having paid for the privilege of sharing in the fun gives it the right, in my opinion, to participate in whatever way it wishes, short of inflicting physical violence on the cast. I seldom laugh out loud myself when at the theatre, but that does not mean that I am not enjoying the performance. Very often, unless there is a handful of strategically-placed loud laughers in an audience, theatre-goers are capable of thoroughly enjoying a show without vocalising their pleasure.

Sometimes they vocalise their displeasure too. In my current play "Corpse!" (Wycombe Swan week commencing 9th June, book now to avoid disappointment!), there is a moment when a shot rings out and one of the characters is propelled backwards into a theatrical skip. At a recent matinee in Mold, North Wales, we heard a Lancashire lady declaim in tones that indicated that he had gone down in her estimation. "Oh my God! Whatever have you brought me to, Norman?"

I hope she stayed to find out; but I'm not sure, as we didn't hear from her again.

It reminded me of the moment in a production of Macbeth when as the words "Tomorrow and tomorrow and tomorrow..." were intoned one Saturday matinee, a woman in the front row declared firmly, "That'll be next Tuesday!"

26th June 1999

When a television company is in negotiation with an actor's agent, the one area in which they always appear to be generous is transport. Even if you only live a couple of miles away from the location, they will happily send a car to pick you up. I thought this was evidence of their consideration for the comfort of the performer, until I realised that it was to make absolutely sure that we get there on time.

Lateness is the most unforgivable crime that an actor can commit. Even an imperfect knowledge of the lines, while not exactly applauded, is less heinous a crime than keeping an entire film crew waiting. When stars become so powerful that they can force a set full of other actors, technicians and production staff to wait for them to deign to step out of their luxury mobile home, then they know that they have made it big time. In their eyes, anyway.

And the stories are legion. Marilyn Monroe even kept Laurence Olivier waiting for endless hours during Prince and the Showgirl.

And whilst the phenomenon is prevalent in the States, it happens here too. I recently heard of an English actor who refused to come on set, as he was distressed because the wrong biscuits had been put in his Winnebago.

The rest of us, who are not terminally selfish and who actually like to work in an atmosphere where everyone is collaborating happily together, are almost obsessive about not being late.

In the summer of 1971, I was cast in several small to non-existent roles in the Chichester Festival season. I settled into my digs and went to bed early, having set my brand-new alarm clock, bought expressly for the purpose of getting me to the first rehearsal washed, dressed and alert, in plenty of time. In the event, the alarm clock was defective. I woke up five minutes after the time at which rehearsals were due to start. Fifteen minutes later I arrived unshaved, unwashed, breathless and terrified as well as mortified.

The entire cast and company, including the star, Sir John Gielgud no less, all came over to me, introduced themselves and sympathised with my evident distress. Apparently, when it was clear that I was late, the director told them all to be nice to me when I arrived, as no actor would be late on purpose and I would therefore be understandably distraught. I will forever revere the name of Robin Phillips, who sadly for us now works in Canada, for this simple and imaginative act of kindness. It is not a characteristic that I have encountered in every director that I have worked with!

The best excuse for lateness that I ever heard was when I was rehearsing a series at the BBC in the mid-seventies. A girl who had been late several times before and who had received stern warnings about the consequences of future lapses was very late yet again. She arrived, sobbing uncontrollably, and told us that her budgie had fallen off its perch that morning and broken its leg. Not wishing to be late for work, she had attempted to mend the tiny broken limb herself using matches as splints. The feathered patient was stumping around the bottom of the cage testing her amateur orthopaedics, when the red heads of the matches came into contact with the sand sheets at the bottom of the cage and ignited. Hey presto – Joey of Arc!

True or false, the tale was just too big to even consider challenging it.

21st December 2001

Today, I earned my living by dressing in black leather, donning a leopard-skin cloak and an elaborate horned Arabian hat. I threatened to cut the Emperor of China into little pieces, if his daughter wouldn't marry me; I shut Joel from Neighbours in a cave, in which he found – oh wonder of wonders - a guitar that he could play while singing a Ronan Keating ballad; and I rather improbably told an otherwise perfectly normal father of two, who was wearing a bright red wig and a spotted dress at the time, that "her" price was above rubies solely to provoke the reply, "How much does Ruby charge?"

And I get to do it three times again tomorrow.

It's panto time again; and this year, I am haranguing the citizens of Canterbury, as Abanazar in Aladdin.

Once again the gods of festive fun and frivolity have smiled upon the efforts of the producers to get together a totally disparate group of people, most of whom have never met before, and within two action packed weeks hone them into a well-oiled – I'm sorry, that should read "finely-tuned" - ensemble that can create a little bit of Christmas magic for family audiences.

I have appeared in shows in years past when the cast have been united only in their common antipathy for the self-absorbed and untalented hero whose moment of fame came when he hosted an afternoon programme on a satellite channel selling trinkets to the unwary, or for the alleged comic whose claim to fame stems from appearing as "Billy Barley – laughter, lunacy and a ukulele, as seen at Cleethorpes Cavalcade of Fun 1964 to 1971".

These are the comics who add 30 minutes to the show over the space of a week in their quest for more, or indeed any, laughs.

This year I am appearing with a hunky (I am told) Neighbour who provokes an alarming volume of noise from hundreds of teenage girls who, having screamed every time he enters, utters or sings then wait in their excited droves outside the stage door for a glimpse of their surfing hero.

Any doubt of the devotion that soap actors can provoke in their young fans is removed instantly by the sight of these thirteen- to fifteen-year-old girls trampling a sixties rock singer, a current quiz show host and your venerable columnist into the mud in their haste to bask in the flash of those white teeth and catch a glimpse of the fit, young bronzed antipodean. Sadly, he is an amiable and talented lad, which makes it impossible to cordially loathe him, which would have made the whole thing slightly more tolerable.

Peter Straker, rock singer celebrated for the 60's iconic musical Hair and a former Phantom of the Opera, Paul Hendy – current host of ITV's Wheel of Fortune, and Colin Baker (whoever he is or was) are viewed only by these fans as possible obstructions preventing them from meeting and blushing furiously in the presence of their Ramsay Street hunk.

It doesn't do to take oneself too seriously in this business.

I remember once being accosted outside a stage door by a couple of rather attractive young ladies who rushed up and breathlessly asked, "Are you Colin Baker?" I modestly acknowledged that I was indeed he. "Could you get us Dennis Waterman's autograph?" they then deflatingly demanded.

3rd October 2003

When I was eleven, I went along with my friends to the school hall one night to find out what this Gilbert and Sullivan production was all about. A term later we were all dressed up as girls (it was an all boys' school) and flirting in innocent Gilbertian style with a bunch of fifth and sixth formers who were being Tower Warders "under orders" in Yeoman of the Guard. The following year I was Phyllis in Iolanthe; then Rose Maybud in Ruddigore. The measure of my talent as a boy soprano can be gauged by the revue in the school magazine. "Colin Baker threw himself with great verve into the part of Phyllis and rarely strayed more than half an octave from the note." At the time I recall being rather proud of what I perceived as being a rather good review. GCSEs intervened (remember them?) and two years later, my boy-soprano glories behind me, I gave the waiting world my Pish Tush in the Mikado. Thereafter, Arthur Sullivan's repose was untroubled by excessive rotation. There are many things that I would have taken good odds that I wouldn't be asked to do on stage – a pas de deux with Darcey Bussell, an elf in Lord of the Rings, the title role in Hedda Gabler. Until recently I would have added a leading role in G & S to that list. And yet…

Next Friday and Saturday I shall be appearing at the Wycombe Swan in HMS Pinafore as Sir Joseph Porter KCB for the Carl Rosa Opera Company. Never one to refuse to take on a challenge, when I was invited to join this prestigious opera company for this production, I agreed first and panicked later. I should point out that there is a world of difference between the demands on a "patter man" traditionally played by actors (Frankie Howard a notable former Sir Joseph) and those facing a soprano, as I purported to be all those years ago. The aria sung superbly by Ann Bourne and Lesley Cox in Act 2 would put the lie to anyone who considers that Sullivan may not have written challenging stuff. I have found the process of working with opera singers a most rewarding and salutary one. Their dedication to their profession and to the development of their voices is unparalleled.

And after many years of doing pantomime with a maximum of four or five musicians in the pit, the joy of hearing an orchestra of twenty-four musicians launch into the overture every night is quite simply inspirational. Since Carl Rosa was reformed in 1998, they haven't received a penny of public subsidy but have to balance their books while touring with a total company of over fifty people. The fact they are succeeding so splendidly is a tribute to the quality of the output.

I am having a wonderful time in the company of such these highly talented and predominantly very young singers and musicians. I have also been delighted to work again with an old friend Brenda Longman – "Little Buttercup" who has moved from the voice of Sue, Sooty's vocal companion with effortless ease into the role of the bumboat woman who harbours a secret.

If you need any further persuasion to come and see us next week – there is a wonderfully uplifting rendition of "For he is an Englishman" sung by Bruce Graham. What more could you ask for?

4th March 2005

Last week's (old fashioned, broadsheet) Free Time included an item about Ellie Pygall, a Wycombe High School student who was on the receiving end of an unusual variation of the theatrical cliché "Is there a doctor in the house?"

Ellie was settling down to enjoy *The Hot Mikado* at the Wycombe Swan last week, when the call came out, "Is there a drummer in the house?" The show's regular drummer had been delayed in traffic. Moments later, she found herself sitting in the pit and sight-reading (with great distinction, it appears) the percussion part of the orchestral arrangement for a show she had never seen before.

Ellie – hats off to you! Indeed, top hats off to you!

There are many seasoned performers who would have sunk down in their seats, pulled up their collars and prayed that no-one would notice them in the face of such a challenge. I include myself in that number. Many years ago, at literally a few hours notice, I was asked if I would step in to a Liverpool production of Alan Ayckbourn's *The Norman Conquests*, which are three interlinking plays, usually performed in repertoire.

They asked me because I had done the plays a year earlier in Windsor. A swift look at the script was sufficient to convince me that 95% of it had departed my brain never to return in order to make room for the next short-term memory intake. The likelihood of my dredging it up by that evening (yes, that's what they asked me to do!) was nonexistent. There are some actors out there who could have done it. My wife, who gave up this silly way of life when we had children, had the immensely irritating ability to learn a play in a couple of days, without letting it interfere with her social life. For me, the process is prolonged, tortuous and debilitating. Each job I do is the one that I think is going to defeat me; mercifully, thus far I have been proved wrong. Once, when Elvira in Noel Coward's *Blithe Spirit* fell ill, my wife was able to step immediately into the role, because while rehearsing her part, the maid, she had by some sort of dramatic osmosis, contrived to learn the whole play. And she's the one who's given up, while I soldier on with sleepless nights and tape recorders. Funny old world.

Sir Ralph Richardson is reputed to have stepped forward in the middle of a play and asked the audience, "Is there a Doctor in the House?"

A man in the stalls called out, "I am a Doctor!" to which Richardson replied, "Isn't this a terrible play, Doctor?"

17th June 2005

This week I complete the tour of Dracula with which I have toured for the last three months. When the curtain comes down in Brighton on Saturday night, the stakes and garlic flowers will be packed away, the coffins broken up and the pools of blood wiped up for the last time; it will be Fangs for the Memories, to employ a pun that no newspaper reviewer has been able to resist using in some form or another.

There are many actors of my age who will simply not tour, usually for the very compelling reason that they don't fancy the idea of living out of a suitcase for months.

Being still responsible for the support and education of four daughters, I have no option but to follow that old Tory Rottweiler Norman Tebbit's famous advice to those in search of employment and 'get on my bike', or in my case into my "G" reg Mercedes. For me, therefore, it's a question of forced to tour rather than a tour de force. But rather than stay in hotels and digs, I opt to commute where I can. It is, in fact, cheaper to do that than it is to stay in hotels; and the old theatrical digs with their infamous landladies of legend, sadly, no longer exist.

Some weeks, like this one, I will cover a thousand miles or more. The last two venues were Southend and Birmingham. Despite the undoubtedly manifold delights of those two places, I had more pressing business at home demanding my daily attention than sampling the delights of those far flung hot spots. So while the younger unattached members of the company having visited the bars, nighteries and cultural attractions are still asleep in their humble lodgings, I am astride my mighty Countax mowing the Baker acre or putting our herd of grass-gulping guinea pigs out to graze (Herd? Don't ask!).

Alistair Darling's proposed road-pricing plan will make touring prohibitive (there are no trains or buses to get me home from Brighton or Birmingham after the curtain comes down). But until that latest motorist-bashing initiative is enacted, I will continue to strive to be both a working actor on the stage and a husband and father too.

My next engagement is as a guest in Little Britain, which I am looking forward too immensely. Teetering permanently on the brink of appalling bad taste, it is a very funny programme indeed.

9th February 2007

The show must go on!

That is the age-old theatrical maxim.

This admirable devotion to duty shown by performers stems from two powerful reasons. If you don't turn up, the show won't go on and the audience will be sent home having been refunded the ticket price by a management who will remember that financial loss for far longer than they will remember the thousands of times that you did turn up and deliver the goods impeccably and on cue. It is also attributable to a fear that, if there is an understudy (which is not necessarily always the case these days), they might just be better than you which, combined with the fact that are also likely to be cheaper, might see you becoming more familiar with the Job Seekers Allowance than you might otherwise have liked. And (all right; three reasons), most performers actually like doing what they do.

As a result, over four decades of earning my living in the theatre and television, there had until recently been only three occasions when, as a professional, I have not delivered the goods. The first was when, as King Rat, I completely lost my voice and missed the final performance of a long run. The second was a farce in the West End when an ill-judged comic leap onto a sofa left me requiring the tender ministrations of an osteopath for a whole week before standing was an option, let alone leaping, comically or otherwise.

And then there was the day I crashed my car and the Emperor of Japan donned my Widow Twankey outfit in Act 1 until I made it to Brighton to take over from him. The audience, as always, seemed not to notice or, perhaps, care.

And then man-flu (as my wife called it) struck. It was in fact the chest and throat affliction that is doing the rounds. I coughed for two weeks and found myself banished to the sofa downstairs at night so that my wife and daughters weren't unduly troubled by my pain and suffering.

As a result, two weeks ago, I failed to honour a commitment to join my favourite local orchestra the Wycombe Sinfonia at John Hampden School to narrate the Dance Macabre.

I was as they say – gutted. All the more so when I heard that the conductor, John Dunnett, multi-tasked superbly and saved the day.

1st September 2001

I recently discovered something that will probably surprise you as much as it did me. Many of you may believe that writing for the Bucks Free Press is about as much excitement as could be crammed into one life, but my principle employment and certainly my principle income is derived from the profession I have stubbornly clung to, against all common sense, for the last three decades. An actor's life is notoriously unpredictable. I spoke to an old colleague last week who, in his mid nineties, has just landed the title role in a major movie as Sir Anthony Hopkins' father.

We worked together at the end of the pier in Weymouth in 1978 and several decades earlier he had been Dr. Dale, the very "Jim" that Mrs. Dale was always worried about in "Mrs. Dale's Diary" on the BBC Radio's post-war Home Service. Readers under the age of 45 - ask a grown up what I'm talking about!

So a jobbing actor can become a star, just as the reverse is also true. I know of one household name of the 70's who has exchanged his former Weybridge mansion for a one-room bed-sitter in Victoria.

Anyway, after six months of masterly inactivity, broken only last week by an episode of the lunch time drama *The Doctors* for the BBC, I was informed by my agent what the reason was for the work famine.

The effects of the threatened strike by American actors have apparently prevented many potential employers from investing any time and money in pre-production on film and television that may never happen.

But the greatest single cause for a significant decrease in drama production in film and television is the Foot and Mouth outbreak. Yes, really!

When it was explained I was able see the logic. Very little drama is now filmed in studios. Indeed, many former productive and state of the art studios are now languishing empty as the combination of internal costing and the quest for "reality" drama drives the production companies out into the real world. I was recently at the BBC in Pebble Mill, Birmingham where the wonderful studio that housed *The Brothers*, *All Creatures Great and Small*, *Angels* and many other series lies not only empty, but gutted, chained up and forlorn.

Everything is location-based, which means large numbers of vehicles and people travelling all over the country. Given the uncertainty about the availability of vast areas of the country over the last months of the still extant outbreak of Foot and Mouth, production companies are declining to get involved in expensive pre-production when they may be unable to maintain tight filming schedules if the countryside becomes a no-go area again.

The end result is that over the last six months there has been an estimated 75% decrease in work offered to actors in film and television in this country. Until I discovered this I had not considered myself as a victim of the same mismanaged blight that has crippled the farming and tourism industries. The full cost of Foot and Mouth 2001 may never be known but will clearly be much more than any of us have realised. It's not just the 2,000 farms that have a combined loss of 4 million animals that are looking at a bleaker future than might otherwise be the case. At least some of them do have the slight silver lining of the possibility of compensation.

5th July 2000

I have recently completed a fourteen-week nationwide tour with a play that ended very conveniently (for me at any rate) at the Theatre Royal in Windsor.

There are many actors of my age who will not tour, usually because they don't fancy the idea of living out of a suitcase for months. Being the father of four daughters, I have to follow Norman Tebbit's famous advice to the workforce and get on my bike, or in my case into my "H" reg Audi. Although I don't tour from choice (tour de force?), preferring to be with my family whenever I reasonably can, I resolve that dilemma, in part, by commuting distances up to 120 miles, to the astonishment of some of my colleagues. It does mean adding a thousand miles a week to my car's odometer and, more alarmingly, huge sums of money to my credit card bill, petrol being dangerously close to the four-pounds-a-gallon mark. Taking into account wear and tear and maintenance, it means that I was probably not much better off financially than Gorden Kaye, also in the play, who stayed at well-appointed hotels in each venue.

Some would envy his relaxed days exploring the delights of Malvern or Bath, if not the somewhat less heady attractions of Stoke-on-Trent or Sheffield, but I preferred to be around for the odd school run and making the lunch boxes. I know some men might disagree with me, but frankly that's their loss. I spent five hours a day driving and three acting – still only an average day's work.

When I started in this business, "theatrical digs" still existed. These were lodgings often exclusively for those working in the entertainment industry, usually owned and ruled with a rod of iron and variable eccentricity by landladies – who were theatrical in both senses of the word.

Stories abound - of the legendary Alma Mackay in Manchester, whose luxurious red wig became less and less secure as evenings progressed, upon which no-one ever commented; of signs in bathrooms reading "One bath per week each. No more than five inches must be run" and in the WC - "No solids after 10pm;" of the actor who played Dracula so convincingly that his landlady, having seen the show, refused to let him into the digs on the reasonable basis that he "couldn't do it if 'e didn't have it in 'im."

During the time of rationing, Derek Nimmo's mother once delivered a sirloin steak and some asparagus to his digs in Bolton, as a treat. He received a note from the landlady saying "I've cooked your steak and put the bluebells in water."

Norman Wisdom once had difficulty finding digs in Barrow-in-Furness. He started knocking on doors at random. One woman took pity on him and told him to return an hour later. During the night, needing to use what he hoped might, according to custom and practice, be under the bed he reached underneath and discovered – a dead body. The landlady's husband had died that day, and not wishing to lose a lodger she had made "temporary" arrangements, pending the arrival of the undertaker.

My favourite story is of Monsewer Eddie Grey, the famous Crazy Gang member who once stayed in digs in Southsea. For the first ten days he had been given fish for his dinner and was longing for some meat.

When the landlady told him that she had read his tea leaves and he was going to meet a stranger, Eddie said: "I hope it's the b***** butcher!"

11th April 2003

I am currently playing the part of a rather seedy, duplicitous Major on the stage. He is an incompetent conman for whom the audience are intended to have grudging sympathy, as everything gradually goes pear shaped around him. I have therefore been intrigued by the public fall from grace of the quiz contestant sharing my temporary rank, together with his wife and his coughing professorial confederate.

Not having followed the case in any great detail, I am unsure how the genius with the dodgy lungs ended up in the audience while, evidently, the demonstrably less gifted officer found himself perched on the unnecessarily high stool. It may well be that the quiz has been cleverly constructed to ensure that the skills required to place the letters D C B A in alphabetical order are intrinsically different to those, say, that enable a contestant to decide which of J D Salinger, Joseph Heller, P G Wodehouse or James Thurber created the character of "Major Major".

In any event, the hapless singular Major, whose character seems even closer to that of the role I am currently playing than might have at first appeared, has been convicted of the grown-up version of writing dates on the back of his hand for the GCSE History Exam. As a nation, we attach a lot of importance to playing fair and generally abominate the cheat, despite our fondness for fictional versions like the characters played by Robert Redford and Paul Newman in The Sting. There has been, though, a general feeling that in this case it is not very easy to find anything that resembles a real victim, apart perhaps from the contestants who might otherwise have had the opportunity to pluck a cheque from the hand of the affable Chris Tarrant, when the Major failed to progress, as he undoubtedly would have done without his consumptive assistant's help. The producers certainly purport to be eager to dish out some of the loot that pours in from the phone calls that the hopeful make in their millions in the hope of getting on to the programme. Therefore, they are not visible losers.

So the question, that may well have more than four possible answers, is: "Why spend even more public money than the miscreants actually failed to prise out of the programme, in order to extract a fraction of that amount in fines from the disgraced trio?" Of course, we all acknowledge that the price of justice should not be an issue in cases where, for instance, a thug has mugged a pensioner for a bag of fish and chips. But this case is not like that. The TV Company had, it appears now, very properly declined to pay out the top prize. This would have left the Major free to sue, if he had the nerve, and expose himself to the financial cost of failure in the civil courts. And should he have declined to sue for his million then that would have been seen to be a more than eloquent confirmation of everyone' suspicions.

I have no sympathy for the greedy trio and their current fall from grace, but wish that you and I didn't have to bear the cost of confirming their seedy duplicity by paying lawyers an amount not dissimilar to that they attempted to plunder from the programme.

(And it was, of course, Joseph Heller who created Major Major in "Catch 22").

22nd March 2002

Actors vary in their approach to the job, from at one extreme those who will spend many long hours on detailed research and try to live the life of their character, insofar as they can legally do so. They will eat, sleep, drink and do everything else in the way that they imagine their character might. Taken to extremes this might mean that an "immersion" actor might well spend weeks learning how to mend shoes, even though the character he is playing – a shoemaker – may not be called upon to ply his trade visibly on stage or before the camera. They feel that the acquisition of this skill enables them more easily to understand the mindset of the characters they are playing.

They may have given their all (or awl in this case) in their quest for truth but, arguably, the only members of the audience who might have even the smallest chance of appreciating their Herculean efforts would be cobblers, and I use the word advisedly.

A certain amount of research is undeniably useful. I am currently touring the country with a play called Flarepath, which deals with the emotional and physical price paid by the airmen who defended us in the air during WW2.

Some of us were indeed given the opportunity to climb inside a Lancaster bomber and see just how vulnerable those nineteen year old boy pilots were in those mammoth, inhospitable tin cans.

But if the writer has done his research (and Terence Rattigan, a serving rear gunner when he wrote the play, certainly had) then that is all there in the script anyway.

There are also what we might term - technical actors. The ones who, according to the old maxim, "learn the lines and don't bump into the furniture." They have any number of professional tricks up their sleeves and drive the character, rather than let it take them over.

The best can play an audience's emotions like a finely tuned harp, whilst giving the other actors a knowing wink with their upstage eye.

I never worked with him, but am told that Laurence Olivier was an example of the technical performer. He worked once, in the film Marathon Man, with Dustin Hoffman, who is apparently a devotee of the research-it/live-it acting style. Just before a take was about start, Hoffman began running violently on the spot. Olvier politely enquired why he was doing this. Dustin replied that the scene that they were about to shoot followed one in which he had been seen running at breakneck speed through the City's streets, therefore he should, logically, be out of breath.

Olivier considered this reply while watching Hoffman's breathing getting increasingly more laboured as he pounded up and down on the spot. Then, with great concern, he asked "Have you ever tried…" he paused, "…acting, dear boy?"

I have worked with actors of the "immersion" type, who like to be in the theatre three hours before curtain up and "get into character," whereas colleagues of the, "just doin' my job" variety like to amble in at the last possible minute, have a cup of tea, chat to the stage doorman and breeze onto the stage with no apparent preparation at all. The work, of course, was done before and during rehearsal. They are the professionals.

Acting, as a craft, is sadly giving way to what at best is simply "behaving" and at worst therapy!

27th June 1997

I suppose that some might envy the trappings of fame. I am not one of them. My boring British lower middle class roots would stop me from ever really enjoying the fruits of the kind of fame that enables you to jump queues and get the best tables in restaurants. I couldn't bear all that hate and would have to do lots of sheepish shrugging, as if it really wasn't my idea, for heaven's sake!

Nor do I envy the goldfish bowl atmosphere in which the real stars live.

(The word 'star' is much abused today. It seems to be applied to anyone who has been in a TV soap for five episodes - so it's hard to find a word to describe The Seans, Clints and Arnolds, without resorting to hyperbole of the super-duper-megastar kind!)

I wouldn't want to have to wear disguise in order to live a normal life. It may sound a bit bizarre, but I would hate not to be able to pop into Asda for the dog food whenever I wanted to. It might seem attractive to be able to pay someone to do that for you for a while, but I suspect the novelty might wear off.

However, even the modest level of television notoriety that I have achieved as a result of being Doctor Who ten years ago has significant disadvantages. But before I list them, I wish to make it quite clear that I am not complaining; I chose the acting profession, for some reason, three decades ago, so must take all the consequences. Indeed, I have little patience with actors who object and become all precious or simply rude when people ask for their autographs and stop them in the street to express appreciation or even simple recognition.

One disadvantage is that you can never allow yourself the luxury of being in a bad mood in public. The one time you complain or mutter an imprecation when you get bad service, is the time that will be remembered by the recipient of your wrath for the rest of their lives. Whenever you appear on the screen, they will inform their friends that you are horrible, unpleasant and arrogant; the friends will seize on this with rapacious glee and pass it on. By the time a few weeks have passed there will be universal amazement that you have not been put on trial for crimes against humanity.

For some reason, I am still surprised when people treat me in an odd way when I meet them. Perhaps that is naive of me. I know that I would probably not behave normally (whatever that means) if I were to meet a sporting hero. But when you are you, if see what I mean, you really do forget that other people see you as HIM. Accordingly people can be impressed and over effusive or ostentatiously unimpressed or downright rude. Sometimes the rudeness stems from simple embarrassment, admittedly. My wife was amazed recently when at a public charity event a total stranger embarrassed her young son who had stopped to get Doctor Who's autograph by saying, "My goodness, you've put on a lot of weight since you were Doctor Who. You weren't as fat back then, were you?"

I am used to this reaction and inclined to be philosophical about it. I can't deny the truth of it, certainly. But I would never dream myself of making such an observation to a friend, let alone a complete stranger. But if I replied in kind, as I did once to a lady in Sweden who detailed all my physical drawbacks, in that forthright Scandinavian style, at length for some minutes, then I would be regarded as appallingly rude.

What did I say?

Well it was twenty years ago and even though I felt good at the time I wouldn't do it again.

I said "How kind of you. Do you know you have a very fat bottom?"

20. Season's Greetings

As I write this I am viewing a Christmas a few months ahead which for a change, I will not be spending in pantomime somewhere a considerable distance from Baker Towers.

Because I am touring with a play the last week of which overlaps with the customary opening period for pantomimes I am allowing myself the luxury of a Christmas with my family this year. I tried it once before as you will read in the following pages. Doubtless, come December, I shall be writing in the newspaper about experience of Christmas 2010.

But it is a special time, whether I just have that one day of high intensity Christmas that I have experienced in my panto years, or the more leisurely experience that I shall be privileged to share this year, I do know that treasure each Christmas I share with my family. Like most families we have our traditional way of experiencing those few days of relaxed sharing and celebration and when the time inevitably comes when the six of us are no longer together, necessarily as our daughters strike out on their own, as they will and should, it will be quite poignant for me and my wife Marion, I suspect.

But here is a glimpse – a la Christmas carol – of Christmases past....

8th January 2010

The Inuit were alleged to have over a hundred words for snow, until it was realised that they didn't all speak the same language. I have two - 'snow' and another word, or indeed series of words, which I cannot include in this article. Enough is enough. We are not a country that expects or is geared up for any more than a light, occasional dusting of snow. It may well be that the Gulf Stream's proximity to our islands has given us ideas above our station (or should that be 'below our line of latitude'?) for several generations; indeed, it is only as recently as 1895 that we have seen the Thames at Oxford frozen to such a depth that a carnival was held on the ice.

All I can say about this current white-out is that, for the first time in the three decades I have been performing in pantomime, on Tuesday we played to a matinee attended by the twenty-eight people who lived near enough to the theatre to struggle through the icy roads. Three schools and scores of other groups that had booked were simply unable to get there. This is undoubtedly the smallest number of people in front of whom I have ever strutted my panto stuff, aside from the last dress rehearsal when you are longing for an audience that contains more than the production team who have seen it a dozen times before and feel no need to react any more.

To their credit, the magnificent Malvern twenty-eight worked even harder than we did to compensate for their lack of company. They clearly felt quite sorry for us and had enough Christmas spirit left over to respond with gusto to every invitation to indicate their loathing of me (I should add here that I am the villain, so booing is okay) or their awareness of who was 'behind' whom. Subsequent performances have sadly been similarly sorely depleted.

All of which is somewhat dispiriting, of course, but when I am prevented from getting home on my day off then this snow stuff is really surplus to requirements. Walking in a Winter Wonderland is okay in songs but when you are trying to get on with your life in a country that is simply not geared up for it, for sound historical reasons that perhaps no longer apply, it is a complete pain!

17th December 2004

So what's the best thing about Christmas?

For some it might be the moment when the all the shopping, preparation and cooking is done and the children are still on a present-induced happiness high and you can sit down for the first time in two weeks and nod off while watching a sentimental movie on TV. For others, perhaps it is watching the children and dredging up bittersweet personal memories of that barely containable excitement on Christmas Eve, desperately wanting, yet at the same time not wanting, to go to bed.

For yet others, it is possibly eating too much turkey, but still having room in the evening for the cold cuts washed down with a glass of something just a little bit more interesting than the usual supermarket Vin Ordinaire.

The more honestly venal amongst you may even admit to deriving the most pleasure from the receipt of copious and lavish gifts; for others it may be the giving, which can often be a less complicated pleasure than that of receiving.

For some it may even be the unalloyed joy of seeing me as Sara the Cook in Dick Whittington at the Theatre Royal in Nottingham!

All these things have their undoubted charms, but Christmas is summed up for me by the nativity plays produced in nurseries and primary schools all over the country.

My daughters are now in secondary and university education, so no more tea towels or gossamer wings for the Baker family, otherwise wild reindeer would not prevent me from being there to witness those unforgettable moments; when the innkeeper forgets his lines and tells the pilgrims from Nazareth that he has plenty of room; or when Joseph picks up the infant Jesus by his head to allow Mary to prepare the straw in the infant crib; or when angels, kings and shepherds scan the expectant audience with screwed up eyes until they spot their adoring mums and dads and then give very un-biblical cheery waves before spending the rest of the performance riveted to the audience and paying no attention to the drama unfolding in the stable; and, inevitably, when the desire to visit the loo compels a diminutive sufferer to seize and hang on to affected area of his anatomy. On one memorable occasion I saw a five year old Mary get quite shirty when a helpful angel tried to replace on her lap the Baby Jesus, when he had tumbled unnoticed to the floor.

But there is something about the charming innocence of all this, that adds to the message of the Nativity play.

It is not always possible to imagine, scanning those infant faces, that from their number will come the adults of the future whose more pressurised lives will take them further away each year from the message of Christmas – which, if it is about anything, must be about hope for the future.

Despite the pressure of providing cards, food, presents and time for everyone at Christmas, most people manage to summon up more tolerance of their fellow man.

Roy Wood sang "I wish it could be Christmas every day" and, though I admit that I heave a very small, private sigh of relief when the decorations are packed away again, wouldn't it be nice if the mutual tolerance and the general bonhomie could last a bit longer?

It's no coincidence that New Year's Resolutions follow so swiftly on the heels of both the generosity and indulgence of Christmas.

24th January 2003

The computer and all its progeny are not providing the relief that we deluded ourselves would follow technology's arrival in every office, shop and home. I'd love to know how many hours are consumed pushing multiple choice buttons on automated "help" lines, so called because of the pitiful cries heard emanating from sufferers from enraged hot ear syndrome.

I am doubly tortured, as I can still cherish that distant image of the bank manager and the grocer (remember them?) who knew you and would never dream of uttering those words that I am convinced will one day result in a judge acquitting a murderer.

"M'lud the deceased shopkeeper told the accused that he not only did not have butter beans but that he would not in the future be able to offer butter beans as… (pause for effect while staring meaningfully at the jury) …there was "no demand for them."

"Case dismissed!"

I know all that boring stuff about prices only being kept low because of economies of scale. But I remember Mr. Sheard. He'd lick his pencil, write a note on the back of a brown paper bag and say "I'll get them in for you. Friday all right?"

Just before Christmas, I was on a mission to buy a specific large cuddly toy that Santa had failed to supply last Christmas. Anticipating his failure this year, I decided to find it myself. I sourced one at Toys R Us, fifty miles or so away. Two hours later I plucked the three foot red plush object off the shelf and presented myself at the check out.

Big Red did not have a bar code. I knew the price. I had been told on the phone and seen it on the shelf. The checkout boy needed the bar code or product number. He sent another young man to the shelf for the number to key in. He returned. He confirmed the price, but there was no number. The till would only accept a bar code or a number. The second young man disappeared with Big Red to consult a computer. Minutes ticked by and my cashier sat passively, avoiding my gaze and feigning not to notice my increasing agitation. The growing queue behind me started to get restless and glared at me balefully or sympathetically, according to their quotient of Christmas spirit. When I asked him to find out what was going on, he told me that he wasn't allowed to leave his till. I went in search, found Red on a counter beside another young man who was consulting a computer for another customer who was at the head of another large queue. Of Boy Two there was no sign. Boy Three was unable to help. I returned to Boy One and a queue that was bonding nicely. I requested an urgent summoning of the manager. He was tannoyed. He was tannoyed in all four times, each at my insistence as Boy One practised his Zen customer avoidance techniques and my queue exchanged addresses and paired off. Forty-five minutes (and I swear I am not exaggerating) after I had arrived at the checkout, the manager strolled up, leaned across the Young Man, keyed in the price that we all knew belonged to Big Red and pressed a few keys. I told him "Cross 'M' I" with Toys 'R' Us. He apologised somewhat less grovellingly than I would have liked.

I was then late for my matinee.

5 December 2003

I have spent the last week in America where it is Christmas with illuminated bells on already. Pity the poor turkeys who survived Thanksgiving. Their reprieve will be short-lived.

Driving from the airport, I passed scores of houses any one of whose external decorations would have put a severe strain on our national grid. How the occupants enter without electrocuting themselves or how they can get fire insurance defeats me. One gets the feeling that if one family were to put a ten foot illuminated all-singing all-dancing Santa in their garden – sorry front yard – within twenty-four hours the next house along would have a twelve foot gigawatt of snowmen juggling Christmas puddings in theirs. Even the weather wants to get in on the Yankee Yuletide Yeehaw – last night it snowed right on cue within hours of the hugest Christmas tree you ever saw appearing in the city square. I can see a snow plough from my hotel window, it has a Rudolph with an illuminated nose on its roof.

I have been grumbling for the last few weeks at home about the steady creep back of Christmas into early November, when they seem to start putting up the Christmas decorations now. It's not that I am a latter day Ebeneezer Scrooge. To the contrary, it is precisely because I want Christmas to be special and exciting that I don't want festivity fatigue to have set in before the advent calendars are even opened. By the time the big day comes, most of us are longing to see the interior of our homes again through the festoons of tinsel, pine needles and holly. And in the States, I imagine they might forget what the exteriors look like without cascades of multicoloured lights obscuring them from view.

But I wish our retailers would follow the example of the American stores. They have their sales before Christmas. The moment they have given thanks for their first harvest in the new territories (a rather nice tradition, actually), then the sales start. And the nation does what it does best – it consumes.

Over here, we spend massively before Christmas buying gifts for our nearest and dearest, as well as our furthest and not so dearest, only to find precisely the same goods massively discounted in the shops before the wrapping has gone to High Heavens (or some other inappropriately named domestic refuse tip). You can't blame the shops, I suppose. Make hay while the wallet's open and all that. But the American companies gamble on shifting such a massive volume at a discounted rate when people are in gift buying mode and awash with generosity and love for their fellow man that they end up making more profit than our retailers do by the UK double-whammy method.

But I was delighted and reassured to find that security at airports is getting better all the time. I was in the States just after the 11th September terrorist attack and was dismayed to find that the only change seemed to be the presence of the military demanding to know if I was carrying any weapons or sharp implements and seeming entirely satisfied with my negative response. Now the checks are efficient, meticulous and purposeful. It is a reflection of the generally gloomy perception of the present world situation that I saw no-one who seemed unhappy with the process. A brave new world?

27th December 2002

For actors who are lucky enough to be in demand at Christmas for pantomime, there is always that moment on Boxing Day when the rest of the family settle down to relax and recover from the after-effects of a day of self-indulgence and you have to force your reluctant legs into the car and onto the roads that lead to Pantoland.

In my case, this year it is as Sarah the Cook at the Wyvern Theatre in Swindon, mercifully a short drive down the M4.

Even clutching turkey sandwiches, it is a moment comparable only with the feeling of returning to school after the long summer break, which I can still dimly remember as not always being entirely welcome. But when you get onstage, hear the orchestra and the sense the hubbub of anticipation in the auditorium, those feelings of being an oppressed worker are replaced by an awareness that you are sharing your Christmas with several hundred excited families, for whom this performance is a Christmas highlight. It makes the enforced brevity of my own family Christmas a little more bearable.

And actors do have it cushy compared to footballers. Playing matches on Boxing Day to entertain us (well, those of us who aren't at panto!) means that they often have to train on Christmas Day and travel to another ground if they're playing away. Now, that really is a sacrifice too far. Everyone should be able to spend at least Christmas Day with their families.

I know that all the emergency and utility services etc. have to work on Christmas Day, but at least they can do so on a rota basis; that means that they get to spend some Christmases with their families and those who would, for whatever reason, prefer to avoid Christmas altogether can always volunteer to work. Footballers and actors have no choice, if they want to remain in their profession and earn a living. Although, I suppose that a footballer could contrive to get a red card in the build up to the festive season and earn himself a convenient suspension! Mercifully, I have never been shown a red card as an actor, although a director did once come on stage and shout at me for laughing during a performance. But that's another story.

For many theatres, panto is a banker that helps to subsidise the rest of the year. The sixty or so performances over the five weeks of December and January can be very good earners, though not to the extent of my childhood, when panto would still be playing in March or April. I once went to see a panto at the Palace Theatre in Manchester only a week or so before Easter. An up-and-coming young pair of comics called Morecambe and Wise was on the bill. And the best dame I have ever seen – Norman Evans. If you had told me then that one day I would be doing precisely the same thing myself, I would have considered you deranged. But then if you had told me than that one day I would own a car I would have felt the same.

Sadly, we will never see the like of those shows again. The advent of home entertainment in all its forms has eased out live entertainment for many people. But, mercifully for this Dame – there are still families for whom Christmas wouldn't be the same without a pantomime.

20th December 2003

If you have sent me one of those Christmas round-robin letters, then, of course, what you are about to read does not apply to you. Yours did not produce a desire to throttle the writer and all their descendants, because yours was not smug and boastful, nor did it contain pages of unmitigated bragging about the prowess of your children. Yours are delightful and their modest but commendable achievements do not eclipse anything my family will ever achieve.

First of all I should concede that I have received two wonderful and interesting letters. One is from an old friend whose epistles I eagerly anticipate every Christmas. He is a witty, acerbic individual who entertainingly catalogues the disasters that pepper his retirement. This year he also recounts the pleasure he has taken from several books that he has read during the year, at least one of which I shall make a point of seeking out myself. That is useful and diverting. The other acceptable letter came from a contemporary who shares the hideousness of his teenage children. He strays only briefly into the murky waters of their talent and achievements but redeems himself by disingenuously detailing their contempt for him, his values and all that he worked so hard to achieve in order to give them the freedom to despise him. These two correspondents made me laugh and are therefore acceptable.

However…

I have received a fair few examples of how it is possible to take self-satisfaction to new and dizzying heights of awfulness. These are the letters that should only be written either to very close relatives who have given a clear indication that they actually give a damn, or to people who do not have children, so no invidious comparisons can be made.

I have decided to write the anti round-robin letter. Maybe I will call it the square-grouse letter.

It will go something like this.

Well, it's Christmas again. This year was much the same as last year. The children ate more and did even less round the house. They're doing okay at school. We decided not to buy a villa in Tuscany or to go sailing around the Aegean with a lovely couple and their delightful children that we met in Barbados last year. Mainly because we didn't go to Barbados and certainly didn't meet anyone with whom we would want to sail round the Aegean.

We went to Cornwall and had a great time without any of us winning a yacht race, qualifying as a parascending instructor or meeting these really wonderful locals who taught us how to do topiary. I didn't get nominated for any acting awards (or literary or journalistic ones). Neither my wife nor I took up Tai-Ken-Pu-Chow (a wonderful physical discipline from the foothills of Indo-China that combines the calm acceptance of flatulence as a manifestation of natural energy with the very gentle massage of the elbow and ankle to release the spiritually disruptive effects of the pressures of 21st Century angst). Nor do we do this every morning in our Tudor Knot Garden (that I have not been creating for the last seven years in between sessions in my workshop where I don't make lutes using traditional methods).

Our children do a bit of homework sometimes and go out with their mates.

I do a bit of work and watch the telly. I'm not sure what my wife does. I must ask her sometime.

27th December 2003

I intended to write a gentle piece this week, celebrating my liberation from pantomime this year. My children have never spent a Boxing Day with their father, so I decided that before they become aware that there may be greater attractions than Baker Towers over the festive season and go off to investigate, I should turn my back on the world of cheesy jokes and ghosts that are always behind you just once, and have a "proper family Christmas." It started well. Another bonus, as a result of not prancing around in an improbable wig on a stage, was that I went to the Wycombe High School Carol Service in All Saints Church in the High Street last week. I can think of nothing else that could have set the tone for a perfect Christmas quite as well! The singing and musicianship were quite simply breathtaking. The church reverberated to the majestic music of Rutter, Britain and Vivaldi, as well as the traditional Christmas carols, and we all left uplifted and ready for the hurly-burly that attends Christmas in the 21st century.

Then I heard that a member of the choir that sings regularly in the very same church had gone to our library in High Wycombe and given them a poster detailing the times of The Christmas Carol Service and Midnight Mass. She thought, with some justification, that people who are not be regular church-goers might like to enjoy the carols. The librarian told Bridget Adams, a local schoolteacher, that she could not display it as the service contained Christian prayers.

One Margaret Dewar, responsible for the council libraries, elaborated, "The aim of the policy is to be inclusive and to respect the religious diversity of Buckinghamshire. This means we tend not to display posters and leaflets concerning religious, political or sexual preference groups, to avoid discrimination."

I'm sorry but, "Eh?"

Leaving aside the fact that we live in a country whose established religion is the Church of England, (and maybe we shouldn't leave that aside), surely the best way to encourage inclusivity is not to stick your head in the sand and pretend that political, sexual and religious differences don't exist, but to tell us about all of the options available. Peter Mussett, the council's "community development librarian" approved the ban. He explained, "We have a multi-faith community and passions can be inflamed by religious issues. We don't want to cause offence to anyone."

Well you've offended me, Peter. And I suspect this decision has offended many more people than would have been offended by seeing a poster for a traditional Christmas concert in a English public library. And I am no sure no sane person would object to seeing Eid posters, Hannukah Posters or Pagan Summer Solstice posters displayed in a building that, if it is about anything, should be about access to information. Shame on you, Bucks County Council!

Political correctness is betraying not just the traditions of this country but will also ultimately fail to serve the interests of the very groups it purports to protect by creating differences were none exist and then highlighting them.

But in a world where a school (in Brighton) has perplexed parents by banning the use of BC and AD as date references, what can you expect?

I apologise to all thin people with a full head of hair and no sense of humour for my existence. I intend no offence.

Happy Christmas!

Afterword

Well, I do hope that as you plucked this book from your shelf, or dipped into in the smallest room of the house, where I have a stack of books that offer snippets and short items of interest, that you found some of my thoughts amusing, enlightening or interesting. It seems overly simplistic to state that you will either agree or disagree with what I have written; but that is undeniably the case. And it is the way it should be, when one write what is essentially an 'opinions' column.

I am very grateful to my publisher Tim Hirst and his colleagues Louise and Elise, for doing the hard work of collating, selecting and arranging the various articles in this book. I was amazed to discover that were still enough unpublished from the first book to justify a further volume.

I would also like to thank those of you who having read the earlier publication were still happy to subscribe to this book, which I can only take as an indication that you derived some small entertainment and pleasure from perusing the first. Should you wish to follow my weekly musings as they unfold in the future, if – as they say – I am spared the axe from the editor – or the higher editing authority – then you can log on to www.bucksfreepress.co.uk/yoursay/opinion/look/ to see what has exercised my dander most recently.

The author and publisher wish to extend their gratitude to the following people, who pre-ordered this book.

Darren Allen
Kade Allen
Richard Black
Sean Brady
Philip Brennan
Darren Chandler
Mike Cook
Steve Duerden
Paul Engelberg
Ross Fletcher
Adam Fronteras
Cynthia Garland
Daniel Humes
David Johnson
Andy Kitching
Christopher Leather
Tristan Maddocks
James C McFetridge
Paul Norman
Marcus Palmer
Matthew Partis
Alister Pearson
Gary Russell
Michael Shakesby
Bryan Simcott
Jan Thomson
Casey Thomas
Cheryl Thorne
Martin Wakefield
Jeffrey Walker
Anthony Zehetner
Alex Wilson-Fletcher

Also by Colin Baker

Look Who's Talking

To many, Colin Baker is the sixth Doctor Who; to some, he is the villainous Paul Merroney in the classic BBC drama The Brothers. But to the residents of South Buckinghamshire he is a weekly voice of sanity in a world that seems intent on confounding him. Marking the 15th anniversary of his regular feature in the Bucks Free Press, this compilation includes over 100 of his most entertaining columns, from 1995 to 2009, complete with new linking material. With fierce intelligence and a wicked sense of humour, Colin tackles everything from the absurdities of political correctness to the joys of being an actor, slipping in vivid childhood memories, international adventures and current affairs in a relentless rollercoaster of reflections, gripes and anecdotes. Pulling no punches, taking no prisoners and sparing no detail, the ups and downs of Colin life are shared with panache, honesty and clarity, and they are every bit as entertaining and surreal as his trips in that famous police box... for a world that is bewildering, surprising and wondrous, one need look no further than modern Britain, and Colin Baker is here to help you make sense of it all, and to give you a good laugh along the way.

www.hirstpublishing.com

Also by Colin Baker

Gallimaufry

For the first time, here is a collection of Colin Baker's short stories, which deal in subjects as diverse as murder, mystery, true love, ingenuity, despair and farcical misunderstandings, with a hint of horror here and there as well as some insight into the minds of some unusual people. If you like your stories with a twist there are some surprises and shocks to be found.

Without Due Care
A car thief gets more than expects when he steals the most beautiful car he has ever seen

Rosita
Ramon and Rosita it is a special day for which the whole of their lives as devout Catholics have been a preparation.

Carter's First Case
When Carter Battersby told the Job Centre he wanted to be a Private Detective he thought that would succesfully protect him from the inconvenience of employment for the forseeable future. He was wrong.

Poison Pen
Jeffery Marsh was a drama critic - a job he executed with savage relish to the detriment of many a career until his untimely demise. Motives to kill Jeffery abounded - but opportunity? That was a different matter.

Ill Gotten Gains
After serving a twelve year stretch for Robbery with Violence, Barney McAteer is released and seems determined to put his criminal past behind him Others however make it difficult for him to go straight.

A Likely Story
A smug and implacably harsh magistrate finds himself in a situation where he has to radically re-appraise his former attitudes.

Hamlet's Ghost
It was perhaps not a good idea to stage two amateur productions in adjacent halls on the same night - particularly when those productions were Hamlet and Jack and the Beanstalk.

A Matter of Form
Martin didn't want to work in the solicitors' office - but his father decided otherwise. However Martin's first day proved more interesting than he had expected.

This is a truly diverse collection of short stories - something for everyone. There are 10 original stories, and a further 3 about the sixth incarnation of Doctor Who - as played by Colin in the mid-eighties, including a key moment in the life of his old friend Brigadier Lethbridge Stewart and a deft piece of negotiation by the Doctor with a very welcome result for the planet Earth.

Released in time for Christmas 2010

Pre-order to get a signed copy, and your name listed at the back.

www.hirstpublishing.com

Also from www.hirstpublishing.com

Single White Who Fan

The Life and Times of Jackie Jenkins

The Life and Times of Jackie Jenkins', as featured in Doctor Who Magazine (1997 - 2000, plus exclusive new material.

Doctor Who Magazine's flirty female diarist is back! Jackie Jenkins: cool, sexy and a little bit naughty. Jackie is a girl who views the world through TARDIS-shaped windows. She loves Doctor Who. She's sassy and holds down a busy PR job, but her real thoughts swim with string-vested sea monsters and silly ideas about who her antiquated Tom Baker doll really looks like (she's long plumped for Starsky and Hutch's Paul Michael Glaser but recently spotted flashes of Michael Sheen). To Jackie, colours come in 'Police Box Blue' or 'Time Warrior Green', a reference to the gorgeous shade of Pertwee's velvet jacket. She loves parties, vodka and belting out Bonnie Tyler numbers. She's never settled the question - Which is better - Inferno or Ambassadors of Death?" or why the only man she's ever fallen for seems to have all the dark-hearted qualities of the Doctor's own arch enemy The Master.

Now the fan-girl with attitude returns to present the best of her popular, funny Doctor Who Magazine column, which began its three-year run in 1997. Re-live the old and enjoy the new as Jackie updates her story with some brand new material. From pub nights out to TV nights in, incompetent friends to entangled relationships, follow Jackie and co as they ponder life, love and the Doctor, and address pressing issues such as "If the Doctors were Spice Girls, which ones would they be?"

Also from www.hirstpublishing.com

Blue Box Boy

By Matthew Waterhouse

As a boy Matthew Waterhouse loved Doctor Who: he watched all the episodes and read all the novels and comic strips. What starts as a heart-warming story, of a boy growing up with Doctor Who as his trusted friend, engaging the reader memories and nostalgia that will be familiar to any Doctor Who fan, takes a sudden twist when he is thrust into an alien and adult world - cast as Doctor Who's youngest ever travelling companion - for two of the series most inventive seasons.

Matthew's sense of wonder with his dream job and his love for the show are palpable; as is his shock at genuine hostilities between cast and crew members and considerable tensions on set, which are counterpointed with poignant reminders that he is just a boy, and still a fan, who finds himself in the absurd, comic world of minor celebrity.

What follows is a story-by-story memoir of his time on the show, peppered with glimpses into Matthew's personal life, tales of conventions, DVD commentaries, and some revealing anecdotes about everyone from fellow actors to Doctor Who's more high-profile fans.

This memoir holds nothing back: written with honesty, warmth, a rapier wit and a good dose self-depreciation, the book is essential reading for any Doctor Who fan.

Finally, we get to hear Matthew's side of a story which has been told and embellished and imagined by fans and fellow actors for years.

This affectionate and darkly humourous memoir is a record of what it was like to make Doctor Who, and to work for the BBC in early 80s.

Also available from www.hirstbooks.com

Shooty Dog Thing

By Paul Castle and Friends

Since the 1970s, Doctor Who fans have written and produced fanzines. Some of the most quirky, passionate and subversive writing is still to be found in the pages of lovingly crafted, home-spun, desktop-published fanzines, and Shooty Dog Thing is no exception. Cool and accessible, Shooty Dog Thing is inspiring a new wave of fandom. This book will make you remember why you fell in love with Doctor Who in the first place; challenging established views, covering The Doctor's travels on TV, in books, comic strips and on audio; and finding reasons to love this very special show just that little bit more than the casual viewer. Shooty Dog Thing is louder, braver, and more loving. The best of the first 10 issues is compiled here for your enjoyment, along with some lovely, juicy new stuff, including contributions from Doctor Who writer Paul Cornell, Doctor Who historian David J. Howe and the original Doctor Who glamour girl, Anneke Wills. If you love Doctor Who, you'll love this.

Also available from www.hirstbooks.com

Flight Risks, by Douglas Schofield

Basel, Switzerland, February 2001: Fifty-six years after the end of World War Two, Switzerland's bankers finally agree to release 21,000 dormant accounts left behind by Jews who died in the Holocaust. Claims from the victims' heirs pour in from across the world...

New York and Washington, September 2001: The Twin Towers fall. The Pentagon burns. Western democracies scramble to meet a deadly new threat...

Victoria, Canada, October 2001: For legal secretary Grace Palliser, the post-911 media circus is just background noise. Grace is too busy with the unholy mess she calls her life. But when she stumbles on evidence of a vast international fraud, her life gets a whole lot messier. Framed for murder and desperately searching for the evidence that will clear her, Grace flees across the continent to New Orleans, then to the Florida Panhandle, and finally to a small island in the northwest Caribbean. Hot on her trail is a corrupt former cop with a simple assignment - to Kill Grace Palliser.

Also available from www.hirstbooks.com

Paddytum

By Tricia Heighway

At one thirty-three in the afternoon, on the second Wednesday in May, something happened which was to change Robert Handle's life forever. At the time, he did not realise it would be a change for the better. Rob is man who has reached his forties without achieving anything at all. To his mother's dismay, he has dug himself into a rut so deep it will take more than a shovel to dig him out. It will take someone...or something, very special. Paddytum is the funny, poignant and heart-warming story of one man and his bear.

Also available from www.hirstbooks.com

Match Day

by Darren Floyd

Cathy is a woman disappointed in life when her dream turns into a nightmare, and mires her with debt which she doesn't have a hope of paying off. Suddenly she is offered a chance of a new life in Australia, but first she must take a desperate gamble...

Martin is a bitter policeman with decades on the job, and a shameful secret in his past. He finds himself wrapped up in events that he could never anticipated.

Leigh is a supporter; he just wants to get into see the match. Unfortunately he gets split up from his mate who has his ticket. He finds himself alone in a city full of sports fans. Now if he can only find a ticket...

Gradually these three people's paths collide, and none of their lives will be the same again...

Also available from www.hirstbooks.com

Cemetery Drive by J.T. Wilson

Death, it's a once-in-a-lifetime opportunity.

Alexa cheated death today. Well, at least that's what she was told, but how can you tell, if the Grim Reaper doesn't show up? Lucky she's got Robbie really, who'll go out and confront Death for her, even if it means going to the furthest corners of the world and killing himself in the process. And given Robbie's suicidal anyway, everyone wins.

Zan's having a bad day. Death's best employee, he's been collecting souls since the day he died, but today one wasn't there for him to collect, and that means a soul's achieved immortality and a serious threat to his job security. Now he's got to hunt that soul down and return it to the afterlife before the universe is torn asunder, before the fabric of space-time is destroyed and more importantly, before his boss finds out.

Featuring steampunk package holidays, demon summoning, sex, violence, casual drug use, possessed technology and technomagic of a universe-threatening nature